Sex Work Now

Edited by

Rosie Campbell and
Maggie O'Neill

WILLAN
PUBLISHING

Published by

Willan Publishing
Culmcott House
Mill Street, Uffculme
Cullompton, Devon
EX15 3AT, UK
Tel: +44(0)1884 840337
Fax: +44(0)1884 840251
e-mail: info@willanpublishing.co.uk
website: www.willanpublishing.co.uk

Published simultaneously in the USA and Canada by

Willan Publishing
c/o ISBS, 920 NE 58th Ave, Suite 300
Portland, Oregon 97213-3786, USA
Tel: +001(0)503 287 3093
Fax: +001(0)503 280 8832
e-mail: info@isbs.com
website: www.isbs.com

Paperback
ISBN-10: 1-84392-096-4
ISBN-13: 978-1-84392-096-0

British Library Cataloguing-in-Publication Data

A catalogue record for this book is available from the British Library

Cover images by permission of Kate Green, a freelance artist who worked with the
authors and Walsall Youth Arts to consult sex workers and local residents using
participatory arts.
Project management by Deer Park Productions, Tavistock, Devon
Typeset by GCS, Leighton Buzzard, Beds
Printed and bound by T.J. International, Padstow, Cornwall

Contents

Notes on the contributors

Laura Agustín (PhD, Open University) currently works for the ESRC-sponsored project 'Regulating the Spaces of Sex Work' and frequently publishes on the connections among migrations, commercial sex, 'trafficking' and the social sector that aspires to help migrants who sell sex. She has worked in *educación popular* in Latin America and with migrants in various parts of the West. She recently received funding for an anti-'trafficking' project with sex workers in Ecuador and has been an evaluator of social programming for the ILO and the European Commission. She moderates an e-mail list in Romance languages for participants in the sex industry (workers, organised groups, supporters) and will edit a special edition of *Sexualities* dedicated to 'the cultural study of commercial sex'.

Rosie Campbell is Project Coordinator of the Armistead Street and Portside Projects, working with street and off-street sex workers in Liverpool, based in North Liverpool PCT. She was a founder member of the UK Network of Sex Work Projects. In her role as Chair of the UK NSWP and of the 'Safety, Violence and Policing Group' she works with sex work projects throughout the UK. Rosie has carried out applied policy research relating to sex work since 1995 and has published widely in the field. Her most recent research involvement was as part of a team of researchers from Loughborough University, Staffordshire University and the University of Strathclyde on a Joseph Rowntree-funded project on communities and street sex work.

Phil Hubbard is Reader in Urban Social Geography at Loughborough University. He has written extensively on the contemporary city, with a particular focus on the identity struggles played out in public spaces. His publications include *Sex and the City: Geographies of Prostitution in the Urban West* (1999, Ashgate), *Thinking Geographically* (2002, Continuum) and the forthcoming *Key Concepts in Geography – The City* (2006, Routledge).

Gillian Hunter is a Senior Researcher at the Institute for Criminal Policy Research at King's College, London. Her work has included evaluations of criminal justice interventions for drug users, sex workers and women offenders with mental health problems. She was the lead author of guidance for meeting the multiple needs of street sex workers, published by the Home Office in collaboration with service providers. She has also undertaken research on the barriers faced by women drug users in seeking drug treatment, on homeless populations and their access to health promotion and primary health care, and the evaluation of various peer education initiatives for marginalised groups.

Hilary Kinnell has worked in the fields of community action and sexual health since 1970. She initiated an outreach project for sex workers in the West Midlands in 1987, and was the UK National Coordinator for the European Network for HIV/STD Prevention in Prostitution (EUROPAP) from 1998 to 2002. Between 2002 and 2005 she was the Coordinator for the UK Network of Sex Work Projects. She has published a number of articles on health and safety in the sex industry.

Ana Lopes is a researcher and sex worker activist. In 2005 she finished her PhD at the University of East London, which was based on a pioneering project that has consisted of setting up an international sex worker organisation and securing official union representation for sex workers in the UK. She is currently undertaking research on sex worker unionisation as part of her post-doctorate studies. She is a well-known international sex worker activist.

Tiggey May is a Senior Research Fellow in the Institute for Criminal Policy Research, King's College, London. Her work has focused on the various aspects of drug markets, including the links between sex work and drug markets, and the impact of pimps on sex markets. Other sex work research includes an evaluation of an arrest referral scheme designed specifically for sex workers. Her more recent work has examined the relationship between drug dealers and local communities, and the policing of cannabis. Together with Gillian Hunter they have published guidance for partnerships and providers of sex work services.

Maggie O'Neill is Senior Lecturer in Criminology and Social Policy, in the Department of Social Sciences at Loughborough University. An expert in ethnography and participatory action research, she has published extensively in the following areas: cultural criminology, street sex work, communities affected by prostitution and forced migration as well as critical theory, feminisms and creative consultation. Research and consultancy have been funded by the British Council, the Arts and Humanities Research Board, Joseph Rowntree Foundation, the Home Office, the Government Office East Midlands and Health Action Zones. Key books include *Prostitution and Feminsim*, *Adorno, Culture and Feminism*, *Prostitution: A Reader* with Roger Matthews, and *Gender and the Public Sector*, edited with Jim Barry and Mike Dent.

Jenny Pearce has worked as a teacher and youth and community worker with young people outside of mainstream school settings. She has researched and published on young women, community safety and sexual exploitation, also running multi-disciplinary training in the field. She is coordinator of the National Working Group on Young People and Sexual Exploitation and is a board member of the UK Network of Sex Work Projects. She is currently based at Middlesex University.

Jane Pitcher is an independent social researcher, affiliated to Staffordshire University and other research organisations. She has been undertaking research for the past 20 years, working in local government, the university sector and for a voluntary organisation concerned with crime, social exclusion and community safety. She has undertaken a number of studies into social exclusion, including research concerning regeneration programmes, disadvantaged young people and women sex workers. As a regular volunteer for a sex worker support service in the West Midlands, Jane was recently involved in a community engagement research project looking at the needs of indoor and street-based sex workers. She is currently undertaking a research study on communities and street sex work, funded by the Joseph Rowntree Foundation, with colleagues from the Universities of Staffordshire, Loughborough and Strathclyde. She is a member of the UKNSWP.

Teela Sanders is a lecturer in the School of Sociology and Social Policy at the University of Leeds and specialises in crime and deviance. Her main research interests are in the female sex industry examining the social organisation of sex work and the management of occupational hazards. She is also interested in qualitative research methods, in particular ethnography. She has recently published in journals such as *Sociology*, *Urban Studies*, *Sociology of Health and Illness*, *Social Science and Medicine* and *Gender, Work and Organisation*. Her first book, *Sex Work: A Risky Business* (Willan 2005) looks at the indoor sex markets in the UK. She is currently working on her next book *Paying for Pleasure: Men Who Buy Sex* (Willan forthcoming).

Marieke van Doorninck (MA) is a historian and currently working as the Advisor Public Affairs for La Strada International in Amsterdam, the Netherlands. The primary goal of La Strada is to improve the position of women and to promote their universal rights, including the right to choose to emigrate and to work abroad and to protect them from violence and abuse. From 1995 to 2004 Marieke has worked as policy consultant and spokesperson for the Mr A. de Graaf Foundation, the national centre for research, policy development and information on prostitution and related issues.

Introduction

Rosie Campbell and Maggie O'Neill

Sex Work Now provides an overview of female sex work and policy in the UK. The book is an edited collection whose contributors include academics, researchers, practitioners and activists who are among the leading commentators on prostitution in the UK. The book addresses a number of contemporary issues and debates. These include: sex worker unionisation, migrant sex work and trafficking, communities and sex work, male clients of sex workers, policing of prostitution, zoning of street sex work, young people and sexual exploitation, drug use and sex work, exiting, violence and sex work. The book will be of interest to those in the field of social policy, sociology, gender studies and criminology and those involved in developing policy and service response to sex work. It will also appeal to a wide general audience who want to gain an understanding of the dynamics and diversity of prostitution in the UK and of current theoretical debates and policy responses.

Women working/sex work now

Eileen McLeod wrote *Women Working: Prostitution Now* in 1982 influenced, in part, by her involvement with the Birmingham PROS (Programme for Reform of the law On Soliciting) campaign. This was a groundbreaking text and a major influence on sex work research in the UK for over a decade. *Women Working* remains a landmark text that interweaves the lived experience of women who sell sex; the role and experiences of clients; a focus upon the law and a call for decriminalisation; and the role and importance of sex worker rights campaigns.

In conceiving this book we selected a title which purposefully pays tribute to McLeod's work but also addresses the changes in both female sex work itself and social policy discourses on sex work in the period since the publication of *Working Women: Prostitution Now*. McLeod's emphasis on sex worker rights and the importance of the 'lived reality' (in all it's diversity) of all those involved in sex work as a basis for theory, practice and policy is something that has shaped our own work on sex work.

In this introduction we explore some of the changes that the intervening decades, research, campaigns, policies, sex work projects and most importantly sex worker rights activism have brought to the debates on female sex work in the United Kingdom. We also, of course, look at some of the continuities.

Before saying more about the shifts and changes that have taken place, and introducing our authors and their chapters, let us first look at some of the key findings from McLeod's research and her analysis of female sex work.

McLeod presented a particular model of the social organisation of prostitution.

> One of the most significant aspects of contemporary heterosexual prostitution is that prostitutes, women are grappling with their disadvantaged social position in the context of a capitalist society. Recruitment to the ranks of prostitute is not appropriately characterised as only concerning a small group of highly deviant women. It is secured by women's relative poverty still being such that for large numbers sex is their most saleable commodity. (McLeod 1982: 1)

Selling sex can bring financial rewards in the context of limited economic choices, it is compatible with domestic labour and childcare and these 'gains' are, in McLeod's words, 'offset by the experience of male domination through superior purchasing power, violence, more developed organisational resources and the ideals embedded in notions of romantic love' (p. 1).

McLeod sets out an analysis embedded in neo-Marxist and feminist interpretations that get to grips with the social organisation of prostitution through an understanding of social structures, agency and lived experience. For McLeod, the role of the client reflects men's advantageous position in gender relations as well as the shortcomings in the institutions of marriage, cohabitation and gender roles under 'existing social orders'. We interpret the latter as structural, cultural and also personal/interpersonal.

In *Women Working* McLeod drew attention to the different ways in which sex workers were victimised; this she connected to the organisation of wider social structures and cultural discourses. The law, media, police, welfare agencies and public opinion are documented as coalescing to protect the face of public morality and victimising 'prostitutes' along social class and sex lines. Street sex workers then, as now, are identified as a stigmatised group. The law shaped by sexist assumptions about women's sexuality, is documented as unjust and futile. This is a theme that has persisted in writings about laws relating to sex work in the UK.

The advent of 'prostitutes' rights' campaigns – from the mid-1970s (a heady time for feminisms and counterculture movements) are documented as challenging and shifting public attention and debate.[1] McLeod, as a founder member of PROS, supports decriminalisation. She advocated for sex workers to have more control over their work. 'Even if law reform comes, unless prostitutes gain greater control over their own work they might simply be exchanging legal harassment for commercial exploitation' (p. 2).

Sex workers' campaigns are of central importance to McLeod because: they oppose the scapegoating of sex workers ('the role of the prostitute is indexical – prostitutes are the end stop in discourses on good and honest women': O'Neill 2001); by speaking out they highlight 'the hypocrisy running through men and womens' relations more generally' (p. 2); they provide examples of feminist efforts to challenge existing structures; and they illustrate that law reform is a 'necessary but insufficient basis for securing humane social conditions' (p. 3). The latter requires more complex and far-reaching changes in social structures. The phenomenon of sex work does however, reflect these wider social problems and structures.

Female sex work and policy two decades on

The chapters in this edited collection retrace many of the arguments and analyses made by McLeod in 1982 and include new issues that have emerged since the early 1980s. They provide a current analysis of contemporary female sex work marked in part by: an increased focus by policy-makers upon children and young people abused through prostitution (McLeod does not discuss 'adolescent prostitution');

changes in drug use particularly among street sex workers; a focus upon residents and the impact of street sex work on neighbourhoods and communities; an increase in awareness, understanding and debate about migrant sex work and trafficking; the development of sex work support services, sex worker rights activism and unionisation, and changes to the law.

From prostitution to sex work

Arguably the biggest change that has taken place is in discourses around prostitution/sex work/commercial sex. The terms 'sex work' and 'sex worker' are now more commonly used by some activists, academics and policy-makers rather than 'prostitution' and 'prostitute' reflecting the impact of sex worker rights discourses and an attempt to challenge the stigma embedded in language use. Moreover, attention is directed to improving sex worker rights by looking at labour law and unionisation. Yet the recent Home Office and Scottish strategies do not make these linguistic or legislative shifts.

Children abused through prostitution

The terms 'adolescent prostitution' and 'juvenile prostitute' have been replaced with 'children abused through prostitution'. At the level of policy there has been a general consensus that the involvement of the under 18 age group in sex work should be treated as exploitation and abuse, with the young people treated as 'victims' not 'villains'. This was reflected in the introduction of Joint guidance, *Safeguarding Children Involved in Prostitution* (Department of Health *et al.* 2000) issued to responsible authorities throughout England and Wales in 2000. Since then they have been obligated to develop local protocols to more effectively identify and respond to children abused through prostitution. The Guidance is issued under section 7 of the Local Authority Social Services Act 1970 and must be complied with unless local circumstances indicate exceptional reasons to justify a variation. Changes in sexual offences legislation have also further criminalised adults who have sex with young people and children, and those who procure. The ongoing research and debates about children abused through prostitution and sexual exploitation are discussed by Jenny Pearce in Chapter 8.

Diversity of sex work

Female sex work is increasingly acknowledged to be a complex terrain and sex workers are not a homogenous group – the sex industry is made up of street and off-street commercial spaces for selling sex as well as a plethora of related activities such as telephone and Internet sex, fantasy and peep shows, and lap dancing/pole dancing venues. During the two decades since *Women Working* was published there has been the emergence of the Internet, mobile phone technology and computer-mediated communication (CMC). This has led to the further development of the commercial sex industry with new means for establishments and independent sex workers to advertise and communicate with clients.[2] New technologies have not only enabled changes in sex work but are a vehicle for communication between sex workers and sex worker activists nationally and internationally. Despite such advances there are some forms of sex working which remain under-researched, for example lorry-park and port-related sex work. Policy debates at a local and national level still focus upon street sex work due to its visibility and more direct impact on residential urban areas and communities living and working in areas of street sex work.

This can deflect attention from much larger sectors of the sex industry such as: massage parlours, escort agencies, independents working via the Internet and contact magazines. In Chapter 4 'Behind the personal ads' Teela Sanders explores indoor female sex work.

Communities affected by street sex work

Yet it is difficult to ignore the policy preoccupation with street sex work and the policy driver at a local level of community responses to street sex work. Community responses were outside the remit of Mcleod's book. We have included in Chapter 2 a discussion from the editors about community responses to street sex work which calls for a more complex understanding within the broader context of social inclusion, active citizenship and renewed methodologies for consulting communities and street sex workers.

Sex work activism and sex work support projects

Developments such as the unionisation of sex workers through the GMB, the ongoing work of the English Collective of Prostitutes and the UK Network of Sex Work Projects continue to highlight and encourage shifts in national attitudes, policy and practice.

For sex workers rights in the UK there has been an important and historic development. Sex workers in the UK came together in 2000 to found the International Union of Sex Workers (IUSW). In 2002 the IUSW became an official branch of the GMB union, a major general workers' union in the UK. By joining the GMB, the International Union of Sex Workers has achieved two of its main goals: establishing the right for any sex worker to join an official trade union, and the acceptance of sex work as legitimate employment by the union movement. The development of UK sex worker unionisation is explored by Ana Lopes, one of the founders of the IUSW, in Chapter 11.

Since the early 1980s the number of health, social care and self-help projects working with sex workers has proliferated and the work delivered has broadened. The diverse work of these projects is illustrated in Chapter 10 by Jane Pitcher. At a national level the UK Network of Sex Work Projects was formally established in June 2002, a non-profit, voluntary association of agencies and individuals working with sex workers. The UKNSWP acts as an umbrella organisation bringing together projects working with sex workers in the UK. Its key aims are: to encourage networking and the sharing of good practice, and to advocate for policies which enhance the safety, welfare and rights of sex workers.

Globalisation and migrancy

The impact of globalisation is experienced in national, European and international responses to migrant sex work. Forced migration also impacts upon the commercial sex trade and so far is under-researched in the literature. McLeod did not touch on the issue of migrant sex work in the UK, i.e. people from other countries who work in the UK sex industry. Often discussions about female migrant sex work are subsumed in discussions about the very serious crime, and human rights violation, of 'trafficking', i.e. women trafficked from other countries against their will and forced to work in the UK sex industry.

This focus on trafficking has at times obscured the experiences of migrant sex workers who travel to the UK to work voluntarily in the sex industry, but who may face a range of exploitations due to their nationality status. High-profile police anti-trafficking operations which have hit the media headlines in the UK have illustrated the complexities linked to migrant sex work. The raid of a massage parlour in Birmingham in October 2005 illustrated these complexities. Police accompanied by immigration officials and BBC cameras entered a massage parlour. High-profile media headlines announced that police had 'rescued' a number of 'trafficked girls'. As the outcome of the raid unravelled some women claimed they had been trafficked, others that they were working voluntarily. Regardless of the women's experiences the authorities showed little sensitivity to the women's rights. A number of the women were placed immediately in a detention centre in readiness for their removal from the country; thus the authorities failed to respect the recommended provision of a window of time for women who may have been 'trafficked' to receive support, advice and time to consider their options. Campaigners protested that in this case immigration agendas outweighed women's rights. To date in the UK the presence of migrant female sex workers is understood to be predominantly an issue within the off-street sector with the highest numbers in London. Yet it is difficult to make hard and fast claims with no national studies of migrant sex work and limited research on this issue. In Chapter 5 Laura Agustín discusses this lack of research and the debates about migrant sex work.

Commonalities

Stigma, taboo and prejudice remain embedded in social structures, processes, the law and the public imagination, although these have been loosened through focused campaigns, the impact of globalization, sex worker rights activism and the impact of feminist and social science research as well media products including a plethora of documentaries about selling sex.

Levels of work-related violence against sex workers is still high (with research highlighting the particular vulnerability of street sex workers) and criminal justice mechanism in many cases continue to fail to prevent or bring justice. The cultural attitudes which form the backdrop for such violence, while challenged by some groups including sex workers themselves, endure. Hilary Kinnell in Chapter

6 makes a forceful argument for policy changes to address violence against women and the murder of sex workers.

There is still a dearth of research focusing upon clients and they remain more or less invisible as a group in policy debates. Where they are present is in arguments put forward by some feminists who argue for the criminalisation of clients either through the existing kerb-crawling legislation or the introduction of new legislation such as adopted in Sweden, which criminalises all men who pay for sex. Chapter 9 by Hilary Kinnell presents a different perspective.

Jurisprudence and policing

Jurisprudence has, in our interpretation, creaked and groaned towards a more 'modern' approach to sexual offences. The campaign to remove imprisonment as a penalty for soliciting in 1983, which McLeod and other sex worker activists were involved with, was successful. Yet sex workers rights continue to be violated in relation to certain criminal justice responses. For example, in 2006 the use of legislation such as Anti-Social Behaviours Orders to address female street sex work has meant the reappearance of imprisonment through the back door without any wide ranging public debate or consultation. A number of these cases have caused great alarm about the violation of sex worker rights and the efficacy of ASBOs in responding to street sex work, and the role of ASBOs in the development of a more 'balanced' policy approach. For example, women have faced bans from areas of towns and cities in which they live, and photographs of women served with ASBOs identifying them as drug users and sex workers have been posted through letter boxes to whole communities. Yet to date few legal challenges have been made and legal provisions which criminalise sex workers (opposed by sex worker rights activist in the early 1980s) still remain, such as the use of the term 'common prostitute' in soliciting legislation. While there is much research evidence that the criminalisation of sex workers heightens their vulnerability, makes it more difficult for sex workers to assert their human and labour rights, and makes it difficult for legal, health and social care services to deliver their interventions, the legal framework enshrining such criminalisation remains intact.

Policing approaches often remain dependent on 'old-fashioned' enforcement with the soliciting legislation still the most used in relation to street sex work. New enforcement-based approaches have emerged since the early 1980s with the introduction of kerb-crawling legislation in the mid-1980s and the anti-social behaviour legislation. Yet the emergence of new policy fora, such as Crime and Disorder Reduction Partnerships and Drug Action Teams, have created a new multi-agency environment within which the police and other agencies must now operate. This has meant the emergence, in some areas of the UK (Manchester for example) of more balanced policing with police liaising with social care and health agencies and in some case being key partners in initiatives to prevent and respond to violence against sex workers and to provide access for sex workers to social care agencies. This has led in some areas to more sophisticated multi-agency partnerships and strategies. Phil Hubbard in Chapter 1 overviews the policing and wider regulatory framework within which sex work takes place.

Some of these multi-agency partnerships and stakeholders concerned with female street sex work have developed approaches within which they have attempted to address the problems associated with street sex work through a 'managed area' or 'toleration zone approach' as pursued in a number of European countries. The debate about 'managed areas' has attracted a great deal of media attention and occupied policy-makers. In Chapter 3 Marieke Van Doorninck and Rosie Campbell discuss the debates about 'zoning' with a focus upon the Dutch experience to which some in the UK have looked.

Drug use and sex work

Problematic drug use was recognised by McLeod as one route into sex work. Since the early 1980s there have been changes in drugs markets and drug use in ways which have shaped some sectors of sex work. Available research would suggest that the proportion of street sex workers with problematic drug use in the UK has increased among street sex working communities. The emergence of new drugs since *Women Working*, particularly crack cocaine, has had considerable impact on street sex work. Tiggey May and Gill Hunter explore the relationship between sex work and problematic drug use in Chapter 7.

Feminist debates

Prostitution has always been an important topic among feminists and debates about the right and wrongs of prostitution became increasingly polarised from the 1960s onwards.[3] McLeod's book was also a landmark text because she focused on the lived experience and situation of female 'prostitutes' and provided an insight into the nature of contemporary prostitution in a way which was sensitive to the pressures and prospects of those who became involved in commercialised sexual activity within the context of capitalism. She showed through the voices of women that 'working as a prostitute is a hard life' (McLeod 1982: 58). Yet she also acknowledged the 'choice' some women made and the agency exercised by sex workers.

In *Women Working* McLeod acknowledged that some women chose to work in sex work as a resistance to poverty, and the issue of choice in sex work continues to stimulate heated and sometimes polarised debate among academics, feminists and sex worker activists. While some argue that sex work can never be a choice for women, is a central pillar of male domination and is in itself violence against women, others contest this as reductionist, denying women's agency, ignoring diversity and silencing the voices of those sex workers who do not feel coerced or exploited in sex work. In taking a methodological approach which prioritised the voices of women themselves McLeod's work acknowledged the diverse routes into sex work and the different ways women experienced sex work.

McLeod's work preceded debates about sex work framed within a labour rights framework that is also situated alongside the emergence of postmodernist debates which focus upon the performativity involved in selling sex, and the multiplicity of the experiences and identities of those involved.

Currently in the first decade of the new millennium the zeitgeist appears to be suggesting a less polarised approach with collaborations and discourses taking place that are more accepting of ideological differences in the interest of women's safety, human rights and addressing sexual and social inequalities, although it is important to acknowledge that at times the consensus and collaborations can be fragile or short-lived within policy debates. At an ideological level, some activist and theorists remain very polarised, some arguing that sex work should be approached within a labour rights framework and others arguing that sex work is sexual slavery synonymous with violence and abuse.

This collection will connect with these debates, not so much through the development of grand theory but through an exploration of the changing empirical reality of sex work. We see the book, therefore, as an important point of reference in ongoing debates between feminists, sex worker activists, researchers and others. Many of the authors in this book acknowledge diversity in sex work and the existence of both choice and coercion and the need for policy responses sensitive to these diversities and complexities. The complexity of the current terrain of *Sex Work Now* is captured, we feel, very well in the chapters in this volume.

Policy change on the horizon?

Throughout the 1980s and 1990s many diverse stakeholders, including sex workers, agencies working with sex workers, local authorities, police forces and communities affected by street sex work, have expressed dissatisfaction with current law and 'prostitution' policy. In July 2003, the then Home Secretary David Blunkett announced that the Home Office would be carrying out a review of legislation and policy on prostitution in England and Wales. A consultation document *Paying the Price* (Home Office 2004a) was published containing findings and recommendations from the review and the Home Office invited responses to the document by the end of November 2004.

At the same time findings from evaluations of 13 Home Office-funded initiatives under the 'Tackling Prostitution: What Works?' were published in *Tackling Street Prostitution: Towards an Holistic Approach* (Hester and Westmarland 2004). Many of the findings from the evaluation documented in the latter report were drawn upon in *Paying the Price*.

Additionally, the Home Office worked with a consultation group with representatives from ACPO, the Probation Service, the Department of Health and Drug Action Teams, Crime and Disorder Partnerships, academic institutions and sex work support projects to develop guidance on responding to drug use in sex work and tackling drug markets linked to sex. These were combined in the document *Solutions and Strategies: Drugs Problems and Street Sex Markets, Guidance for Partnerships and Providers* (Home Office 2004b). The academics commissioned to pull together the work of this group and review the research evidence contribute their expertise in Chapter 7.

The Scottish Office carried out its own review and adopted a different process. They announced that they would have a staged review process: in the first stage street sex work would be examined, the second stage would explore off-street female sex work and the third stage would examine male sex work. This contrasted with the Home Office review which reviewed the whole of 'prostitution' in one go. In Scotland an expert group on prostitution was established to carry out the first phase in contrast to the Home Office model of an internal team. In July 2004 the expert group published *Being Outside* which not only contained findings but also recommendations for a future policy framework for street sex work in Scotland.

The Scottish Executive responded to 'Being on the Outside', produced by the expert group, in October 2005. The executive defined female street sex work as a 'survival behaviour' and a form of abuse of women and stated that policies to 'eradicate' street sex work should be in the context of broader policies of tackling violence against women. The Executive identified a long term object of eradicating street sex work but stressed that harm reduction was critical and not in conflict with this objective. The Executive tasked all areas to develop; multi-agency partnerships, with planned responses tailored to local needs and an integrated approach to allocating resources. They announced that they would provide authorities with guidance on dealing with street prostitution. The Executive pointed out that sexual health and drugs policies should address sex work and support harm reduction and routes out interventions. They announced some new legislation which would establish an offence focusing on harm and nuisance caused to communities from prostitution-related activities, whether by 'sellers or purchasers' (to replace the existing offence of soliciting). The stated intention of creating this offence was to criminalise 'men who cause nuisance or alarm when attempting to purchase sex'.

As we go to press with this book the Home Office published a strategy document (January 2006) 'A coordinated prostitution strategy' that sets out proposals for addressing prostitution that focus upon: prevention of involvement; fostering routes out; protecting communities from street based sex markets and a greater enforcement focus on men who pay for sex. Prostitution is defined as 'commercial sexual exploitation' and whilst promoting zero tolerance to street based sex work, the report recommends that prostitution off street can be tolerated where 2–3 women are working together. Greater measures to address trafficking are advocated by wider issues of migrant sex work are not addressed. The strategy does not support zones of tolerance or managed areas for street sex work. At the very least, many stakeholders hoped for some sort of strategic framework based upon the recognition and rights of sex workers, the needs of residents living in areas of street sex work, and attention to the endemic levels of violence against sex workers including pimping and procuring. It is our hope (and our research is based on these principles) that responses to the strategy will be developed in the light of critique and further reasearch that will foster processes of inclusion, participation and valuing all stakeholder voices thus facilitating dialogue that will usher in policy reform based upon a politics of inclusion.

Notes

1 See the excellent collection on the feminist 1970s edited by Helen Graham, Ann Kaloski, Ali Neilson and Emma Robertson, published by Raw Nerve Books, York University (www.rawnervebooks.co.uk).
2 Such as Internet technology and 3G phone technology.
3 The central ideological tension for feminisms is that the exchange of money for sex is seen as the exchange of equivalents – this marks a situation that is unacceptable to many feminists as this equivalence is a socially created illusion and is central to the commodification of women and our use as body objects of desire and oppression. This central tension complicates the possible range of responses ideologically and in law (see O'Neill 2001: chapter 1 and p. 31).

References

Hester, M. and Westmarland, N. (2004) *Tackling Street Prostitution: Towards an Holistic Approach*, Home Office Research Study 279. London: Home Office Development and Statistics Directorate.
Home Office (2004a) *Paying the Price: A Consultation Paper on Prostitution*. London: Home Office Communications Directorate.
Home Office (2004b) *Solutions and Strategies: Drugs Problems and Street Sex Markets, Guidance for Partnerships and Providers*. London: HMSO.
McLeod, E. (1982) *Women Working: Prostitution Now*. London: Croom Helm.
Scottish Executive (2004) *Being Outside: Constructing a Response to Street Prostitution: A Report of the Expert Group on Prostitution in Scotland*. Edinburgh: Scottish Executive.

Chapter 1

Out of touch and out of time? The contemporary policing of sex work

Phil Hubbard

Introduction

Although sex work essentially involves a private contract negotiated between two consenting individuals, in Britain this contractual interpretation of sex work has traditionally been rejected by the state and the law in favour of legislation designed to express moral condemnation of sex work as well as to protect 'respectable' populations from the sight and sounds of those engaged in sex work. In addition, British 'vice law' has generally sought to offer some level of protection to sex workers by punishing those who seek to control or exploit them. Yet, as has been the case in other nations (Symanski 1981; Lowman 1992), the interpretation and enactment of British prostitution laws has been somewhat inconsistent and uneven, and it is clear that the police have not enforced all vice laws with the same vigour and vigilance. Rather, there has been a sense in which the police have treated the law as a resource which they are able to deploy as and when particular issues or problems arise. Vice law, in this sense, needs to be understood not as an instrumental force, but as produced in and productive of the social world (Blomley 2005). Hence, while it is instructive to analyse the laws surrounding sex work as abstract legal discourses, it is more meaningful to explore the way that legal relations of power are constructed and reproduced through police practices that code, exclude, enable, locate and repress particular forms of sex work in particular places at specific times. Above all else, it is clear that the policing of sex work produces a differential and striated landscape of sex work, evident in the contrast between 'red-light' (inner-city) districts where street sex work has traditionally been tolerated by the state and law and those wealthier, whiter and more politically articulate residential neighbourhoods, where any manifestation of sex work is routinely repressed and removed (Hubbard 1999).

Challenge.

Recently, however, dominant modes of regulation have been inexorably unravelling in the face of critiques of British vice laws and policing strategies. Specifically, vice legislation has been repeatedly exposed as of dubious value in offering a meaningful, long-term solution to the 'problem' of prostitution and publicly criticised by many senior police officers as entailing a huge outlay of resources for little demonstrable return (Sharpe 1998). Moreover, vice laws have also been opposed on broadly humanitarian and libertarian grounds by a growing number of campaigners – including sex worker unions, legal experts and feminist groups – who argue for the liberalisation of prostitution laws. Recognising that some women and men will always want to work in the sex industry – albeit not always under circumstances of their own choosing – advocates of liberalisation suggest it offers a more pragmatic way of dealing with the problems associated with sex work and would offer more protection to sex workers, clients and those living in the vicinity of sites of sex work. In effect, some have gone so far as to suggest that the modern forms of policing have actually exacerbated the problems associated with street sex work by attempting to contain prostitution in specific areas and applying the law in uneven and contradictory ways. Latterly, the fact that the police have adopted a more repressive and draconian mode of enforcement in particular locales has further highlighted the uneven and iniquitous impacts of vice laws – and the need for reform of those laws.

The fact that there has been no radical overhaul of vice laws for nearly fifty years in the UK means that dominant modes and practices of policing now seem badly out of touch with the needs of sex workers, communities and even the police themselves. In this chapter, I want to scrutinise this argument, detailing the way that the police deploy the law in different contexts and situations, and noting the gendered injustices wrought by this process. The chapter hence begins by detailing the current legislative situation in the UK, describing the way that the dominant logic of common and statute law in the UK has remained essentially unaltered since the deliberations of the Wolfenden Committee in the 1950s. It then turns to explore the enactment of these laws at 'street level' through a scrutiny of the way that the police seek to control or intervene in specific sex work markets. The fact that this mode of intervention is seen to be breaking down and that there is a need for a new form of policing is then highlighted. Accordingly, significant attention is devoted to the rhetoric and practices of zero tolerance which are beginning to impact on the policing of sex work in many areas of the UK. The chapter concludes by outlining the possible consequences of going down this more repressive route, contrasting this with possible modes of regulating sex work that might involve the police working collaboratively alongside a wide range of agencies.

The criminalising of sex work

Currently, prostitution itself is not criminalised in Britain, and is legally regarded as a private transaction conducted between two consenting adults. However, there are many pieces of legislation that still seek to regulate and punish a wide variety of acts associated with sex work. In general, these laws focus on those aspects of the sex industry which impinge on the 'wider public' and, as such, may be considered as public order offences. Under the terms of the Street Offences Act 1959 and the Sexual Offences Act 1985, such offences may include soliciting in public or quasi-public spaces, kerb-crawling, advertising sexual services or conducting sexual practices in public view (with the Criminal Justice and Police Act 2001 adding new powers to arrest those who place advertisements for sex work in a public place – see Hubbard 2002).

Simultaneously, the Sexual Offences Acts 1956 and 2003 allow for the prosecution of those who are seen to benefit from other people's prostitution, such as pimps, procurers and the owners of brothels. As such, British vice laws (which differ slightly between Scotland and England and Wales) have the twin aims of preventing 'the serious nuisance to the public caused when prostitutes ply their trade in the street' while simultaneously penalising the 'pimps, brothel keepers and others who seek to encourage, control and exploit the prostitution of others' (cited in Edwards 1997: 928). In practice, this creates a paradoxical situation where, although prostitution may not be illegal, it is impossible for female sex workers to work without breaking a number of laws in the performance of their work. Moreover, as soon as any third party becomes involved in any transaction between sex worker and clients (whether as owner of the premises where sex is being sold, a pimp or agent) they are immediately subject to arrest on the basis that they must be exploiting the sex worker.

3

The Sexual Offences Act 1956 thus penalises 'the procurer' – any pimp who knowingly lives wholly or in part off the earnings of prostitution (Edwards 1997: 63). However, this definition has been taken to include the partners or boyfriends of sex workers, and has sometimes led to a situation where the sex worker is both isolated or criminalised (the penalty for pimping is up to seven years in prison). Equally, section 33 of the same act makes it illegal to run a disorderly house, defined as a house used by more than one woman for the purposes of prostitution (Sharpe 1998), again encouraging women to work alone.

Yet if British vice laws often proclaim a concern for the working conditions and safety of sex workers, the low number of prosecutions for living off immoral earnings or encouraging women into prostitution suggests that such concerns are currently given a low police priority: for instance, in 2002 there were 2,678 women found guilty of soliciting compared to just 31 incited for procurement offences (Home Office 2004b). Hence, it has been suggested that the police are most concerned with responding to pressure from residents and politicians who wish to reduce the 'nuisance' experienced by people living in areas of street prostitution (rather than intervening in off-street sex markets). According to the Wolfenden Report (1957: 23), which preceded the introduction of the 1959 Street Offences Act, the main justification for intervening in sex work markets was to maintain 'the right of the normal decent citizen to go about the streets without affront to their sense of decency'. Hence, while many of the attitudes underpinning contemporary British vice laws can be traced back to the 1824 Vagrancy Act, which instigated the power of arrest for women behaving in a 'riotous and indecent manner', it is the Wolfenden Report that provides the moral justification for current laws. Significantly, the Wolfenden Committee was established at a time when street prostitution, while largely contained in deprived inner-city districts, was implicated in a wider process of postwar moral decline that was leading to family breakdown and social disintegration. With the ascent of the new queen to the throne, an attempt was made to redefine women's and men's role as homemakers, with support for family values often made with reference to the Christian values of the British monarchy (Self 2003).

Outwardly, the attitude of the Wolfenden Committee was dogmatically moralistic, claiming that 'prostitution is an evil of which any society that claims to be civilised should seek to rid itself of'. Referring to 6,829 arrests for street soliciting in 1953, the committee further suggested that London's prostitution population was 'without parallel in the capital cities of other civilised countries' (cited in Matthews 1997: 1). Such claims were informed by a detailed mapping of the capital's sexual topography, a strategic mapping that isolated some of Soho's notorious streets and landmarks as belonging to London's more recalcitrant citizens, a sexually immoral population that was seen in need of isolation and re-education (Mort 1998). However, alongside this desire for order was a concern that it was not the law's role to interfere in the private lives of citizens or to seek to enforce any particular pattern of behaviour:

> If it were the law's intention to punish prostitution *per se*, on the grounds that it is immoral conduct, then it would be right that it should provide for the punishment of all the men (clients) as well as women (prostitutes). But that is not the function of the law. It should confine itself to those activities which offend against public order and decency or expose the ordinary citizen to what is offensive and injurious, and the fact is that prostitutes do parade themselves more habitually and openly than their prospective clients, and do by their continual presence affront the sense of decency of the ordinary citizen. (Wolfenden Report 1957: 14)

This judgment may well have been informed by the fact that many of those among London's elite continued to be dependent on prostitution, either financially or as a sexual outlet. Nonetheless, this distinction between prostitution as a public offence and prostitution as a private *consensual* transaction was important in subsequent British legal debates which demonstrated the law's ostensible acceptance of sexual liberation while simultaneously actually strengthening the legislation which could be enacted against sex workers.

For example, by recommending the national introduction of a cautioning system first employed in Edinburgh and Glasgow, whereby the police were merely empowered to caution women who they considered to be soliciting on the first and second occasion, the Wolfenden Report appeared to express a concern that female sex workers should not be punished without being given the chance of 'redeeming' themselves. Once charged in court as a common prostitute though, the new legislation stipulated that prostitute women need not be cautioned again, and, under section 1 of the 1959 Street Offences Act, could be charged with loitering or soliciting in a street or a public place for the purpose of prostitution *without* caution. Lopez-Jones (1990) points out the absurdity of this position by stressing that the guilt of the prostitute is assumed once she has been labelled as a common prostitute, with the purpose of her presence in public space presumed on the basis of her previous conviction. Nonetheless, if a woman is charged with an offence she may incur fines and court costs which may simply force her to work extra hours to pay off, instigating a vicious cycle of arrest–fine–arrest. In this context, it has been suggested that the role of intermediaries becomes more important too, and some prostitute women may look to their pimps to pay off the fine or pay bail costs as appropriate (Edwards 1987).

Moreover, although the Wolfenden Report made reference to the nuisance of kerb-crawling, it was not until the (hastily drawn-up) 1985 Sexual Offences Act that British law sought to criminalise those men who solicited women in addition to those women who solicited men. Under the provisions of this act, a man commits an offence if he solicits a woman for the purpose of prostitution from a motor vehicle while it is in a street or public place or in a street or place while in the immediate vicinity of a motor vehicle he has just got out of (Edwards 1987). Those convicted of kerb-crawling are normally subject to a fine which varies from around £50 to £300 depending on local court procedures (Benson and Matthews 1995). However, the criteria for prosecution normally requires proof that the kerb-crawlers acted persistently or in a manner likely to cause annoyance to the solicited woman or to other persons in the neighbourhood. This need for proof of persistence places a burden on the police which they are often unable to meet, and instead they may prefer to adopt methods where warning letters are sent out to the kerb-crawler's address (presumably in the hope of 'shaming' him). In cases where such cases proceed to court, names (and sometimes photographs) of kerb-crawlers are published in the media to try to deter further offences. Kerb-crawling legislation has consequently been the source of much controversy and while it was designed to bring equality in terms of how women soliciting men and men soliciting women are treated, in 2002, the number of men found guilty of kerb-crawling was 993 against 2,678 for soliciting. Here, it should be noted that these figures refer to a period when kerb-crawling was a cautionable and not an arrestable offence, with the 2003 Sexual Offences Act also allowing judges to demand the confiscation of persistent offenders' cars. Enactment of the law has been described as a 'fiasco' by some commentators (Lopez-Jones 1990).

Avowedly created to both protect sex workers and the public at large, it has therefore been suggested that British laws effectively serve to criminalise all sex workers. The way in which such legal

6

discourses contribute to this stigmatising process is particularly pronounced in that women convicted of soliciting are labelled as a 'common prostitute', a term that dates back to the Contagious Diseases Acts. Through this label, Lopez-Jones (1990) contends that the current prostitution laws effectively distinguish between the civil rights afforded to sex workers and those offered to other women (once labelled as a 'common prostitute', the guilt of sex worker is assumed in eyes of the law, with any legal protection sought by the prostitute with respect of violence or exploitation undermined by the court's awareness of her status as common prostitute). In this sense, the dominant discourses encoded in prostitution laws appear to combine with political, medical and religious narratives to construct the sex worker as separate from 'decent' women. As such, it has also been suggested that prostitution laws reproduce certain assumptions about sexual power, and thus reproduce dominant *male* discourses:

> The law creates potential offences in every aspect of the prostitute's life, raising the spectre of an offence for everyone she comes in contact with, constituting her as a pariah … Beyond the surface of order and innocence, prostitution laws create and extend the power which underpins male sexuality by facilitating the buying of women on their own terms. (Duncan 1994: 25)

The English Collective of Prostitutes (1997: 93) sums the position up by suggesting that the prostitution laws continue to divide women between the good/moral and bad/immoral, signalling to men that female sex workers are criminals. In turn, they argue that this has major implications for sex worker's safety, with men thinking that violence against prostitute women will be dealt with more leniently by the law. In sum, this type of reading backs up Duncan's claim that there is no legal approach to prostitution that is not abusive and does not exploit women, stressing that 'all legal approaches to prostitution are masculinist systems that yield to the market demand and concede to the misogynist myth that prostitution is a necessary and inevitable sexual service required by men'.

Surveillance, territoriality and police control

While the implicit gendered moralism of prostitution laws has been a cause of major concern to pro-feminist and sex worker groups in Britain, the operation of these laws has been subject to similarly cynical scrutiny. In particular, the way that the law has been interpreted and enacted by the police has been shown to be, at best, arbitrary, indistinct and confused, and, at worst, sexist and racist. Far from being panoptic and permanent, police surveillance is better described as elliptic and ephemeral. Concurring, Sharpe (1998) contends that the police response to both female prostitute sex workers and kerb-crawlers in England and Wales is essentially uncoordinated and largely ineffectual. In her analysis of the policing of prostitution, she highlights how police tactics and strategies for policing vice differ markedly across space dependent on a number of factors including levels of staffing, financial constraints and the discretion of senior police officials. Moreover, her study also stresses that these strategies are negotiated through specific understandings of the unwritten 'rules of engagement' between police, punters and sex workers, rules which are applied differently across time and space.

Sharpe's (1998) investigation of police, punters and sex workers in Kingston-upon-Hull provides perhaps the clearest description of how contemporary cultures of policing impact on sex work. Describing police culture as centred on 'beer, sport and women', she contends that the Divisional Enquiry Team (vice squad) in Hull gave prostitution a low priority and pushed it to the back of queue when other issues, particularly drugs offences, cropped up as pressing concerns. Many officers obviously thought such offences were more worthy of their attention, and Sharpe contrasts their 'fight' against drugs with the laissez-faire attitude police developed towards prostitution, which they appeared to accept as an inevitable feature of the urban landscape. As one of the team claimed:

> We could put a lot of pressure on them and move them on but where do we move them to? If you continually keep moving them the only thing left for them is to work from home and then somebody ends up with a neighbour who is using the house as a brothel which isn't a good thing, so perhaps it's better the devil you know. (Cited in Sharpe 1998: 135)

Noting the existence of a predominantly non-residential area where the police largely tolerated prostitution, Sharpe recounts that it was only when the sex workers moved beyond this area that public complaints would reach the ears of local councillors and MPs who might pressurise the police to take steps to stamp out prostitution in these areas. According to Sharpe (1998), the overwhelming belief that prostitution could never be removed from the street thus dictated a policing policy in Kingston-upon-Hull which aimed to monitor, control and contain prostitution in a designated area so that it would not raise wider public concern and create more work for the police.

In this sense, it appears that the police employ their own specific understandings of spatial and sexual morality in order to decide how they ought to enact specific vice laws. In response, sex workers learn to recognise the rules of the game, and tactically adjust to work in times and spaces where they do not attract the unwelcome attention of the police (Hubbard and Sanders 2003). They may also develop working relationships with police officers whereby they share information about the comings and goings at street level in exchange for being left to work (Sanders 2004). Indeed, although there are fewer and fewer specialist 'vice' police units in the UK (Benson and Matthews 2000), it is common for police forces to maintain a close working contact and knowledge of street sex work markets. This necessarily involves a level of fraternisation that some local residents find puzzling. In addition, it is clear that many police are broadly sympathetic to the plight of some sex workers and are reluctant to arrest them. Nevertheless, the relationship between sex workers and police is not as cosy as some imagine, and there have been publicised instances of police intimidation of sex workers. Developing this, Lopez-Jones (1990) contends that most sex workers do not object to being arrested when they are caught breaking the law, but do object to the sexist and racist forms of police behaviour which may entail false arrest, insults, threats and violence, demands for free sexual services or information on other sex workers in exchange for immunity from prosecution. For example, one Liverpool street sex worker interviewed by Campbell *et al.* (1996: 78) stated that some of the police 'are bad news, they call us all cows' while another stated that 'the abuse I've heard them give when I've been arrested you just wouldn't believe'. In this case, the situation was complicated by the fact that there was no established vice squad and the women didn't know what to expect 'from one day to the next'. In particular, police from one local division were regarded as much more sympathetic and friendly than those from a neighbouring area, so that the relations between police and sex workers were variously described as supportive and respectful or harassing and hostile depending on which police were involved. It is this variation in attitude that seems to unsettle many street sex workers, knowing that their presence on the street may by tolerated for months on end, but that there is always the threat of a police purge in which they might be arrested several times in one week.

As such, it appears that the private (police) and public (legal) moralities intertwine in a complex manner to create a distinctively uneven geography of prostitution. The overriding factor appears to be the level of public complaint about sex work, which appears to be prompt periodic 'crackdowns' in which sex workers and/or their clients are cautioned or arrested. Such crackdowns fulfil a variety of functions, serving to deter sex workers and kerb-crawlers (at least in the short-term) while placating residents' fears that the police are unconcerned about street sex work. Indeed, Matthews' (1993) study of Streatham suggests that residents are concerned about the fraternisation of police and sex workers, albeit some recognise that a close relationship between 'vice officers' and sex workers is important in maintaining public order (see also McKegany and Barnard 1996). Highly publicised crackdowns thus provide a clear indication to local residents (and community representatives) that the police are dealing with perceived problems, while sending out a message to new sex workers and clients that the area is 'off-limits'.

Assessments of such campaigns are mixed. Clearly much depends on the nature of the crackdown, and whether the police target kerb-crawlers, sex workers or both. Post-1985, the emphasis in England and Wales has increasingly been on the former given sex worker advocacy groups contend that the cautioning, arrest and fining of street workers for soliciting instigates a cycle of 'reoffending' whereby sex workers are forced to work to pay off fines (Self 2003). This is reflected in arrest and caution figures for soliciting, which have steadily declined since the introduction of new powers to arrest and caution kerb-crawlers for 'causing annoyance to women or to other people in the neighbourhood or where it is persistent behaviour' (Sexual Offences Act 1985). As well as using section 1 of the 1985 Street Offences Act, section 71 of the Criminal Justice and Police Act 2001 and clauses in the 2003 Sex Offences Act which allow for the caution, arrest and banning of kerb-crawlers from driving, the police may also use stop-and-search powers to warn 'cruisers' that they are in a known area of sex work (sometimes sending letters to their home address to this effect). In some areas (e.g. Leeds) re-education programmes have been used for first-time offenders. Typically these courses outline the nature of street sex work (including the drug use of many of those involved, the health risks and the risks of prosecution). Attendance can be reinforced by the use of police cautions (see Campbell and Storr 2001, for a critical assessment of kerb-crawler rehabilitation programmes).

Although such crackdowns on sex workers and kerb-crawlers are highly publicised, more routinely, the police are involved in strategies

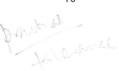

of restraint and order maintenance rather than any concerted and vigorous process of law enforcement. Indeed, evidence suggests that the concentration of street sex work in particular locales facilitates the task of order maintenance and surveillance, and amounts to a system of de facto tolerance (Hubbard 1997). For example, a survey of the 39 'vice squads' established to monitor prostitution in England and Wales revealed that 80 per cent of these squads focus their activities on an area of no more than one square mile where they concentrate on routine surveillance and street patrol (Benson and Matthews 1995). In part, this spatial concentration results from a strategy of deliberate containment, and when sex workers exceed the boundaries of this space it may be that they are targeted by police under soliciting and vice laws. This process has been described in McKeganey and Barnard's (1996) exhaustive ethnographic study of street workers in central Glasgow. This study revealed that the changing definition of a permissible working area is at the heart of the everyday negotiations between police and street sex workers, with workers who transgressed beyond boundaries deemed acceptable by the police undoubtedly charged if caught. Often, these boundaries coincide with the police's own administrative boundaries. For instance, O'Neill and Campbell (2001) report that Walsall police did not regard policing sex work as a high priority, with the local police force allocating the lead in 'vice' policing to those in Sector C (one of eight operational sub-areas in the city). This means that when sex work shifted beyond the boundaries of this sub-area, it creates logistical problems, with the police preferring to contain it in one locale. In practice, however, this proved difficult in Walsall, and Sector C ultimately took responsibility for sex work in both areas.

In the final analysis, the idea that sex work is inevitable and cannot be prevented (or *eliminated*) through the application and enforcement of established prostitution legislation appears to be a key factor shaping police practices and attitudes towards prostitution. Indeed, the police concede that it is difficult to ensure that those charged with soliciting will not return immediately to the same area (given a system where many prostitutes can only pay off their fines by returning to the streets), while kerb-crawling legislation has been frequently adjudged as a poor deterrent for those looking to buy sex (with powers to disqualify drivers also difficult to enforce). Perceiving that current laws cannot be used to prevent individuals buying and selling sex, the principal tactic adopted by the police in the UK was to contain sex work in specific areas so that they might restrict its visibility to those residents who protest most vehemently, reduce their surveillance costs and attempt to gather intelligence relating to those who exploit or attack sex workers. However, this model of policing was to come under fire in the 1990s as media and political espousal of zero tolerance tactics threatened to undermine this 'softly, softly' approach and encourage more repressive modes of policing.

The impacts of zero tolerance policing and the attack on anti-social behaviour

Given public perceptions of rising crime in the UK, and recognising the need for more cost-effective modes of policing, the dominant trend in Britain under the Labour government has been for policy-makers to espouse tactics of zero tolerance. Following the initial use of this term by William Bratton (the then commissioner of the New York Police Department) in 1994, zero tolerance has become something of a buzzword in crime enforcement circles, travelling across the Atlantic to inform police strategy in many European nations, and particularly the UK (Raco 2003). The logic of this approach is deceptively (and perhaps dangerously) simple. By refusing to tolerate even minor incivilities such as begging, public drinking, graffiti, litter, public urination and busking, police authorities hope that more serious crimes like assault, burglary and arson will be avoided. The precise way in which these minor incivilities are supposed to encourage major crimes is not spelt out, although Wilson and Kelling (1982) famously drew on ideas of defensible space to suggest that they act as environmental cues which send out a message to potential criminals that the area is an easy target. In this sense, there is a growing focus on *situational* approaches in which the focus is on reducing the opportunities for criminal behaviour through design measures. On the other hand, zero tolerance policing also involves the creation of orderly subjectivities, i.e. making subjects conduct themselves in an appropriate manner. In practice, emerging policing tactics often represent a *hybrid* approach which seeks to modify the design of urban spaces and behaviour at the same time (Raco 2003).

In practice, zero tolerance policing is intensive of time and resources, so it is an approach that has mainly been applied in known 'hot-spots' of crime in a high-profile manner. Bratton's campaign against so-called 'quality of life' crimes in New York is perhaps the most (in)famous example, notable for targeting sex workers alongside panhandlers and graffiti merchants. Supported by Mayor Rudolph Giuliani, zero tolerance policing was used to drive street sex workers from Manhattan, especially Times Square at a time when the Disney Corporation was simultaneously seeking to reinvent the area as a site of 'family' entertainment. Long-notorious as a marketplace for commercial and illicit sexuality, 'anti-porn' resolutions were effectively used to force sex shops and cinemas from the area, while increased enforcement by the NYPD and stricter sentencing at the Midtown Court resulted in a 50 per cent decline in sex work between 1993 and 1995 (Weidner 2001). The net result has been the creation of a sanitised theme park where traces of burlesque and risqué Broadway life are now hard to find: as Merrifield (2000) relates, the square is now dominated by Disney Corporation and its partners in the Times Square Business Improvement District (e.g. HBO, Marriott, Virgin, Sony *et al.*). Hence, Papayanis (2000: 351) contrasts the contemporary consumer landscape of Times Square with the memory of a district that was 'the antithesis of productive social space ... shunned by developers, the middle-classes and mainstream retailers'.

While many politicians in the UK have avoided the term, zero tolerance has become a widely espoused tactic. Importantly, the Labour Party endorsed such policies through its promise to be 'tough on crime', with successive Home Secretaries Jack Straw and David Blunkett having espoused tough policing as a way of 'reclaiming the streets'. Frequently, the experience of New York has been cited as an exemplar of successful policing, with Giuliani's visits to the UK having been used as opportunities to share best practice. Furthermore, enthusiasm for such punitive policing goes right to the top: in 1997, Tony Blair (then shadow leader of the House of Commons) threw his weight behind Operation Zero Tolerance, a high-profile policing initiative that involved 25 officers removing the homeless, 'squeegee merchants' and sex workers from Kings Cross (a district that Blair described in the press as 'frightening'). Given the initiative was acclaimed as a success, with a dramatic fall in anti-social behaviour in the area, similar campaigns were enacted by the Metropolitan Police in tandem with the London boroughs. For insistence, in an eight-week programme in 2000, Westminster City Council and the Metropolitan Police cooperated to tackle a series of 'nuisances' including prostitution, unlicensed taxi drivers and 'bogus' portrait artists (the latter being blamed for a spate of handbag thefts).

This casual labelling of sex work as a nuisance and its identification as a threat to community safety marks a significant shift in the logic of policing vice in the UK. In the past, the police have tended to pursue a programme of containment whereby they have sought to contain, survey and manage sex work in geographically concentrated

13

areas. Furthermore, the Home Office has generally asserted that current legal powers are sufficient to deal effectively with a wide variety of nuisances associated with prostitution. However, in the wake of the perceived success of zero tolerance campaigns, successive Home Secretaries have nonetheless argued that a number of additional (non-legal) measures could be employed to reduce opportunities for prostitution to be practised in specific districts. Such measures include the use of closed-circuit television cameras in areas of street soliciting, traffic management schemes designed to close off the 'scenic routes' often taken by kerb-crawlers, lighting schemes designed to 'reclaim' the streets from sex workers and the use of community watch schemes to gather intelligence on sex work. In the one area of Britain particularly associated with zero tolerance (Cleveland), these tactics have been combined with a 'name and shame' approach as clients and kerb-crawlers from Middlesbrough have been simultaneously prosecuted as part of a highly publicised crackdown on street prostitution, with the local police promising 'no hiding place for those who prey on those drawn into vice' (*Daily Telegraph* 27 July 1997; *Middlesborough Evening Gazette* 5 August 1998).

What is particularly interesting about these new forms of enforcement is that they often amount to a form of social exclusion that marginalises sex workers within the communities that they live and work. This is clearly illustrated with reference to Street Watch, an offshoot of Neighbourhood Watch introduced in 1994 and endorsed by the Labour government as a means of enhancing community safety through citizen participation. Piloted in several rural locales, it was used by a group of residents in Balsall Heath, Birmingham, solely as a means of targeting sex workers and their clients. From 1995 onwards, this involved police-sanctioned street patrols walking around the areas known for soliciting and kerb-crawling and monitoring the activities of sex workers. Placards and banners were used to inform kerb-crawlers that their registration number was being passed onto police. This persistent patrolling (and the publicity it created) had a noticeable and immediate effect on numbers of clients visiting the area and resulted in sex workers moving to work at different times and in different areas. However, there were accusations of intimidation and violence against sex workers, and service providers such as outreach workers also experienced difficulty in accessing the area. Further, it was clear that not all members of the community supported the protest, which was organised through the local mosque: some local residents felt the protestors were more intimidating than

14

the sex workers as a presence on the street, and others pointed out that several sex workers had been part of the community for many years (see Hubbard 1998). Rather than promoting inclusion, the Street Watch campaign clearly allowed participants in this case to impose their moral values on the neighbourhood, irrespective of the views of others. Conceived as a crime reduction measure, here Street Watch allowed for the effective scapegoating of sex workers for a host of problems, and endorsed actions that ultimately did little to enhance community safety. Reviewing a similar initiative in Grangetown, Cardiff, Sager (2005: 108) suggests that the actions of Street Watch 'do not represent the collective will of the community', 'increase tensions in the community' and 'do not sit comfortably alongside existing policy measures' designed to support sex workers and improve their health and safety.

Similar questions about who in the community the streets are being made safe for are raised by the widespread use of Anti-Social Behaviour Orders (ASBOs) served on sex workers effectively banning them from working in particular areas. ASBOs were created by the Crime and Disorder Act 1998, enabling the police or local council to apply to magistrates for an order to control 'anti-social' behaviour, defined as that 'likely to cause harassment, alarm or distress to one or more persons not of the same household'. Though rarely served on sex workers at first, they have quickly become recommended as a means 'to protect communities from the harassment, alarm and distress caused both by those soliciting and those kerb-crawling' (see http://www.crimereduction.gov.uk/asbos9.htm). In some areas of the UK, it appears that the police prefer ASBOs to prosecuting under the soliciting or kerb-crawling laws because the standard of proof needed to obtain an ASBO is lower than in a criminal trial, while breaching an order can result in up to five years imprisonment rather than a fine. Further, ASBOs may be used to target particular individuals identified as the cause of complaints from local residents. Though ASBOs have been served against kerb-crawlers (the first being in Middlesbrough, May 2000), the vast majority have targeted working women. No ASBOs have been served on pimps to date. Recent orders have thus included demands that a worker should not go to a particular area (e.g. Edinburgh has banned several women from the Leith Locks area), not associate with particular people and even not to purchase more than twelve condoms at a time. Though normally applying to named areas in specific cities, there have been examples of ASBOs which seek to prevent sex workers soliciting anywhere in England and Wales.

15

One significant feature of ASBOs is that they tend to be publicised through courts records and the local media. Some authorities have adapted a 'name and shame' approach in relation to workers served with ASBOs: for instance, in Reading, ASBOs have been served on seven women, whose name, address and picture appeared on a police website. This strategy clearly poses issues concerning civil liberties, but in this case the local Labour MP, Martin Salter argued:

> We are enthusiastic users of the antisocial behaviour legislation in our communities and on our estates. We have used acceptable behaviour contracts to quieten youth disorder. Innovatively, we have used seven ASBOs on the most prolific street sex workers. Fining drug-addicted prostitutes £40 for soliciting is plain stupid – what on earth will they do other than to go back on the streets to earn the money? I am proud that our approach to using the welcome powers that the Government have given us – if you like, tough love – has resulted in five of the seven most prolific prostitutes engaging in treatment programmes. (*Hansard* 29 November 2004, col. 447)

In some locales, local authorities have sought civil injunctions against sex workers and kerb-crawlers, while some magistrates have granted ASBOs at the end of criminal trials ('CRASBOs'). Despite some criticisms of the difficulty of enforcing such notices, and the problems geographically specific injunctions may create for women seeking to access social services, ASBOs and CRASBOs are increasingly common in zero tolerance styled campaigns designed to tackle problems surrounding sex work. For instance, a police-led initiative in Nottingham (funded as part of the Crime Reduction Programme) used covert operations to effect 350 arrests, served six ASBOs on sex working women, used street signs to highlight the number of arrests of kerb-crawlers during the operation, issued press releases publicising successful enforcement action, displayed posters in pubs, bars, clubs, men's toilets and bus shelters, and sent letters to over 200 suspected kerb-crawlers based on vehicle registration numbers. However, this period of repressive policing was carried out without appropriate reference to other relevant agencies (e.g. Nottingham's sex worker street outreach team, social services, etc.). Given such organisations did not have protocols in place prior to the police crackdown, increased policing was not accompanied by increased advice and help to sex workers. In one instance, an ASBO served on a sex worker actually prevented her from accessing suitable housing and exiting prostitution. Overall, this campaign was therefore judged to have had only a limited impact on sex work, with just 10 per cent of residents perceiving the sex workers had declined following intervention, as against 31 per cent who thought the numbers had risen (see Hester and Westmarland 2004). Despite the Home Office issuing 'Solutions and Strategies' guidance that ASBOs should only be used after diversionary interventions have been put in place, several forces and local authorities are continuing to issue them without making such arrangements.

This type of cooperation between local authorities, police and community groups is thus a hallmark of many campaigns designed to reduce 'problems' associated with sex work in residential areas. Though not part of the Nottingham scheme, situational or environmental interventions intended to 'design out' street sex work are integral to many of these. For example, road closure and the introduction of CCTV may be introduced to steer sex workers and their clients away from areas where they cause distress to (some) residents, while gating off alleyways denies access to areas for sexual activity (see Scott 2001). Matthews (1997) cites instances where such interventions have been deemed effective, including Toxteth, Finsbury Park, Streatham, Luton and Southampton. An early example of a road closure system took place in Toxteth, Liverpool in the 1970s. This area comprised several roads of terraced housing arranged in rows with main roads at either end, with a regular stream of kerb crawlers. Police and the local authority transport department devised a scheme where most of the affected roads were closed at alternate ends to create a series of cul-de-sacs. This was very successful in almost eliminating prostitution and kerb crawling in the area. It also had the added benefit that community spirit was improved, non-local vehicles became easily identified by local residents and there was a significant reduction in all crimes in the area. However, such interventions are expensive, and can be disruptive for some local residents and businesses (for instance, Nottingham residents rejected a scheme as it would disrupt their school run). Their overall effectiveness is also in question: for instance, blocking one end of Cheddar Road in Balsall Heath in 1992 did not markedly decrease the amount of traffic in the street but merely turned it into 'Britain's busiest cul-de-sac'. In other instances, it may simply result in sex work moving from one street to an adjacent one. The effectiveness of CCTV systems in discouraging sex work has also been questioned given that the presence of cameras may provide reassurance to sex working women. Likewise, improved street lighting has not always discouraged sex work, but can provide sex workers and clients with a better working environment.

More controversially perhaps, some local authorities have been using planning powers to prevent sex workers working from private residences. The use of such powers was first explored by Southampton City Council in 1991 as a way of dealing with window workers in Nicholstown and Newtown, as a single woman operating from a private premises did not constitute an offence under existing British vice laws (Hubbard 1999). Utilising the powers of the Town and Country Planning Act 1971, the council served a number of enforcement notices on the owners of those houses which were being knowingly used for prostitution. A similar strategy was later pursued in Balsall Heath in 1993 when 14 enforcement notices were served on the owners of houses on Cheddar Road and Court Road which were being used for commercial sex, suggesting that this represented a material change of use from their normal residential purposes to that of a 'business'. Although an appeal was bought by one occupier against the notice, the planning inspectorate fully supported the local authority's use of planning powers to shut houses being used for sex work, thus setting an important precedent. According to the decision letter, the inspector paid no regard to moral issues, but was merely concerned that the number of clients visiting the house did not constitute 'the usual comings and goings of neighbours, friends and domestic visitors' and hence was 'disturbing local residential amenity' (*Planning* 25 November 1994). In 2004, Westminster City Council pursued a similar course of action, compulsorily purchasing two flats used by sex workers in Soho on the grounds that they were an environmental and health risk (despite contrary evidence presented by the sex workers, who enjoyed the support of the local Soho Society). However, viewed alongside the ongoing Westminster City Council's role in pushing through anti-carding legislation (with sections 46 and 47 of the Criminal Justice and Police Act 2001 making it an offence to place advertisements relating to prostitution in, or in the immediate vicinity of, a public telephone box) it appears that this is part of a concerted attempt to 'clear up Soho' and remove the last vestiges of sex work in the area (Hubbard 2002). In many ways, this exclusionary approaches chimes with the debates on the removal of homeless populations, squatters and 'street' people from areas considered ripe for corporate investment: in the neoliberal city, the divide between liberal and illiberal subjects finds sharp geographic expression (Smith 1996).

By tacitly and explicitly supporting these preventative measures, the British government has thus responded to criticism of existing vice laws by advocating the increased use of multi-agency solutions intended to 'design out' prostitution:

> Police success has come when they have worked with local authorities to design out prostitution through street lighting and traffic management designed to make the area as unattractive as possible to prostitutes and their clients. (MacLean, cited in *Hansard* 1994, col. 289)

This type of solution, embracing the technocratic logic of New Right law and order policy, implies that simplistic engineering responses may be sufficient to tackle a complex social problem. Specifically, rather than trying to address the causes of sex work, or providing 'exit' routes for women wishing to leave the industry, this behavioural discourse implies that sex work can be eliminated through measures which reduce the *opportunity* for sex workers to ply their trade. In essence, by seeking to reduce crime at the level of deterrence, not at the level of causation, such opportunity-reduction measures have been accused of changing behaviour patterns, not underlying social conditions (Fischer and Poland 1998).

One major issue here is therefore that attempts to eliminate prostitution in specific areas through campaigns of punitive policing (coupled with the use of CCTV, traffic management and other environmental interventions) run the risk of *displacement*, with sex work disappearing from one neighbourhood simply to resurface in another as prostitutes and clients react to changing environmental conditions. Accordingly, while some criminologists have suggested that prostitution is an opportunistic crime that can be designed out of existence (see especially Scott 2001), the overwhelming evidence suggests that authoritarian policing and increased surveillance in red-light districts merely serves to displace sex work. This usually takes one of two forms: *spatial* – where street beats move to an adjacent or nearby area – or *functional* – where sex workers resort to criminal activities including shoplifting, cheque fraud, robbery and so on. Though the latter does occur, the former is a more common response, and it is evident that periods of protracted anti-sex work activity encourage women to work in established beats in different towns or move their beats en masse to a new area of the same town. The anti-prostitution campaign orchestrated by the Muslim community in Birmingham is a case in point, displacing sex work from Balsall Heath to Rotton Park (Hubbard and Saunders 2003).

19

However, there are several examples where repressive policing has been combined with effective multi-agency intervention in street sex markets. Agencies involved in such strategies typically include local authorities, health trusts, Drug Action Teams (DATs), Drug and Alcohol Teams (DAATs) in Wales, the police, the criminal justice service, voluntary organisations, social services and probation. For instance, Birmingham City Council formed an inter-agency Partnership Action Group in December 2001, reporting to the member-level Street Prostitution Panel. The Partnership Group has met monthly and has implemented a wide range of measures designed to address the adverse effects of street prostitution on the local community in the North Edgbaston and Ladywood areas of the city. This group developed a Legal Proceedings Chart detailing legal action against kerb-crawlers, pimps and street prostitutes in collaboration with the police, the probation service and Birmingham magistrates court. Nuisance injunctions (using powers provided by section 222 of the Local Authority Act 1972) were taken against 20 street workers, permanently forbidding them from soliciting for the purposes of prostitution and entering the local area in question for one year. The civil legal proceedings were issued in Birmingham County Court during December 2002 and heard in February 2003, with a further court hearing in July 2003, when three women received a suspended sentence on condition that they obey the original order. The council also claims that it encourages street workers to self-refer to appropriate voluntary agencies for support and help to exit prostitution (http://www.together.gov.uk/article.asp?c=121&aid =1098). Birmingham claims its actions have resulted in a reduction in sex workers in the area from 50 to 10 on any given night.

As such, it seems more inventive programmes of community engagement where sex workers and community advocates seek to resolve issues may offer more sustainable solutions to resolving conflicts (O'Neill and Campbell 2003). The possibility that these might become integral components of a new approach to policing sex work is considered in the final section of this chapter, which explores the possibility that more sex worker-centred forms of policing and regulation may emerge to become dominant in the twenty-first century.

Towards the progressive policing of prostitution?

The weight of evidence suggests that punitive policing strategies and

(rethinking policy?)

coordinated zero tolerance campaigns appear to be of dubious value in offering a meaningful, long-term and balanced approach solution to the 'problem' of prostitution, entailing a huge outlay of resources for little demonstrable return. Moreover, such measures have also been opposed on broadly humanitarian and libertarian grounds by a growing number of campaigners – including sex worker unions, legal experts and feminist groups – who instead support the reform of prostitution laws. Given the constant campaigning of such groups, it is perhaps not surprising that comprehensive Home Office and Scottish Executive reviews of prostitution policy were begun in the UK in 2003–04, marking the first major re-examination of the issue since the Wolfenden Report in the 1950s. In contrast to Wolfenden, where the focus was initially on resolving issues of public morality (Self 2003), the role of legal regulation is currently being revisited in light of wider concerns about sex work in the UK. These concerns, *inter alia*, include:

- an increased concern amongst health care practitioners about the negative impact sex work has on the physical and mental health of prostitutes (Church *et al.* 2001);

- a growing awareness of the complex interaction of street drug and sex markets (May *et al.* 1999);

- increased anxiety among some residential communities about the negative impacts sex work has on quality of life (with cited nuisances being noise, increased traffic via kerb-crawling, discarded condoms, etc.) (Hubbard 1998);

- a heightened concern about the participation of children and minors in the sex industry, with media concern centring on issues of sex trafficking, enforced prostitution and migration (Phoenix 2002);

- an awareness that new communication technologies (i.e. the Internet, mobile telephones) allow for increased flexibility in working practices among prostitutes, with sex workers advertising their services online and in public spaces in ways that cause offence to some groups (Hubbard 2002);

- a rise in the number of so-called 'respectable' corporate entertainment clubs and US-style lap-dancing clubs being used by (female) prostitutes as spaces from which to sell sex (Hubbard 2002);

21

- a concern that existing vice laws are implemented in an ad hoc fashion, with many police forces seemingly unwilling to now enforce vice laws that they regard as inoperable or morally indefensible (as evidenced in official statistics for soliciting, whereby arrest, prosecution and conviction rates dropped from around 10,000 in 1990 to less than 3,000 by 2002).

In the words of the then Home Secretary, David Blunkett, the Home Office review was thus intended as 'a starting point for the development of a realistic and coherent strategy to deal with prostitution and its serious detrimental consequences for individuals and communities' (Home Office 2004a: 3). Beginning with the assertion that 'many of the laws relating to prostitution are outdated, confusing and ineffective', this document has provided a much-needed platform for discussing possible changes to legislation.

While the flurry of publicity created by the Home Office consultation *Paying the Price?* provoked some unfortunate media reaction, it did stimulate a large number of public and private responses. Among these, it was interesting to note submissions from the police themselves, not least the submission from the Association of Chief Police Officers (ACPO), which effectively sets prostitution policing priorities in England and Wales. In their submission, it was noted that 'Police Forces … are currently operating in a policy vacuum', not least in relation to the increased number of street sex workers addicted to class A drugs and the increased involvement of criminal gangs in trafficking and exploitation (ACPO 2004: 7). Yet ACPO continued to assert the need for vice law, suggesting that:

> Prostitution is often seen, erroneously, as a victimless crime [but] the most obvious, but generally the most neglected, victim is the prostitute. Prostitutes may be exploited, abused and physically and mentally harmed. Too often individual damage has been seen as an 'occupational hazard', but such an attitude can have no place in modern Britain, and especially not in any police strategy seeking to address the problems caused by prostitution. (ACPO 2004: 13)

The fact the police themselves have become outspoken critics of sex work policy suggests that legal reform is imminent. At the very least, it appears there is a need for a simplified approach to policing and regulating vice, given there are actually currently around 35 pieces of legislation that can be invoked in relation to sex work.

Yet in spite of an emerging consensus in favour of reform, there is considerable disagreement as to the most appropriate policy solution. Some have argued for legalisation and point to the experiences of Nevada in the US or German Eros Centres, where prostitution is regulated according to labour laws (see Hubbard 1999). Others have lobbied for the outright decriminalisation of the selling and buying of sexual services (as in New Zealand) or its selective decriminalisation introduced through the establishment of carefully managed 'toleration zones' (an idea proposed in Lothian member of the Scottish Parliament Margo Macdonald's Prostitution Tolerance Zones (Scotland) Bill 2003). Yet others have argued for a more interventionist approach (often termed *regulationism*) that would offer multi-agency support to sex workers, offering 'routes out' of sex work alongside an increasing criminalisation of clients. Sweden, where clients purchasing sex have been outlawed in an attempt to eradicate prostitution, is often cited in this context (Kilvington *et al.* 2001; Scoular 2004).

Weighing up these different approaches, the Scottish Executive Group (2004) concluded the law should be changed to repeal the criminalisation of soliciting per se and replaced with an offence targeting offensive behaviour or conduct arising from a prostitution-related sexual transaction (whether caused by purchaser or seller). However, the Home Office consultation for England and Wales is considering a wider range of policy options (outlined in Table 1.1). Though the Home Office is careful not to discount any particular possible policy change, the thrust of the document suggests that decriminalisation (meaning all reference to prostitution would be removed from criminal law) is unlikely and that legalisation would be difficult to implement and enforce. Against this, much of the publicity surrounding *Paying the Price?* makes play of the allusion to the adoption of managed areas or toleration zones, following the Dutch model of *tippelzones*. While successive British governments have claimed that they have no intention of decriminalising or legalising activities connected to prostitution either 'as a matter of general application or in specific geographical areas' (MacLean, cited in *Hansard* 1994, col. 289), the idea that managed zones might become a key part of the legal framework surrounding sex work is becoming a real possibility. In essence, the aim of a managed zone is to physically restrict street prostitution to an agreed non-residential area. It should be designed to minimise any harm to communities (residential and business) while maximising the opportunity to provide protection and support services to women working on the streets. Supporters argue that a managed area should help address the causes of prostitution

Table 1.1 Policing street prostitution: the Home Office view

	Outcomes	Problems
Continue to enforce laws prohibiting soliciting, kerb-crawling and pimping	Temporarily removes sex work from the streets – long-term impact if combined with follow-up programmes to educate clients and/or help sex workers exit	May displace sex work to new locations and compel sex workers to work more to pay fines; kerb-crawling legislation has little deterrent or rehabilitative value; expensive (c. £176m per annum)
Increased enforcement and a highly visible police presence	Discourages both prostitutes and clients from negotiating on streets; increased surveillance would reduce all types of criminality in a locale	Intensive use of time of police, CPS, courts, probation services, etc.; possibly create the perception that the area is unsafe
Serving restraining orders/ civil injunctions against sex workers and kerb-crawlers	Effectively controls and deters the activities of large numbers of sex workers and clients in a particular area	Labour-intensive and costly to document individuals and activities; legality questioned in some cases; may prevent workers accessing key services
Closing streets and alleys, diverting traffic or introducing lighting	Increases the difficulty for clients to find and negotiate with sex workers	Potential disbenefits to local car-owners; slowing traffic may be conducive to kerb-crawling; expensive to implement; results in displacement
Relaxing the regulation of indoor prostitution venues via licensing	Gives street workers incentive to relocate to indoor venues; reduction of sexual trafficking and exploitation; improved data on number of working women	High compliance costs could result in businesses remaining outside the legal system; may be perceived as condoning prostitution; shifts burden of responsibility to local authorities

Treating sex work establishments as legitimate businesses (decriminalisation)	Should encourage improved working conditions; benefits for the taxpayer through increased national insurance contributions	High compliance costs could result in businesses remaining outside the legal system; loss of anonymity for workers; businesses could fall into hands of criminal gangs
Mediating conflicts between prostitutes and the community	Keeps sex work away from the areas of highest citizen complaints, or from engaging in the most offensive behaviours	Difficult to get sex workers, clients and communities to adhere to agreements
Increased preventative measures	More systematic provision of general information to raise awareness of the dangers of prostitution and the ways in which young people can be 'groomed' into it; more specific provision for those who may be at particular risk	Resource implications for social services; significant costs attached to meeting the needs of children and young people in terms of refuge accommodation, health care, and other services required to prevent them from becoming vulnerable to coercion into prostitution
Managed areas	Reduces nuisance complaints; increases the police ability to monitor street prostitution and related crime	Remoteness might reduce demand for sex work; costs borne by members of the community where a managed area is designated; possibly ineffective in reducing nuisance complaints or harm to prostitutes; implies that police condone prostitution

Adapted from Home Office (2004b), with reference to Scott (2001).

and assist those involved with returning to legitimate forms of work. Of course, in order to work, the implementation of a managed zone requires a zero tolerance approach to prostitution taking place in any area outside of the zone, meaning that there may not be major savings in terms of police time and resources (Clark *et al.* 2004).

While managed zones have many advantages, their siting remains critical, with many attempts at designating such zones having been thwarted by local opposition. However, after a protracted period of consultation, Liverpool City Council designated a managed zone in 2005, and pressed the Home Office to officially recognise the concept of a managed zone (see Chapter 3). While the Liverpool example suggests that managed zones offer potential for a more cost-effective and woman-centred form of policing, it needs to be noted that previously designated zones (most notably that in Edinburgh) have been abandoned in the face of local pressures, and that the stability of a zone cannot be guaranteed as its socio-spatial character changes over time. Given this, it may be that managed zones will not become a key feature of the urban landscape of the UK, and that the Home Office continues to argue for rigidly enforcing – and even toughening – the laws around sex work and sexual exploitation. However, it appears that there may be a move towards a more sex worker-centred form of policing, involving closer liaison with service-providers (particular those providing exit strategies) (Aris and Pitcher 2004).

Some of these multi-agency approaches have been funded by the Home Office through specific sex work initiatives. One example was the Liverpool Linx Project (2001), which was designed to address the needs of street sex workers. This involved the appointment of a community liaison and mediation officer who worked to negotiate between the community and sex workers over points of conflict (for instance, by brokering an agreement whereby women agreed not to work near a school and to disposes of sharps and needles responsibly). This officer also communicated the needs of sex work women to the police, providing training sessions to the police where sex work issues were considered. Via the same initiative, information on violent or coercive punters were passed onto the police from sex workers via 'Ugly Mug' sheets (Penfold *et al.* 2004). In Manchester, two prostitution referral workers funded by the local council encourage access to drug treatment, liaise with local colleges to provide basic education to sex workers, offer information on debt, benefits and other services and have set up a mentoring and befriending programme. Between January and December 2003 these outreach referral workers made over 1,700 client contacts, seeing 300 individual street-based sex workers.

Significantly, this programme (and ones like it) are made available at the point of arrest. Moreover, there is increasing scope for the police to refer those workers charged with soliciting (or breach of the peace offences in Scotland) to Diversion from Prosecution Schemes, with the introduction of conditional cautions under the Criminal Justice Act 2003 allowing police to consider striking cautions from a worker's record if she attends named services.

Here, it is notable that the Crime and Disorder Act 1998, as amended by the Police Reform Act 2002, placed a duty on specific agencies to work together to tackle crime and disorder and the misuse of drugs in their local areas. Working in partnership the responsible authorities are required to undertake a triennial audit to identify the extent of the problems within their community, and to develop strategies that deal effectively with them. Such strategies should address the needs of the community through the enforcement of the civil and criminal law to reduce the anti-social behaviour and criminality associated with sex work, including exploitation through pimping, and also through the provision of support services, to help individuals off the streets and out of prostitution. ACPO (2004) hence argue that there is little case for managed zones but, on the other hand, there may be a case for creating 'priority action zones' where partnership resources are concentrated; prostitutes are given welfare and health support and environmental resources are implemented to reduce the harmful effects on communities. At the same time, ACPO (2004) also stresses the value and importance of gathering intelligence against organised exploiters, noting that policing strategies that simply displace sex work from one locale to another actually play into the hands of pimps and traffickers. They go on to argue that 'prosecution should usually only be used where there is evidence of a persistent and voluntary return to prostitution after exit opportunities have been provided', stating that the principal aim of policing prostitution should be to ensure workers receive the normal protection in law for crimes committed against them, and normal opportunities to receive healthcare and therefore minimise harm to themselves (ACPO 2004: 19).

The fact that ACPO recognises the need to work inventively with other agencies to prevent exploitation and violence against women suggests that the police may become only one of a series of agencies who work collectively to address issues of individual and social harm connected to sex work. Instances of inter-agency working between outreach agencies and the police funded through the Crime Reduction Programme suggests such that such cooperation can produce significant outcomes for little financial outlay. For instance,

27

Penfold *et al.* (2004) review the formalisation of the Ugly Mugs scheme in Liverpool through the cooperation of the police and sex work outreach teams on Merseyside, suggesting that this has proved an extremely cost-effective way for the police to reduce violent attacks on workers, gather intelligence and better understand the needs of the sex work community. It remains to be seen, however, whether successful long-term cooperation between the police and other agencies can be developed across the gamut of services so vital to providing support to sex worker women, including drop-in centres, safe-houses, outreach workers, vocational training, health and educational welfare schemes and probation services.

Conclusion

British vice law – like that extant in many other nations – is contradictory and complex. Avowedly constructed to serve the public and protect the vulnerable, it nonetheless stands accused of constructing gendered imbalances which reaffirm men's right to buy sex while organising the terms on which sex is sold. Moreover, this chapter has suggested that policing is implicated in a number of significant ways in the production of sex worker vulnerabilities. Indeed, while one of the main roles of vice policing is to offer sex workers protection, many sex workers fear and distrust the police. In such ways, the policing of sex work in the UK reproduces sex workers' status as second-class citizens: while citizens fear criminality, sex workers fear both police and criminals. Irrespective of these critiques, the legal position of sex work has remained consistent for nearly fifty years. Yet while the law regarding prostitution is clear, the *application* of the law is not. Accordingly, it is possible to detail discrepancies in the way sex work is policed between different police forces, towns and even beats. This inconsistency and variation serves to create a series of difficulties for those working in the sex industry, who may find their activities tolerated in an area one week, yet be persistently arrested the next. Likewise, this inconsistency puzzles those residents who live in areas of sex work, particularly those who feel sex work blights their everyday life. Though pressures for an overhaul of the law have mounted for decades, in the absence of serious legal reform the dominant trend has been for the police to pursue high-profile 'crackdowns' on sex work as and when pressures dictate, cooperating with local authorities to 'design out' sex work. The increased use of anti-social behaviour legislation (notably

ASBOs) against sex workers is yet another symptom of the uneven yet often highly repressive approach being adopted by the state and law. Though this type of approach accords with the logics of zero tolerance and urban neoliberalism, its efficacy has been increasingly brought into question by sex work advocates and policy-makers alike. As such, recent moves towards legal reform hint at a new era of policing in which cooperation and multi-agency working become the norm. If this is the case, the role of the police in shaping practices and patterns of sex work may be diminished: instead we will see a situation where police intervene in sex work markets only to prevent the real crimes of client violence, sexual exploitation and coercion – not consensual sex between clients and workers.

References

ACPO (2004) *Policing Prostitution: ACPO's Policy, Strategy and Operational Guidelines for Dealing with Exploitation and Abuse through Prostitution*. Gloucester: ACPO.

Aris, R. and Pitcher, J. (2004) *Evaluation of Coventry SWISH Arrest Referral Scheme for Sex Workers: Final Report*. London: Terrence Higgins Trust.

Benson, C. and Matthews, R. (1995) *The National Vice Squad Survey*. Middlesex University: Centre for Criminology.

Benson, C. and Matthews, R. (2000) 'Police and prostitution: vice squads in Britain', in R. Weitzer, (ed.) *Sex for Sale: Prostitution, Pornography, and the Sex Industry*. New York: Routledge.

Blomley, N. (2005) 'Flowers in the bathtub: boundary crossings at the private-public divide', *Geoforum*, 28 (1): 28–49.

Campbell, R. and Storr, M. (2001) 'Challenging the kerb crawler rehabilitation programme', *Feminist Review*, 67 (1): 94–108.

Campbell, R., Coleman, S. and Torkington, P. (1996) *Street Prostitution in Inner City Liverpool*. Final report of the Abercromby Prostitution Project, Liverpool Hope University College, Applied Research Centre.

Church, S., Henderson, M., Barnard, M. and Hart, G. (2001) 'Violence by clients towards female prostitutes', *British Medical Journal*, 322: 524–5.

Clark, P., Bellis, M., Cook, P. and Toque, K. (2004) *Consultation for a Managed Zone for Sex Trade Workers in Liverpool: Executive Summary*. Liverpool John Moores University Centre for Public Health.

Duncan, S. (1994) 'Disrupting the surface of order and innocence: towards a theory of sexuality and the law', *Feminist Legal Studies* 2 (1): 3–28.

Edwards, S.M. (1997) 'The legal regulation of prostitution: a human rights issue', in G. Scambler and S. Scambler (eds), *Rethinking Prostitution: Purchasing Sex in the 1990s*. London: Routledge.

English Collective of Prostitutes (1997) 'Campaigning for legal change', in G. Scambler and S. Scambler (eds), *Rethinking Prostitution*. London: Routledge.

Fischer, B. and Poland, B. (1998) 'Exclusion, risk and social control: reflections on community policing and public health', *Geoforum*, 29: 187–97.

Hester, M. and Westmarland, N. (2004) *Tackling Street Prostitution: Towards an Holistic Approach*, Home Office Research Study 279. London: Home Office Research Development and Statistics Directorate.

Home Office (2001) *Circular 27/2001 – Criminal Justice and Police Act 2001 Section 46 and 47: Advertisements Relating to Prostitution*. London: HMSO.

Home Office (2004a) *Paying the Price?* London: HMSO.

Home Office (2004b) *The Development of a Coordinated Strategy on Prostitution*, Partial Regulatory Impact Assessment. London: HMSO.

Hubbard, P. (1997) 'Red-light districts and toleration zones: geographies of female street prostitution in England and Wales', *Area*, 29: 129–40.

Hubbard, P. (1998) 'Community action and the displacement of street prostitutes: evidence from British cities', *Geoforum*, 26: 269–86.

Hubbard, P. (1999) *Sex and the City: Geographies of Prostitution in the Urban West*. London: Ashgate.

Hubbard, P. (2002) 'Maintaining family values? Cleansing the streets of sex advertising', *Area*, 34: 353–60.

Hubbard, P. (2004) 'Revenge and injustice in the neoliberal city: uncovering masculinist agendas', *Antipode*, 36: 665–82.

Hubbard, P. and Sanders, T. (2003) 'Making space for sex work', *International Journal of Urban and Regional Research* 27: 75–89.

Hughes, G. (1997) 'Policing late modernity: changing strategies of crime management in contemporary Britain', in N. Jewson and S. MacGregor (eds), *Transforming Cities: Contested Governance and New Spatial Divisions*. London: Routledge.

Kilvington, L., Day, S. and Ward, H. (2001) 'Prostitution policy in Europe: a time of change?', *Feminist Review*, 47: 78–93.

Lopez-Jones, N. (1990) 'Guilty until proven innocent', *New Law Journal*, 140 (8): 658–59.

Lowman, J. (1992) 'Street prostitution control: some Canadian reflections of the Finsbury Park experience', *British Journal of Criminology*, 32: 1–16.

Manchester City Council (2004) 'Anti-social Behaviour Order Prevents Prostitute from Soliciting Anywhere in England and Wales' 15 June. Online at: http://www.manchester.gov.uk/news/2004/june/wales.htm.

Matthews, R. (1993) *Kerb-Crawling, Prostitution and Multi-Agency Policing*, Police Research Group Crime Prevention Unit Series Paper No. 43. London.

Matthews, R. (1997) 'Developing more effective strategies for curbing prostitution', in R.V. Clarke (ed.), *Situational Crime Prevention*, 2nd edn. New York: Harrow & Henson.

May, T., Edmunds, M. and Hough, M. (1999) *Street Business: The Links between Sex and Drug Markets*, Police Research Series Paper 118. London: HMSO.

McKeganey, N. and Barnard, M. (1996) *Sex Work on the Streets, Prostitutes and their Clients*. Buckingham: Open University Press.

Merrifield, A. (2000) 'The dialectics of dystopia: disorder and zero tolerance in the city', *International Journal of Urban and Regional Research*, 24: 473–89.

Mort, F. (1998) 'Cityscapes: consumption, masculinity and the mapping of London since 1950', *Urban* Studies, 35 (5): 889–907.

O'Neill, M. and Campbell, R. (2000) 'Love for sale: the politics of prostitution in Stoke', in T. Edensor (ed.), *Reclaiming Stoke-on-Trent: Leisure, Space and Identity in the Potteries*. Staffordshire University Press.

O'Neill, M. and Campbell, R. (2001) *Working Together to Creat Change – Report for Walsall South HAZ*. See www.safelysoapbox.com.

O'Neill, M. and Campbell, R. (2003) *Working Together to Create Change: Conducting Participatory Action Research (PAR) with Communities Affected by Prostitution*. Paper presented at British Sociological Association Conference 2003: Social Futures, York University. (See also http://www.safetysoapbox.com for full report and executive summary.)

Papayanis, M. (2000) 'Sex and the revanchist city: zoning out pornography in New York, *Environment and Planning D – Society and Space*, 18: 341–54.

Penfold, C., Hunter, G., Campbell, R. and Barham, L. (2004) 'Tackling client violence in female street prostitution: inter-agency working between outreach agencies and the police', *Policing and Society*, 14 (4): 365–79.

Phoenix, J. (2002) 'In the name of protection: youth prostitution policy reforms in England and Wales', *Critical Social Policy*, 22: 353–75.

Raco, M. (2003) 'Remarketing place and securitising space: urban regeneration and the strategies, tactics and practices of policing in the UK', *Urban Studies*, 40 (8): 1869–87.

Sager, T. (2005) 'Street Watch: concept and practice', *British Journal of Criminology*, 45 (1): 98–112.

Sanders, T. (2004) 'The risks of street prostitution: punters, police and protestors', *Urban Studies*, 41 (9): 1703–18.

Scott, M. (2001) *Street Prostitution*. US Dept of Justice, Dept of Community Oriented Policing.

Scottish Executive (2004) *Being Outside: Constructing a Response to Street Prostitution*. Edinburgh: SEEP.

Scoular, J. (2004) 'Criminalising "Punters": evaluating the Swedish position on prostitution', *Journal of Social Welfare and Family Law*, 26: 195–210.

Self, H. (2003) *The Fallen Daughters of Eve*. London: Frank Cass.

Sharpe, K. (1998) *Red Light, Blue Light: Prostitutes, Punters and Police*. London: Ashgate.

Smith, N. (1996). *The New Urban Frontier: Gentrification and the Revanchist City*. London: Routledge.

Symanski, R. (1981) *The Immoral Landscape: Female Prostitution in Western Societies*. London: Butterworths.

Weidner, R. (2001) *'I Won't Do Manhattan': Causes and Consequences of a Decline in Street Prostitution*. New York: LFB Publishing.

Wilson, J. and Kelling, G. (1982) 'Broken windows', *The Atlantic Monthly*, 29 March: 29–38.

Wolfenden, J. (1957) *Report of the Departmental Committee on Homosexual Offences and Prostitution*, Cmnd 247. London: HMSO.

Chapter 2

Street sex work and local communities: creating discursive spaces for *genuine* consultation and inclusion

Maggie O'Neill and Rosie Campbell

The impact of street sex work on 'communities' and associated complaints from sections of residents and neighbourhoods is a key factor cited by authorities and national government for developing policies and strategies to address street sex work. In *Paying the Price: A Consultation Paper on Prostitution* published by the Home Office in 2004 the [then] Home Secretary David Blunkett states

> The consultation paper is intended as the starting point for the development of a realistic and coherent strategy to deal with prostitution and its serious consequences for individuals and communities ... forced to suffer the unwanted approaches of kerb crawlers, and the antisocial behaviour and drug dealing street prostitution attracts. (2004: 4)

Blunkett goes on to locate the issues in the context of wider policy-making and the promotion of civic renewal and community safety. Yet, despite this salience, the research literature on communities and street sex work is very much a developing one (Hubbard 1999; O'Neill and Campbell 2001; O'Neill *et al.* 2004; Sanders 2004; Sagar 2005).

A more complex understanding of community responses and consultation with communities is important particularly in the light of Home Office-funded research (Hester and Westmarland 2004) which found that community mediation and liaison models could have some success in addressing community concerns. This chapter argues that more constructive and inclusive consultation is required to develop policies and practices that promote civic renewal and active citizenship. Our argument is supported by drawing upon research we conducted in Walsall in 2001–02.

Walsall South Health Action Zone (HAZ) commissioned the research having identified street prostitution as a significant issue for residents in terms of their well-being and community safety. A range of concerns were expressed by residents including: women working outside of residences; women working outside of places of worship; the volume of cars in the area; children being exposed to inappropriate behaviour and practices; the 'shame' of the area being labelled a 'red light area' and the overall physical/environmental 'decline' in the area over the last few years; the presence of pimps and drug dealers in the area; the erosion of community safety: fear and not feeling safe (especially for some women and children). Residents also expressed concerns for the safety and welfare of street sex workers themselves.

The commissioners hoped the research would provide: baseline data to better understand street sex work in Walsall; and a strategic action plan in consultation and collaboration with the local communit(ies) for 'managing' sex work. Over a period of twelve months, the research team[1] met and interviewed local residents and community groups, and women and young women working both on- and off-street using participatory methodologies including participatory arts. The combination of participatory action research and participatory arts has been defined by O'Neill and Webster (2005) as 'creative consultation' and by O'Neill (2001) as 'ethno-mimesis'.[2]

The report, *Working Together to Create Change*, and related exhibition launched at the New Art Gallery Walsall (see www.safteysoapbox. com) provide an example of the representational appropriation of neighbourhoods by the inhabitants themselves as an oppositional political movement to reappropriate and redraw their neighbourhood spaces (O'Neill *et al.* 2004).

In the process of the research, we sought to provide safe spaces for sex workers and residents to contribute their experiences, and hopes for managing sex work in their residential spaces. In the process of this work, they/we developed greater understanding of the scale and politics of the neighbourhood, but also particular issues both ideological and material that surround the sex work economy.

Most importantly, the work served to develop reflexive knowledge and understanding across the resident–sex worker divide that marks much of contemporary research on sex work in urban residential areas.

Communities affected by prostitution

In many communities, residents have felt that the impact of street sex work has reached intolerable levels and have canvassed agencies, predominantly the police or local authorities, to take measures. Some residents/communities have taken more direct forms of action (Campbell *et al.* 1995; Hubbard 1999; O'Neill *et al.* 2000). In response attempts have been made by agencies to assess objectively the impact of street sex work on residential communities. Matthews (1993) reported that increased street sex work and kerb-crawling in Streatham, London was associated with a growth of incivilities such as noise and volume of traffic – but also that 'various areas of private space were regularly infringed and defiled. These issues came increasingly to dominate everyday life in the neighbourhood – particularly for women – more than anything else, most noticeably harassment on the street intensified' (Matthews 1993: 1).

The All-Party Parliamentary Report on Street Prostitution (Matthews 1996) stressed the adverse effects that street sex work can have on communities:

> We have become increasingly aware in the course of listening to the evidence, of the ways in which street prostitution, as currently practised, has adversely affected a number of communities … For those who are affected, the price they pay in terms of nuisance and public safety is enormous. (p. 39)

The Group heard evidence from several residents associations who reported the negative impact street prostitution and kerb-crawling had on their communities. The South Yorkshire Standing Forum on Prostitution community consultation survey (1995) collected information about residents' and employees' feelings regarding street sex work in their areas. Two-thirds felt uncomfortable about sex work in the area where they work/live and some felt it to be a continual public nuisance with significant environmental effects such as noise, traffic and litter. Yet a majority of respondents stated that they were not affected or affected only a little by street sex work in the area where they live/work.

Benson and Matthews (1995), as part of a survey of vice squad activity in England, found that residents were primarily concerned with noise, litter and the activities of kerb-crawlers, especially in relation to the harassment of female residents.

Hubbard (1999) identifies protests in Balsall Heath against sex work as NIMBYism ('not in my back yard' syndrome) as part of the need to purify and order public spaces and exclude the 'threatening others' (p. 152) and as a way of 'managing risk' (p. 155).

Reports from residents groups nationally who have been affected by street sex work identify a similar range of problems and risks associated with street sex work and kerb-crawling. These include:

- noise: from cars, kerb-crawlers and disputes between different parties;
- litter: used condoms, tissues, discarded syringes;
- increases in traffic;
- intimidation of residents and fear of victimisation;
- increase in associated criminal activities: drug dealing, pimping, robbery;
- harassment of female residents;
- male residents constantly solicited by prostitutes;
- disregard for private and communal property, e.g. use of public and private spaces such as gardens or alleyways for doing 'business'.

More recently, the Home Office consultation document *Paying the Price* (2004) and the Scottish Executive document *Being Outside* (2004) reproduce these concerns by residents and communities affected by street sex work.

Contingent communities: renewal, regeneration and impact of media discourses

Before we explore the responses and experiences of residents it is useful to take a moment to define what we mean by 'community'. In *Paying the Price* and *Being Outside* the concept of community tends to be used in a homogenous, solid sense – set against the prostitute or sex work. However, the complexities of what we mean by 'community' and prostitute/prostitution/sex work need to be unpacked to generate a better understanding and to inform social policy. We focus here upon generating a better understanding of 'community'.

The ideal type of community is marked by a shared sense of place, shared interests and shared identities – 'even though the precise nature of the sharing could vary considerably between regions and over time' (Crow 2002: 71). However, researchers concur that the ideal type of 'solid' community (typified, for example, in mining communities) no longer exists and that the communities in which we live and to which we belong are contingent, due in part to processes of labour reorganisation and restructuring, individualisation, globalisation, the processes of migration both forced and free, and the constitution of later modernity/postmodernity.

For Ulrich Beck community is less tied to place and he provides a hopeful reading of this development through new 'niches of activity and identity', allowing a 'new mode of conducting and arranging life' (1998: 35). For Bauman (2001) the paradox of the contemporary world is that there is a fascination with community while at the same time people are increasingly aware of the fragmentary nature of community relationships. 'Togetherness' has become fragmentary and episodic, and so contemporary communities become more contingent. Beck and Bauman direct us to new ways in which both individual and collective identities are formed, and Bauman problematises 'community' to arrive at 'forms of togetherness'. The forms 'togetherness' takes can be mobile (such as in a busy street); tempered (through common purpose); manifest (unloading the burden of individuality, for example a football crowd/disco); postulated (imagined community of nations/races/classes); and matrix – like (marked by impermanent sociability). Communities are also defined through the concept of neighborhood as a defined geographic space or ward where residents live, for example, in our study, the Caldmore, Palfrey and Pleck neighbourhoods (wards).

The communities, neighbourhoods and groups we worked with in Walsall could be mapped onto Bauman's categories as tempered, manifest, postulated and matrix-like. Their concerns around street sex work were pivotal – some members no longer lived in the geographical area but had businesses or worked there. Some had lived for generations in the specific area of street sex work; many were migrants of South Asian origin. Some of the sex workers we interviewed lived in the area, others travelled in from Wolverhampton, Stoke, Birmingham and other areas in the Borough. Many people identified strongly with the geographical area in spatial terms as the area they lived or worked in with a sense of pride as well as the need to reclaim some sense of control over both public and private spaces and places.

Urban renewal and regeneration

A central issue for residents was the importance of urban renewal and regeneration initiatives to improve and reclaim spaces that were used for street sex work. However, sex workers were not considered as being possible contributors.

Sex workers are a marginalised, stigmatised and relatively muted group in urban renewal initiatives – they are not consulted but seen by local authorities and criminal justice agencies as 'out of place', described by Hubbard and Hall (1998) as 'displaced and excluded from the reconstruction and re-imagining of urban spaces by an idealized white middle-class hegemonic notion of urbanity' (p. 110). Residents,[3] on the other hand, are more likely to be consulted in plans to redesign and regenerate urban spaces in current times. For example, in Stoke-on-Trent in 1999 a key task of the city council's original Single Regeneration bid was to respond to the demands of the local community to improve street lighting and reduce the levels of prostitution and street crime (O'Neill *et al*. 2000: 11).

Bianchini and Ghilardi (2004) discuss the concept of 'neighbourhood' culture stating that 'neighbourhoods are understood to be the result of collective work reflecting the processes of appropriation and production of social and cultural space by the groups of which they are made up' (p. 238). To what extent are the 'out of place' a part of this process? Sex workers are of course members of neighbourhoods, sometimes the very neighbourhoods they work in. As a marginalised 'group' operating in liminal urban spaces they are rarely if ever consulted in the process of the collective work taking place to renew and regenerate urban spaces as part of New Labour's vision for the future of multi-ethnic Britain, marked by Neighbourhood Renewal, the development of local strategic partnerships as the drivers behind local and regional social policy and Community Cohesion initiatives (see www.neighbourhood.gov.uk and www.homeoffice.gov. uk/comrace/cohesion/).

Media discourses and attitudes to sex workers

Residents' perceptions and attitudes to sex workers working in their area are heavily influenced by local and national media reporting. Media messages inevitably feed into the local imagination and media reports can provide powerful symbolic representations of 'prostitutes' and 'prostitution'. Representative examples include labels for female sex workers such as 'women of the night,' or 'vice girls', who work in 'the vice ridden area' or 'street of shame' adding to a 'soaring vice epidemic' or 'the sex for sale racket' in the 'capital of vice' (see O'Neill *et al*. 2000). Simplistic notions of sex workers are often reinforced, i.e. that all sex workers have pimps and that all residents are hostile to sex workers. There is little space for complexity. Media representations such as these help to establish in the public imagination an approach to understanding and thinking about sex work as a social problem, in Hubbard's words 'polluting the moral order of the community' (1999: 164). The prostitute is an abject 'other', a body object of fascination and disgust.

Thus the sex worker is deemed a problem to be controlled, regulated and kept under continual surveillance (Corbin 1990). The rise of the prostitute's rights movement and the unionisation of some sex workers (see Chapter 3 by Ana Lopes) has challenged these unidirectional discourses to create a space for considering the social inclusion and citizenship of sex workers within the context of social policy and practice at local and national levels. Researchers and activists have helped to further these debates by using participatory methods and respecting and valuing the voices and lived experiences of sex workers across the trajectory of sex work from street to 'salon' (see Chapter 6 by Laura Agustín).

Working together to create change in Walsall: the local context

It is perhaps important to say a few words about the local context in terms of indicators of poverty and social exclusion. Street sex work is synonymous with poverty; research has shown throughout history that economic need is the bottom line for routes into street sex work. The urban spaces in which street sex work takes place are distinctive in their demographic and topographic make up. The Walsall Poverty Profile (Griffiths 1999) commissioned by Walsall Metropolitan Borough Council and Walsall Health Authority provides a very clear picture of poverty and indicators of social exclusion in the borough.[4] The major agencies are actively involved in combating these indicators through various activities, research, measures and the working of the Anti-Poverty Strategy. Geographically, the profile found particular concentrations of deprivation in Caldmore/Pleck, Birchills through to Blakenhall and Beechadale (p. 19). Our consultation research was conducted in relation to the Caldmore, Palfrey and Pleck areas.

The authors are committed to research that seeks to develop processes of social inclusion for sex workers as well as residents affected by sex working. Our chosen methodology for the research was participatory action research (PAR). PAR develops social knowledge that is interventionary in partnership with communities; it seeks to promote social change. Challenging prostitution inevitably involves challenging the causes of sex work that are embedded in poverty; the role and position of women in society (women's bodies sell, and men will always find money for sex); the ability and possibility for adults (usually men) to coerce young people and women into sex work; and, for some sex workers, the need to fund drug use.

Spaces of sex work

There was a consensus in our interviews and ethnographic work that historically the Caldmore area has been the area where street sex work has taken place and been concentrated over time. Local people's views varied but on the whole the view was that street sex work had taken place there for at least 30 years. It was reported that street soliciting had, between 1998 and 2000, been dispersed into the Palfrey area and to a lesser degree into Pleck. Very recently the authors are aware that street sex work has reduced dramatically due in part to the impact of ASBO legislation.[5]

While specific corners were worked, some women moved around the area. Residents pointed out that it was not simply the immediate locations where women stand to pick up clients that is of concern but also locations in the area that were used by some sex workers and their clients to 'do business'. These locations included, for example, car park areas, gardens and alleyways.

Methodology: participatory action research and participatory arts

Using PAR methodology, the research sought to develop a strategic action plan to look at ways of managing street sex work in the borough through consultation and collaboration with all those involved and affected by street sex work – residents, community groups, women and young people involved in sex work, statutory and voluntary agencies.

The research aimed to work with all local people, including sex workers, and was committed to principles of community governance and partnership development which are at the heart of the principles underpinning Walsall South HAZ. Involving local communities is vital to ensure the sustainability and progress of the research outcomes in order to take forward the recommendations.

A key recommendation was that the community(ies) (and this includes sex workers) should be included in the future progress and outcomes of the research.

PAR is rooted in the following principles:

• Partnership responses to sex work includes all those involved, thus facilitating shared ownership of the development and outcomes of the research.

• Innovative ways of consulting local people are devised, for example through community arts workshops.

• Processes of monitoring and evaluation are built into the research outcomes.

Participatory arts (PA) or community arts 'attempts to give people the tools to be active, confident participators and creators, to help communities and individuals to discover, develop and use their abilities to express themselves through creativity' (O'Neill and Webster 2005). The combination of PAR and PA defined by O'Neill and Webster as 'creative consultation' is an approach to research and consultation that aims to incorporate the voices and views of communities directly into the process of policy-making and service delivery.

How did we carry out the research?

We assembled all local data and research on sex work and identified relevant local agencies in order to obtain existing research and policy documents relating to sex work in Walsall. We designed our research tools, trained the community researchers (residents who had volunteered to help us conduct the research) and conducted the fieldwork phase of the research with our group of community co-researchers. Fieldwork was made up of agency interviews; involvement from communities and residents that includes community networking and interviewing ethnographic principles; sex worker involvement, networking and interviews; focus groups; and creative consultation using art workshops. Art workshops were led by Kate Green, an arts worker based at Walsall Youth Arts. Three sets of workshops took place with residents, street sex workers and young people who were residents. The authors were present at workshops documenting as well as supporting the arts worker and participants. The outcomes of the arts workshops were exhibited at the Walsall New Art Gallery and are currently archived there.

Findings: living with street sex work in Walsall

Key agency responses included both enforcement and environmental approaches. The police took a three-pronged approach:

- Respond to residents.
- Prosecute kerb-crawlers.
- Prosecute women.

Responses from local area committees in collaboration with Crime Prevention Initiatives included:

- locating CCTV cameras in the Caldmore area;
- designing out the risks and littering by putting up fences and gates on some car parks and other security measures.

Together these key strategic responses had contributed to a dispersal of sex work to a wider area encompassing the Pleck and Palfrey areas as well as the 'traditional' Caldmore area.

Alongside these responses there was an investment in welfarist approaches – health and social care for street sex workers. A sex work support project was commissioned by the health authorities to carry out outreach on two evenings a week. The service adopted a harm reduction approach and offered safer sex supplies/advice, safety advice and a violent attackers report scheme, drugs harm reduction information, sexual health information/advice, a listening ear, housing information and referral to a range of services. The project worked with a local drug service to offer a beat-based drop-in one evening per week. At the time of the research further follow up and support work was commissioned. A voluntary sector service based on Christian principles also delivered outreach and support.

Consultation with residents

The researchers took the view that residents and sex workers were the 'experts' in the local area. Moreover, there was an ethos that through processes of consultation and inclusion of residents' voices all researchers could work in partnership with statutory and voluntary agencies and dedicated sex work projects to reach a pragmatic strategic response to better 'manage' sex work in the Walsall South HAZ area, thus also preventing processes of displacement that simply lead to moving the 'problem' from one area to another.

This section is organised into a series of subsections that describe and analyse our findings. The issues that are raised in each subsection are dealt with in the order of priority given to them by residents. Levels of priority are based on the extent of feeling with which residents describe a particular issue and the number of times the issue is raised.

The following subsections emerged from the combination of ethnographic work (participant and participant observation), focus groups and in-depth interviews with residents. The research findings are organised under these headings:

- changes in the dynamics of street sex work through time;
- perceptions of community safety and specific impacts of street sex work;
- satisfaction with responses from the authorities;
- community responses and pragmatic possibilities for change.

Changes in the dynamics of street sex work through time

Increased and dispersed

All residents that we met and interviewed stated categorically that sex work had increased and dispersed, especially between 1995 and 2000. The increase was seen to include a greater volume of women working over a larger space, a greater number of kerb-crawlers; and an increase in the volume of traffic.

There's been an increase since they blocked the town off, because the prostitutes used to hang around the bottom of the town. But since they've let no traffic through the town then they come out to the areas where the traffic can come through and this is one of them, I'm afraid. So we have got more prostitution than we had five years ago. (FG1)

The numbers of prostitutes is volatile according to external factors. In the summer one would see more prostitutes than in the winter; or when there is a police 'crackdown' in another town such as Wolverhampton, there's an influx in Caldmore. (Written evidence from a Caldmore resident)

Increase in the hours women work

Research has shown that women will adapt to attempts to design out or prevent them working by reorganising their working patterns (Lowman 1992; Hubbard 1999). This may be a result of local authority attempts to design out sex work, or clampdowns in other areas, or heavier policing. For example, one of the women we interviewed said she preferred working in the early hours of the morning to avoid being arrested. Additionally, some of the 24-hour working patterns were interpreted as a response to drug use needs.

> I've had them still working right opposite me when I go to work at half past eight in the morning, and I've actually had to go over to them and say, 'Look, I've got kids coming to school now, do you mind just…?' And, I mean, give the ladies their fair due, they have moved on, you know what I mean. (FG3)

> I think the increase is drug-related … I could take you to four places, five minutes from here and you could get whatever you wanted … This encourages more drug dealers. (FG3)

Increase in younger women – more under-age girls working on-street

Many residents were disturbed at the perceived ages of some of the young women they see soliciting on street.

> They're definitely a lot younger. I saw a girl a few weeks ago and she was definitely of school age, she was really young, as you got nearer to her you could tell she was about 15. The ones that I saw last night were probably late teens. (FG4)

Perceptions of community safety and specific impacts of street sex work

The researchers asked residents: 'Do you feel your community is a safe area to live in?' Overwhelmingly, for the majority, the response was No. Understandably, there were levels or degrees of feeling 'safe'. Some individuals felt safe in the day and less safe at night. Some people felt safe on the streets (participants in Focus Group 4).

> Yes. There is always someone on the streets. (FG4)
> Yes…our community feels safe. (FG4)

A few residents felt safe on street but not in their homes due to the risk of burglary; they also felt the risks had increased over the past five years.

> When local residents work with the police and press we see a reduction ... but in the last two years it has increased ... certainly it has increased during the last five years. (FG4)

The majority of our respondents stated categorically they felt unsafe, insecure and were concerned about break-ins at home, risk of burglary and especially drug-related crime. Some residents spoke about the fear of their homes being attacked or vandalised when there are arguments or fighting on the street.

> Greater feeling of intimidation and fear ... they are more in our face now. (FG6)

> It has invaded our homes. (FG6)

> I think there's more chance of ... rather than violence against you yourself on the streets, there's more chance of your home being raided, broken into in that way, than the safety aspect. I think there's a greater degree of break-ins. (FG4)

For the majority of residents this erosion of a sense of safety was shaped by the perceived presence and impact of street sex work.

Concerns and community impact of street sex work

In answer to our question 'What are the concerns/problems you have regarding sex work in your area and how are you affected?', residents talked about how much they liked living in the area and the sense of community that exists there, but that they were angry and frustrated at the responses from the authorities. On the whole they feel let down, but overwhelmingly the incivilities associated with the area such as litter, harassment, fear of crime, exploitation and violence against sex workers, drug use and dealing, and the untimely introduction to these matters for children were their key concerns. A resident in Focus Group 5 expressed great concern and gave a list of problems that she faced:

> No safety, harassment, being asked for business, explaining things to children and making up lies to protect them. You can't

walk out in a night at all now because someone might come up to you, a client or something and they might say this and that so you can't, you don't feel safe walking anymore. (FG5)

Fear and concerns for children
The majority of residents were very concerned about how witnessing the selling of sex will impact on children and also whether they are vulnerable to involvement and abuse. It was felt that children were witnessing street sex work at inappropriate ages and this could lead to a loss of innocence and untimely introduction to sexual matters.

When they come from the mosque and they see them again and sometimes they ask their mum, like 'Is she still standing there?' 'Why, mum? What is she doing?' And they are going to say why? Well it's so cold … We left her at five o'clock and we're coming back from mosque at seven o'clock, and she's still there, and then it's so hard to explain to your children. (FG5)

We have to look at the influence the girls on the street have on young people … they will see it as the norm … the right words in the wrong ear. 'This is an easy way to earn money' … and they are lost forever. (FG4)

There is no safety at all … our children, daughters are not safe … they go out and see prostitution … they are frightened. (FG2)

Harassment from kerb-crawlers
Harassment from kerb-crawlers was documented by residents of all ages. Harassment includes: the volume of cars driving around the area; the temporal dimensions of street sex work as residents feel that the beat was more or less 24 hours; the noise and litter; the fear of being approached by a kerb-crawler and mistaken for a prostitute. All of the residents we interviewed felt that the kerb-crawlers seeking 'business' are more visible and more open. Some respondents reported that women residents were being approached for 'business' during the day even though they were not sex workers. Some of the young people we interviewed living in the area reported harassment from kerb-crawlers.

The big problem for our community is that soon after the dark our sister and daughter wouldn't go and walk on the road because the people passing are shouting, 'Are you in business?'

I feel shame for us when this happens. (FG1)

Well, I'm not very safe to go out at night ... because when you're walking through the streets, or even to the corner shop, which is about 50 yards from our house, you've got cars pulling up and saying, you know, 'what are you charging'. I mean, it only takes one of those to drag you into the car and you're gone, aren't you? (FG3)

A couple of weeks ago, three weeks ago, I was running a taxi and about 8 o'clock I came round to pick up a girl and she was resident (...) Street, flats, and she was standing there crying and I picked her up and I said, 'What's the matter?' She started screaming, 'Why you come late?' I said, 'Well, I was stuck in the traffic,' and she said, 'You know what happened?' She said, 'Nearly six cars stopped near me, they thought I'm a prostitute.' (FG2)

Some men mentioned the risks associated with the area such as being approached by sex workers for business, and feeling nervous when slowing down in their cars over speed bumps in case they were mistaken for punters. Some men reported a fear of being approached.

Personally, I am affected by girls approaching me and asking for 'business'. After a while it becomes irritating and uncomfortable. (Written evidence from Caldmore resident)

Negotiating harassment

Some residents spoke about the way that sex work affected the way they move around the area, not daring to look people in the eye, walking with their head down. A woman described how her 16-year-old son told her to make 'no eye contact ... no engagement' (FG6). A family with two teenage daughters reported that they budgeted for taxis after dark.

Health and safety: condoms and needles

Health and safety were of pressing concern. Residents identified litter such as condoms and syringes as associated with street sex work and drug use. The additional problem of having to pay for collection seems to be incongruous with the local authority's duty to provide 'streetcare'.

I take my dog for a walk in the cemetery – it is like a condom shop ... and empty fuel cans and needles ... this is where kids play. (FG3)

If you find a used condom ... you also find used needles ... a needle stick injury could lead to a major tragedy. (FG5)

We moved out because it has driven us away ... I couldn't sleep ... the noise ... the litter ... the condoms ... it drove me crazy ... residents are suffering ill health. (FG6)

Pimping
The issue of pimps and pimping is a difficult subject. It represents a relatively hidden dimension to street sex work illustrated very clearly by the lack of official statistics and the lack of research and literature on the subject. Some residents were very concerned about this aspect of sex work and they are uncomfortable with the fact that they ignore ('turn a blind eye to') certain incidents near their homes because they are too frightened to get involved and are fearful of reprisals from pimps. Residents witnessed the following examples of the violence meted out to women controlled by pimps: a man who collects his money using a golf club; verbal abuse; kicking and punching; a woman being ordered to take her clothes off in the street. Another female resident reported witnessing an assault on a young woman living in Caldmore because she would not get involved in street sex work activities.

While sex workers' interviews showed that not all women were controlled by 'pimps', research evidence from sex workers and residents demonstrated that a section of women were.

There is abuse and violence as well ... I have had 4–5 years of misery ... and we are allowed to live like this. (FG2)

Examples of 'pimp'-related violence described to us by women working as street sex workers in the area include: being controlled and watched; being beaten up and verbally abused; being held hostage in the flat and beaten and kicked; being left for dead after a serious assault.

Pimps and related violence were of concern to residents because they felt that this further emphasises the poor reputation of the area and association with lawlessness and crime. For some residents, pimps were giving women more pressure and they felt that drugs and drug use have a great influence and are responsible for introducing some women into sex work, and some men to pimping. The interaction between street sex work and drug cultures was a great concern for residents:

> Oh yes, very much, because these pimps, the situation this town or this area also bring the drugs as well, and they're very dangerous people, very, very dangerous people. (FG1)

Drug use and violence

The interrelation between sex work and drug misuse was described by residents as a specific problem. The problem of an increase in violence in the neighbourhood and a decrease in community safety was linked very clearly, for residents, to drug misuse:

> Because you hear like fighting, yeah you're just a bit worried about drugs and also what if they like try and break into people's houses and stuff like that for money and stuff like that and if someone gets caught up in the argument and it gets serious … (FG5)

Residents were angry and upset by what they felt was increased drug dealing and drug dependency in their communities. Drug dealers, in particular, were identified as problematic to community safety; many residents felt some dealers were also involved in pimping and other criminal activities. Indeed some residents could name and point out specific men who they believed had been or were involved in pimping and dealing. Also, residents pointed out to researchers examples of visible drug dealing in the community and were particularly angry with this continuing to take place seemingly uninterrupted.

Violation of personal and private space

Residents reported particular distress and anger when street sex work came 'close to home'. Some of those residents we met who felt most affected were those for whom soliciting or the actual exchange of sexual services took place very close to their homes, in some cases right in front of them. Some residents complained about back alleys near their homes being used for business. In one case a resident witnessed sexual intercourse in her back yard and was extremely upset and concerned for her children. These residents felt that some sex workers, their clients and pimps disregarded the residents' rights. In such circumstances tolerance was eroded.

Some residents distinguished between those women who worked in a way that was discrete and respected, to a certain extent, the neighbourhood and 'didn't upset anybody', and women they perceived as inconsiderate and blatant in their soliciting behaviour. In these cases there was a sense that street sex work was taking over. As a policy approach it is important to explore means of reducing such intrusive practice. It is important to work with sex worker projects to communicate areas of residential concern and encourage less invasive working (see a forthcoming report by Pitcher *et al.* 2006 for the Joseph Rowntree Foundation: 'Living and Working in Areas of Street Sex Work'). In some areas environmental measures have been adopted to physically prevent such nuisance, for example gates across back alleys and 'alley gating' only accessible to residents.

Soliciting near places of worship

Members of faith groups were particularly concerned about soliciting near places of worship. Street sex work activity near Mosques is experienced as substantially affecting the quality of life of parents and children.

> There are about three or four mosques in one road you see all the children, and the children are sort of like going round them, their mothers are sort of like going round them. (FG1)

> I mean … we send children to the mosque, right, to learn good things, and now when they go there they see girls standing there with even, you know, not very much clothes on them, right, and it looks really bad. We try and teach our children good things, right, and when they go out they see bad things there, and it's really a shame. (FG2)

Reputation of the area

A problem experienced by the majority of the residents was the reputation and perception of the area. This was experienced at a number of levels; some residents felt it misrepresented the 'community', leading to a negative labelling of the area by the wider communities in Walsall. Some of our participants believed it deterred people from visiting and living in the area. For some home owners there was concern that the reputation could lower house prices, and for some small retail businesses there was a concern that it could put people off coming into the area. This they felt is exacerbated by bad publicity and irresponsible press coverage:

We need a positive representation of the area. (FG3)

Specific concerns for businesses
Small retail businesses in the area reported being affected to different degrees by street sex work depending on their hours of opening, location and nature of their business. Some businesses stated that they were not affected. Some pointed out that their trade took place during the day when there was little visible activity and/or they were not located in sight of a specific location affected. Businesses open in the evenings, including restaurants and other food outlets, reported being affected to differing degrees. Those businesses that did feel affected raised the following issues:

- Presence of on-street sex work deterring customers: one publican felt that the soliciting near her establishment deterred some customers from coming to the pub. One shop felt that, particularly during winter months and dark evenings, customers might be put off from coming to the area.

- Reputation of the area deterring customers.

- Safety of staff: one owner was concerned about staff who had to open the shop early in the morning, particularly as they had encountered a woman and her client doing business in the back yard area.

- Litter in back alleyways/yards: some owners and other staff complained about condoms and discarded needles in shop yards.

- Some small business owners lived above their businesses and hence shared the wider concerns of other residents.

- Some small business owners felt some other businesses were happy to tolerate the sex trade because it gave them a certain amount of business.

Safety of women and young people involved in sex work
Some residents reported their concerns about the safety of young people and women involved in sex work and wondered why they are involved. A section of residents described the women to be victims of social conditions or exploitation.

There was particular concern about vulnerable people involved in sex work and the violence they experienced from pimps and kerb-crawlers. Many residents assumed there were high levels of violence against the women involved and were concerned about this. Residents made suggestions about responding to this issue that we have incorporated into our recommendations.

A minority of the residents we interviewed were aware of the issues which lead women and young people to be involved but were so angry and frustrated by their current situation that they did not want to focus upon routes into sex work and welfare responses to prostitutes. For them to do so would serve to take the emphasis off their experiences and their feelings of being the victims of sex work:

> I am angry. I feel we (the residents) are the victims ... A lot of people take an interest in prostitution ... but residents are pushed to the end of the queue ... we are the victims. (FG6)

> We know it is bad and vicious ... we know they are beaten ... but I have had enough ... I have no sympathy left. (FG2)

Residents said that routes into sex work are a response to involvement in drug use and abuse or a response to poverty and single parenthood. The majority of residents focused upon the pimping of vulnerable young women and also the demand for sex workers by kerb-crawlers or punters. Routes in from 'broken homes' and local authority care and by young offenders were highlighted, as was the low self-esteem of the young people and women, and their vulnerability. Lack of love and lack of care was also mentioned as a precipitating factor along with the opportunity to get involved. Some residents mentioned 'choice' – that is to say women can choose their involvement, often as a response to lack of other opportunities or options.

> There are many reasons for routes in. I often think 'There goes me or my daughter'. (FG6)

> It's circumstances that has those women on the streets and nothing else. (Resident, public meeting)

> They are victims of debt, early programming and men. (FG1)

> We should find out why women prostitute themselves. Young women are being abused sexually and physically! These people

have got to eat. They couldn't live on my pension. But don't blame the women, look at the men! (Resident, public meeting)

One resident described those involved as 'young people who are brutalised and de-sensitised'. 'They are victims and we de-humanise them' (FG6). The majority of residents described those involved as victims. They also described the kerb-crawlers as 'just normal men ... any man' (FG3).

Responses to street sex work

An additional concern was that although the *police* are seen by residents as the key agency in dealing with, and responding to, sex work (and residents show a good understanding of the role of the police, i.e. they can only enforce what is enshrined in law), they feel frustrated when they see the police talking to the women and then driving away. Some residents feel that the police don't respond quickly enough to their complaints.

It looks bad when you see them standing on the corners and the police are not bothering ... prostitution is not addressed in Walsall ... clients come from everywhere. (FG1)

We log car numbers, but nothing gets done. (FG1)

Some participants suggested that in responding to sex work 'the law needs to be changed'. They felt that one response is to leave the area, and one side effect of this is that the area may then attract people who are drawn to the area because of sex work, drugs and lawlessness.

One reaction from residents to the problem of street sex work is to develop residents' action or residents' patrol groups. Yet the majority of residents in our study were not in favour of this response as it may move into vigilantism, and is risky, potentially dangerous and time-consuming.

Satisfaction with responses from the authorities

Overwhelmingly residents were not satisfied with responses from the authorities. The major agency they focused upon in the interviews was the police. There was a limited degree of awareness of work conducted by the health authority and even less awareness of social services responses.

> There appears to be a lack of organised action by the authorities, whoever those authorities may be, whether it's the Council, whether it's the police or the local authority. (FG1)

> We know that the health authority and social services are looking at the welfare responses, but they are not doing anything for the residents. (FG6)

Residents were unhappy that the local authority was not doing more to respond to their complaints about environmental issues (poor street cleaning, uncollected condoms, needles and lighter fuel cans, unlit alleyways, alleyways not cleaned). They were also unhappy that local politicians were not more active on their behalf:

> The local authority and the biggest landlord are not bothered … the police and the courts do their bit but the local authority needs to put their house in order. (FG1)

> Local politicians have not taken this up on behalf of their constituents … we are disappointed. (FG1)

However, at the same time, residents did show an understanding of the role and limitations of policing measures in relation to street sex work within the context of the current law, performance indicators and police resources. Responses to policing were therefore mixed. All residents wanted the police to do more but some understood the limitations:

> The police response is poor … they blitz, but not often enough … they can't be here 24/7. (FG3)

> Policing is limited as a response and actions so far have led to displacement. (FG5)

Residents were frustrated when they did give specific information about pimping and nothing appeared to happen:

> We have told you about the pimps and who they are – night in, night out we see them. [The resident then talked about one man they saw every night sitting in his car with a golf club.] What have you done? (Resident, public meeting)

Ultimately residents felt that there is a lack of interest in the concerns residents have regarding sex work and in the area generally from the major authorities:

> The police response seems to be to arrest the girls, they arrest her, they take her to court, she gets fined, she goes back on the street to pay her fine, what have you achieved, nothing. (FG1)

> All the authorities are absent from the local area. They come in when we organise a meeting. (FG1)

> We have a tolerance zone in Walsall and it is in a residential area. (FG6)

Many residents – whatever their views – felt that their voices were not heard, or if they were heard, were not acted upon. In the light of this we recommend in the report that local authorities and community groups consider developing the role of a community liaison officer.

Long-term sustainable responses are required
Residents were very clear that they wanted long-term sustainable responses that included more police in evidence in the area, more of a focus on kerb-crawlers and pimps and for some more extensive health and welfare support for sex workers. Residents were very aware of the dynamics of displacement and even the most frustrated residents who experienced sex work outside their homes wanted measures that would work long term and were sustainable. Residents felt that the fining system does not work as it does not prevent involvement, that no one is really taking their concerns seriously, that the action to date such as clampdowns and traffic calming are simply serving to displace sex work. The majority of residents wanted to see a change in the law. Finally residents felt that:

> If the powerful lived in the area we might get change. (FG2 – all focus groups expressed this sentiment)

> We want to see a response ... we pay taxes ... we want them moved on. (FG6)

Community responses and pragmatic possibilities for change
Residents' views on street sex work represent the diverse attitudes and values towards street sex work that exist in society more

generally. Some residents were anti-sex work and felt it should be outlawed. Others felt it was a 'necessary evil' in that there would always be men who were willing to pay for sex and women needing to supply this desire, and that sex work was centuries old. The latter group felt that there was therefore a need to better manage sex work. For some, this included the need for a 'zone of toleration' and/or enabling women to work in off-street premises. Many residents felt that legalising sex work was a step in the right direction.

In relation to the impact of street sex work, some residents felt safe on the streets and others did not. Some people felt it was a minor nuisance in comparison to burglaries, theft and violent crimes. However, the majority view was that street sex work has a serious impact on the quality of life of the community and conflicts with neighbourhood living. Of major concern was the impact on children including social, emotional and health concerns for children. The incivilities associated with sex work include nuisance and harassment from kerb-crawlers, disregard for private and communal property, and associated noise and litter. The issue of pimps and pimping was also a major concern. Residents were frustrated when they gave specific information about pimping to the police and nothing appeared to happen.

What do residents want?
Residents, whatever their views on sex work, were very unhappy with existing measures to 'manage' sex work. They felt that the police can respond in too limited a way within the context of current legislation and policing policy. In responding more pragmatically to sex work residents suggested that coordinated multi-agency responses should be developed that include all major agencies, including residents, as sex work should not be addressed in isolation. Suggestions included the following:

- A safety (tolerance) zone: it was felt this might ease the current situation for residents and provide a safer place for women to work.

- Pimping and kerb-crawling should be addressed as a matter of urgency.

- Better support services were needed to address drug use and abuse as a matter of urgency. (Drugs have made a serious impact on routes into sex work and maintaining involvement in sex work.)

- Education and prevention should begin in schools as an aspect of children's basic education. (This includes working towards improving children's self-esteem and ability to say no.)

- Support services which focus upon routes out of sex work as well as harm reduction – education, training, health and harm prevention should be developed.

This section has illustrated that many residents feel their diverse concerns are not heard or are rarely acted upon. We recommended, in the report, that the authorities and community bodies consider the possibility of developing a community liaison and mediation role. This role would include identifying on an ongoing basis the specific community safety and other concerns of residents, businesses and other statutory and voluntary sector agencies; liaising and mediating between 'community stakeholders', sex workers, the police; and brokering agreed solutions to alleviate specific problems associated with street sex work in affected neighbourhoods. Such a role had been established and evaluated in Merseyside and Stoke for a period (funded by the Home Office) and could act as a model.

We also recommended the integration of community representatives into the multi-agency structure via a community working group. Our understanding is that the community liaison/mediation role was taken up by police officers located in a house in the 'beat' area, hence it became tied in with enforcement, which was not the model proposed. Also the introduction of community wardens meant community liaison and mediation regarding sex work was part of their wider role. The integration of community representatives on the multi-agency forum did not take place.

Ultimately all participants agreed that all stakeholders have to work together to create change. This was evident most clearly in the exhibition at Walsall New Art Gallery.

Concluding summary

In the process of conducting the research our findings problematise the complex relationship between state, local authority, agencies of social control and communities/neighbourhoods affected by street sex work. Amid a shift in government policy to 'participation', 'consultation' and 'inclusion' of citizens, sex workers are 'out of place' (operating in liminal urban spaces) in neighbourhoods and are not included in consultation agendas.

The relationship between neighbourhoods, communities and local governance are key issues to work with in order to explain and seek to manage street sex work. Safe spaces for dialogue are important here. The discursive spaces that were formed in the art workshops and focus groups and among the research team are examples of discursive formations that can better inform and understand, challenge and help to form policy. In the process of this work, we developed greater understanding and some real options in responding pragmatically to street sex work. These strategic recommendations included safety zones, community mediation/liaison, and greater involvement of resident's representatives in the strategic groups such as the sex work themed implantation group.

While our research appeared to have a reasonable impact – in that some of our recommendations were actioned (outreach services to sex workers were increased to two nights per week, a drop in service was extended to two nights per week, and the police developed a service to residents in the most affected area that included a police presence via a police house/base and two dedicated officers available to residents), other more strategic recommendations did not materialise. Ultimately, the work conducted by Walsall South HAZ, residents, agencies and research team was not integrated particularly well at the strategic level. This lack of fit between horizontal and vertical processes of social inclusion is not limited to work in the area of street sex work in the context of the current government's commitment to citizen participation and inclusion – or progressive governance (see O'Neill *et al*. 2004). Disturbed by this, the community researchers (independent of the research team) were moved to produce a pamphlet to ensure the issue and the report's recommendations were not forgotten and were kept in the public sphere and on the agenda of local agencies and residents in neighbourhoods affected by street sex work. The pamphlet *What you told us about prostitution* was launched on a website (www.safetysoapbox.com) and was hand-delivered to all houses and relevant agencies in the affected areas.

We can conclude that the research and the participatory approach adopted was valued in terms of developing a more evidence-based knowledge base about the nature/extent of street sex work in the area and local and national policy. It built capacity among communities, agencies and sex workers and included all voices, not privileging the more powerful or loudest. The participatory action research led to greater awareness and understanding for residents, some bridging of the gap/barriers between residents and street sex workers, and a platform for greater levels of participation that led to suggestions for policy and practice in the local area, with a proposed strategic framework for a future multi-layered strategy. Thus, our collaborative work served to develop reflexive knowledge and understanding across the resident–sex worker divide that marks much of contemporary research on sex work in urban residential areas, a testimony to the possibilities for participation in local governance that can shed light on broader structures, practices and processes. Of course, sex worker voices need to be added to balance the narrative and our wider research included sex worker voices. The Joseph Rowntree 'Contested Spaces' research published in February 2006 reflects this and also provides updated commentary, findings and analysis on the contested spaces of street sex work in residential areas and a more complex understanding of communities' responses and possibilities for policy and practice.

We have demonstrated in this chapter how 'sex workers and community residents can come together [through participatory action research including participatory arts methods] to establish ways to introduce effective urban policy that is neither punitive, moralistic nor biased' (Sanders 2005: 1715).

Notes

1 The team was made up of Maggie O'Neill, Rosie Campbell and community co-researchers.
2 O'Neill developed the concept of 'ethno-mimesis' to articulate the combination of ethnographic research and artistic representation of lived experience through sensuous knowing. See publications since 2001. Maggie O'Neill and Mark Webster have contributed a section on 'creative consultation' to the NIACE toolkit *Rise Up and Become* edited by Jane Thompson in 2004. Available from NIACE.
3 Of course sex workers can also be residents – the stigma and lifestyle of street sex workers is likely to impact negatively upon their involvement in 'community' regeneration initiatives.
4 Walsall (at the time of our research) was reported as having the lowest full-time wages in the seven West Midlands local authority areas. The lowest tenth of full-time workers in Walsall earned less than £160.40 per week. In the UK the earnings of the lowest tenth were £166.90 per week. Violence was a key feature in the research on housing and homelessness. Almost half of the families presenting as homeless during the research period had been involved in domestic violence. Griffiths (1999) reports

that in the year to March 1998 there were 1,359 incidents of domestic violence reported to the police. In the year to June 1998, 637 families with 1,268 children were referred to the Women's Refuge, and 698 families were accepted as unintentionally homeless as a result of domestic violence. In 1998 the Hostels Working Group was reported to have considered the needs of 177 young homeless people.

5 Findings from a Joseph Rowntree Study 'Contested Spaces of Street Sex Work' conducted in five cities and led by Jane Pitcher was published in February 2006. The research deals in part with the impact of ASBOs. The authors are part of the research team.

References

Bauman, Z. (2001) *Community: Seeking Safety in an Insecure World*. Cambridge: Polity.

Beck, U. (1998) *Democracy without Enemies*. Cambridge: Polity.

Benson, C. and Matthews, R. (1995) *National Vice Squad Survey*. Middlesex University, Middlesex.

Benson, C. and Matthews, R. (2000) 'Police and prostitution: vice squads in Britain', in R. Weitzer (ed.), *Sex for Sale*. London: Routledge.

Bianchini, F. and Ghilardi, L. (2004) 'The culture of neighbourhoods: a European perspective', in D. Bell and M. Jayne (eds), *City of Quarters: Urban Villages in the Contemporary City*. Aldershot: Ashgate.

Campbell, R. and Hancock, L. (1998) *Hearing Loud Voices and the Silencing of Dissent: Commercial Sex in a Climate of Zero Tolerance*. Paper presented at 'Sex Work Reassessed: A National Day Conference', University of East London, 9 September.

Campbell, R., Coleman, S. and Torkington, P. (1996) *Street Prostitution in Inner City Liverpool*. Liverpool City Council.

Corbin, A. (1990) *Women for Hire: Prostitution and Sexuality in France after 1850*. Cambridge, MA: Harvard University Press.

Crow, G. (2002) *Social Solidarities: Theories, Identities and Social Change*. Milton Keynes: Open University Press.

Griffiths, S. (1999) *A Profile of Poverty and Health in Walsall*. Birmingham: Public Management Associates.

Hester, M. and Westmarland, N. (2004) *Tackling Street Prostitution: Towards an Holistic Approach*, Home Office Research Study 279. London: Home Office Development and Statistics Directorate.

Home Office (2004) *Paying the Price: A Consultation Paper on Prostitution*. London: HMSO.

Hubbard, P. (1999) *Sex and the City: Geographies of Prostitution in the Urban West*. Aldershot: Ashgate.

Hubbard, P. and Hall, T. (1998) 'Introduction', in T. Hall and P. Hubbard (eds), *The Entrepreneurial City*. Chichester: John Wiley.

Lowman, J. (1992) 'Street prostitution control: some Canadian reflections on the Finsbury Park experience', British Journal of Criminology, 32 (1): 1–17.

Matthews, R. (1993) *Kerb Crawling, Prostitution and Multi-Agency Policing.* London: Home Office.

Matthews, R. (ed.) (1996) *All-Party Parliamentary Group on Street Prostitution.* Middlesex University, Middlesex.

O'Neill, M. and Campbell, R. (2001) *Working Together to Create Change.* Staffordshire University, Stoke-on-Trent, and Liverpool Hope College (also available on: www.safetysoapbox.com).

O'Neill, M. and Webster, M. (2005) 'Creativity, community and change: creative approaches to community consultation', in J. Thompson and C. Turner (eds), *Rise Up and Become …: A Toolkit to Put Learners at the Heart of RISE.* Leicester: NIACE.

O'Neill, M., Campbell, R., James, A., Webster, M., Green, K., Patel, J., Akhtar, N. and Saleem, W. (2004) 'Red lights and safety zones', in D. Bell and M. Jayne (eds), *City of Quarters: Urban Villages in the Contemporary City.* Aldershot: Ashgate.

O'Neill, M., Campbell, R., Webster, M. and Green, K. (2001) 'Prostitution, ethno-mimesis and participatory arts: processes and practices of inclusion', in J. Swift *et al.* (eds), *Disciplines, Fields and Change in Art Education*, Vol. 3. Article Press, School of Art, University of Central England.

O'Neill, M., Stoke, L., Giddens, S. and Jayne, M. (2000) 'Love for sale: the politics of prostitution in Stoke-on-Trent', in T. Edensor (ed.), *Reclaiming Stoke-on-Trent.* Stoke-on-Trent: Staffordshire University Press.

Sagar, T. (2005) 'Street Watch: concept and practice', *British Journal of Criminology*, 45: 98–112.

Sanders, T. (2004) 'The risks of street prostitution: punters, police and protesters', *Urban Studies*, 41 (9): 1703–71.

Scottish Executive (2004) *Being Outside: Constructing a Response to Street Prostitution. A Report of the Expert Group on Prostitution in Scotland.* Scottish Executive, Area 3.

South Yorkshire Standing Forum on Prostitution (1995) *Report of Findings from the Community Consultation Survey.* South Yorkshire Police Authority.

Chapter 3

'Zoning' street sex work: the way forward?

Marieke Van Doorninck and Rosie Campbell

Introduction

A number of government reviews and local and national research have demonstrated considerable dissatisfaction with current UK approaches to street sex work and the ineffectiveness of current polices to address the safety, well-being and rights of street sex workers and the nuisance and incivilities reported by some communities living in areas where street sex work takes place (Benson and Matthews 1996; O'Neill and Campbell 2002; Home Office 2004). Some researchers, local and national stakeholders/policy makers and sex worker activists have called for the 'zoning' of street sex work, and looked to countries where the formal management of street sex work via an 'official street walking zone' has been adopted, for example the Netherlands. There remains strong opposition from others and little indication at a national level for support for 'zoning'. Debates about 'managed areas' or 'tolerance' zones have often dominated discussions about policy options for responding to street sex work in the UK. This chapter will consider what is meant by 'zoning', the debates about zoning street sex work in the UK, areas where a policy of 'unofficial zoning' has been adapted and the lessons that can be learnt from the Netherlands experience. We conclude that a policy framework should be developed which enables those areas which have carried out inclusive consultation and wish to pilot 'zoning' to be able to do so. We caution that the model of zoning adopted should have at its heart improving the safety and rights of street sex workers and not compound their marginalisation. Zoning should not stand alone but be part of a multi-layered strategy to address street sex work. Areas in the UK have the option of looking towards countries such as the Netherlands and Germany for guidance regarding the critical factors for more successful 'zoning'. While 'zoning' does not offer a panacea we argue that as part of a holistic strategy it has the potential to offer a way forward to improved sex worker safety and rights, accessible services and reduction in community impact.

What's in a name?

Within the context of sex work 'zoning' is a term which is used to indicate a policy approach whereby within a (mostly) urban area sex work is more or less tolerated. It does not indicate what sort of sex work nor what degree of toleration. In New South Wales, one of the three Australian states where prostitution businesses are decriminalised, zoning means restricting brothels to industrial areas (ACON and SWOP 2000). In several cities in the UK and on the European Continent zoning means toleration either from just the police or from the police and the municipal council of street prostitution in a specific area. So the term zoning does have a different meaning in different contexts.

In policy and media discussions about the management of street prostitution in a specific area in the UK several terms are in use to describe such a model, e.g. 'safety zone', 'managed area', 'tolerance zone' and 'official red light area'. We will clarify the terminology that is being used when dealing with street sex work and specify the terms that are used in this chapter.

The places in a town or city where women solicit on the streets in the UK without any kind of 'official' or informal tolerance are usually and often colloquially known as *the beat*. The term red light area is often used to describe an area or areas in a city that are know for a concentration of sex work (be it street based or off street), sometimes in combination with other sex industry venues like strip bars and sex cinemas, whether it is hidden or conducted very openly. For clarity we will not be using the term 'red light area' to describe a street beat.

In the Netherlands the term *tippelzone* is used for an appointed area designated for street prostitution between specific hours. Soliciting is legal in the zone as stated in the local bylaws (Lamboo 1995). 'Tippelen' is the Dutch word for soliciting for prostitution on the street. The correct translation that also covers the legal status of a *tippelzone* would be 'official street walking zone'. In this chapter we use the term 'official street walking zone' to describe an official policy of allocating an area for street soliciting and the provision of a place where sexual services can be carried out, responsibility for the management of which is taken by the police and local responsible authorities.

In the UK such a model with formalised status and responsibility being taken by local authorities is increasingly being referred to as a 'managed area'. Such proposed zones don't just permit street soliciting but present a model for actively managing street sex work in an allocated non-residential area at permitted times, with health and social care services on site and policing focused on sex worker safety and addressing exploitation.

In some areas of the UK there is an approach in which a number of agencies work together to manage and geographically 'contain' street sex work. Some of the elements of an official street walking zone may be in place, e.g. support services on site and a prostitution liaison officer working with support services to respond to any violence against street sex workers. Agencies may even meet in a multi-agency forum and coordinate management. Among those areas which adopt such a model rarely is it declared an official street walking zone and/or written into local council bye-laws or other official policies as in the Dutch case. Here we refer to this model as an 'unofficial street walking zone'. At a local level agencies involved in managing the zone may purposefully choose to use other terminology to describe their approach – this may be to avoid the charge that they are 'tolerating sex work' or to avoid accusations that they are not enforcing current legislation. In such cases terms such as 'strategic enforcement' or 'area of lesser complaint' may be used.

Also, in some UK towns and cities, an area can emerge whereby street prostitution is unofficially tolerated by the police who conduct a no prosecution policy. This is often the toleration of an existing beat or part of an existing beat. Other agencies may be aware of this arrangement and encourage sex workers to adhere to any informal conditions that apply. We refer to this as a 'toleration zone'.

The different meanings and uses of zoning can often pose a barrier when the general public, local communities, sex workers, local authorities and other professional groups in the UK enter into informed discussions about establishing 'zones'. The tendency in the UK has been for policy-makers, local communities and the media to refer to 'tolerance zones' without careful definition of what this means. Some locally based research and consultation exercises in the UK have found that when discussing 'tolerance zones' different stakeholders envisage different models of 'zoning' and have differing knowledge levels about zoning policies in other places (O'Neill and Campbell 2002).

Unmanaged street sex work and the call for piloting zoning

The traditional approach to the 'management' of street sex work in the UK has been the periodic enforcement of the 'soliciting' and kerb-crawling legislation (see Chapter 1). Some police forces in the UK, recognising their obligation to offer protection to all citizens and deal with all crime, have also put police time into policing violence against street sex workers with close liaison with sex work support projects (Penfold *et al*. 2004). Since the mid-1980s many areas have also made some sort of investment in support services for street sex workers to address the range of health and social care needs of street sex workers. These projects vary in the services they offer, but can offer prevention, harm reduction, exit support, court diversion and community mediation (see Chapter 10). Some areas have established some form of multi-agency forum to bring together the different agencies and stakeholders and enable greater coordination between these and the different elements of their approach. Yet despite a shift to a more coordinated, multi-layered approach some areas have been frustrated with the enduring 'problems' that they seek to address including the following.

- The social exclusion, criminalisation and marginalisation of street sex workers. The continued criminalisation of street sex workers sits uneasily with the increasing recognition of street sex workers as a vulnerable, victimised or socially excluded group with a wide range of issues to face such as problematic drug use and homelessness (Home Office 2004; Hester and Westmarland 2004).

- The general failure to break the 'revolving door' syndrome, with the enforcement of the soliciting legislation, leading to a court appearance and fining, leading to greater pressure to work, creates much frustration. The use of ASBOs and CRASBOs in some areas of the UK has added another layer to this cycle with some women breaching and serving prison sentences (see Chapter 1).

- High levels of violence against street sex workers and low levels of reporting to the police. There is now a considerable body of research that shows that violence against sex workers continues to be alarmingly high, seriously under-reported and that the vulnerability of sex workers is often compounded by current policies (see Chapter 6).

- Difficulties providing street sex workers with access to drugs, health, social care and employment and training services. The criminalisation of street sex workers and the dispersal of street sex workers creates adverse conditions for the provision of support, health, drugs, social care and exit support projects (Campbell 2004; UK Network of Sex Work Projects 2005).

- The vulnerability of street sex workers to exploitation by certain groups, e.g. drugs dealers and coercers.

- The existence of various forms of criminal activity in and around some street beats, e.g. drug dealing.

- Street beats spread over considerably large unmanaged areas in some cities (Clark *et al.* 2004) with dispersal into new areas.

- Adverse impact on residential communities. Research with residential communities living in areas where street soliciting takes place has illustrated a range of adverse impact reported by local residents (see Chapter 2).

In some towns and cities interventions have rarely seen long-term reductions in the level of street sex work and have more usually simply displaced or dispersed street sex workers into new areas or over larger areas (Clark *et al.* 2004). Hence there is continued impact on residents living and working in 'street walking' areas with a range of responses and concerns. While some areas have developed more coordinated multi-agency approaches to addressing street prostitution which constitute a mix of initiatives, they have been unable to remove street prostitution from the streets via enforcement or exit support measures, or to provide safe areas for sex workers to work. This has in some areas led to an examination of alternative approaches which are seen to have the potential to offer more effective 'solutions'.

Some municipal authorities have looked to official street walking areas and specifically to the Dutch experience as a potential way forward. This has included fact-finding missions to the Netherlands and Dutch officials visiting the UK to report on their work.

Looking to and learning from Dutch experiences

For over 20 years some cities in the Netherlands have established official street walking zones. Some Dutch commentators, while clear that others can learn lessons from the Netherlands, have cautioned against simply transferring models to other countries without considering local factors (Visser 1998). The Dutch approach towards these social phenomena is pragmatic. The principles informing the approach are perhaps best labelled 'harm minimisation', aiming to reduce the problems associated with prostitution. A society needs a certain degree of tolerance to implement policies based on pragmatism. The specific policies on street sex work are part of a wider approach in which the Dutch government has accepted the distinction between voluntary and involuntary sex work, brought voluntary sex work into a legal employment rights framework and strengthened legislation to address the exploitation of prostitution (Visser 1997).

Establishing zones in the Netherlands

Although not in the penal code, street sex work was prohibited under city ordinance in the Netherlands and until the 1970s streetwalking was more or less condoned in red light areas as long as public order was not disturbed. In the 1970s and 1980s in the bigger cities women with problematic drug use started to work the beats in order to earn the money needed to pay for their habit. Their presence, and that of drug dealers and boyfriends, on the streets caused more nuisance to the neighbourhood. The circumstances in which the women with problematic drug use had to work and live attracted a lot of media attention. Indignant about these images and stories and the fact that these women were only regarded and treated as a nuisance, a group of catholic nuns in Amsterdam sought a way to assist. In 1982 they opened a shelter for street workers in the neighbourhood of the beat. The shelter was called a 'living room' to indicate that it had to be a safe haven where women could feel 'at home' for a short while in between clients, where they were not judged for their addiction nor for their work (Viet 1996). Two years later a similar project was funded in Den Haag. The government of Den Haag planned to tolerate the beat near the shelter but ongoing, sometimes hostile, protests by the residents prevented this. In 1984 the council appointed a non-residential area behind one of the city's railway stations as an official streetwalking zone in the local by-laws. Two years later the shelter moved to the zone.

The council of Utrecht decided to install an official zone in the same year as Den Haag. The establishment of a living room was to be an integrated part of the new prostitution policies. The city funded the new project, Huiskamer Aanloop Prostituees (HAP), which was responsible for the function of the living room. HAP chose a mobile living room so it could be removed during daylight hours in order to prevent vandalism. Another advantage of a mobile unit was that during the day nothing in the area indicated that at night this was the place where women and transsexuals were soliciting. Although the zone had liberated the residential areas from soliciting, the people in the neighbourhood of the zone were now complaining about the fact that sex workers and their clients were doing business nearby and leaving their litter. This was the reason the city chose to create a 'working area' (where sexual services were performed) a distance of one kilometre from the zone. The area consists of car parks and a parking place for (motor) cyclists (Municipality of Utrecht 1999). Although the 'working area' was established to protect public order, it benefited the safety of the street workers greatly as they no longer had to leave the surroundings of the zone for desolate places to make sexual contact. The police are nearby in case of danger. The official streetwalking zone in Utrecht was the first to have the 'whole package': an official zone, a living room and a working area. These three elements are now seen as vital for a functioning zone.

General characteristics of the zones

In the late 1980s and 1990s a total of eight zones were set up in the Netherlands. In each case the set-up was the result of a complicated, sensitive and sometimes long process (Visser 1998). In the early days the actual political decision to have an area where street prostitution was allowed was a tough one. Political consensus was hard to reach because of moral opposition. Later on, after tolerance or official zones in other cities had proven to be an effective instrument against nuisance and provided a safe working place for sex workers, the most difficult part was to appoint a location (Visser 1998; Van Doorninck 2004).

Fierce and in some cases violent protest from residents against street workers and the living room accompanied those processes in some areas (Bovenkerk *et al.* 1993). In some areas the zones have been relocated due to these protests. Yet research has shown that, in general, the installation of an official streetwalking zone has reduced the nuisance and disturbance in residential areas.

The main criteria for finding a location for a zone is that: it is not in a residential area, it can provide a reasonable degree of safety for sex workers and it is easy to access by car and by public transport. All zones have been located away from residential areas. Four out of the eight zones were located in an already existing urban street environment that during the daytime has another function and shows no evidence of the activities that take place at night. The other four were especially designed for the purpose of street prostitution. The opening hours for the zones are set in the local by-laws.

In every zone there is a shelter called a living room where sex workers can have a break, drink a cup of coffee, eat something, talk with their colleagues (for instance exchange the features of the cars of dangerous clients), talk to the staff and buy or get condoms for free. On a number of nights a medical doctor can be consulted on STIs and on general health issues. Drug use is prohibited in all the living rooms, except in the Rotterdam zone which has a special 'tolerance place for users'.[1]

The zones are managed and funded by the municipalities. This means that the city is responsible for the environment of the zone, the (in some cases daily) cleaning and the financing of, for example, the parking meters and the employment of the dedicated police team.

The police have a key role in the functioning of the zone. In most cities a special 'tippelteam' was formed: this is a small group of policemen and women who control the zone. Because these tend to be a stable team in terms of personnel, who are known by the sex workers and the project workers, mutual trust is developed. The team checks the zone a few times a night and are on call if the project or sex workers need them. They can visit the living room as guests according to the rules of the living room. This is extremely important for the credibility of the living room as a safe haven for sex workers who do not always have a good relationship with the police in general. The presence of the police in the zone is a very strong signal to the clients but also to pimps and drug dealers. Outside the zone, the police warn and fine sex workers who solicit.

Drug dealing is prohibited in the zone but because the possession of a small quantity for own use is not forbidden in the Netherlands, in some zones these amounts of drugs are bought and sold in the zone. The advantage of this is that sex workers don't have to leave the zone to go into residential areas to buy their drugs and perhaps start soliciting on their way back to the zone. The police have to maintain the balance between toleration of some dealing and keeping dealers out of the zone.

Results and opinions about the zones

In the first ten years of their existence the reports on the zones were positive, despite all of them starting in the context of considerable protest from residents and businesses. The zones have caused less nuisance than was expected and indeed in most cities the installation of the zones marked a decrease in nuisance (Viet 1996). The safety and health of the street sex workers improved following the installation of the zones. The only violent attacks committed on sex workers have taken place outside the zones and there have been no murders in the zones. In several research evaluations the women themselves confirmed they felt much more secure working on the zone than in the former situation (Viet 1996; Van Doornick 2003, 2004; Visser 1998).

There are some differences between the eight cities, however. The earlier zones (Utrecht, Den Haag and Nijmegen) encountered less problems than the other zones. The first zones were situated in an existing area, whereas the others were especially built for the purpose of streetwalking. The areas where the first zones are located function as normal streets during day hours. In a sense the first zones are more integrated into society whereas the others were specially created for the purpose of street sex work and placed outside 'normal' life. This major difference in approach does have an impact on the functioning of the zone.

A general complaint from sex workers about these designed zones is that they are too small which heightens competition between sex workers (Ten Dan *et al.* 1999). These zones are also far away from city centres and it is either expensive (taxi) or dangerous (walking through a desolated area) to get to the zone.

Also the (over-)regulation itself is problematic. Street prostitution by nature offers a certain amount of freedom – for the sex workers as well as for the clients. The autonomy, speciality and the excitement of street work can be lost in the strongly regulated areas. The zone of Heerlen is the most over-regulated. The sex workers need a licence to work in the zone. As a result a lot of the drug-using sex workers still solicit in the 'old beat' to the anger and frustration of the residents.

The location of most of the zones has been an issue. The zone in Amsterdam is situated in an industrial area outside the city, which by some is seen to be a key factor in why it was less successful. The zone was far too remote from the city and was not accessible by public transport. Sex workers with an addiction would not work in the zone because of the distance but also because drugs couldn't be bought in the neighbourhood. Whereas the drug scene was too far away from the zone in Amsterdam, it was too near in Rotterdam. The zone had an attraction for drug use and drug dealers. The zone was situated near a socially vulnerable residential area where a number of dealers were based. The sex workers made money in the zone to spend in the drug houses in this neighbourhood, and often used the walk back to the zone for soliciting. Residents had been complaining for some years.

Recent developments

Not withstanding the difficulties, the zones have on balance proven to be successful in the last 15 to 20 years in terms of meeting their original objectives. Yet there is continued criticisms about the functioning of the zones.

Opposition to the zones has included moral criticism and also is linked to a shifting political climate. Because of the existence of legal zones the working and living conditions of addicted street sex workers have become highly visible for a larger audience. There have been a number of TV documentaries about the zones that show the daily reality of the lives of people living on the margins of society. Although the zones offer women a relatively safe place to work, the circumstances of street sex work are far from ideal. The public is confronted with images of women who suffer from physical and psychological problems, images of women who have stories about rude and sometimes violent clients and images of women who, suffering from withdrawal, sell their services for very little money and take risks concerning their health and safety. Being confronted with this reality some journalists and politicians pose the question whether this is something that local government should facilitate. These critics generally accept sex work as labour for women and men who choose to do the job, but they argue that most drug-using women are not voluntary sex workers but forced by their circumstances, i.e. their addiction. Some even call the reality of the zones 'state controlled rape or sexual abuse', arguing that the actual existence of zones condones these sexual abuses and that the zones should be closed as they cannot be accepted as part of a contemporary civil society. Some critics use this as an argument to call for free or prescribed heroin, others recommend (non-voluntary) rehabilitation programmmes.[2]

Following the legalisation of the Dutch sex industry,[3] migrant sex workers, whose presence had been tolerated for years in the prostitution businesses, were no longer allowed to work. As a result some migrants moved from the window brothels, sex clubs and private houses to the zones. Because the zones were meant to be a safe place for predominantly marginalised women, the police in most cities conducted a policy of not checking IDs in the zone. Within a short period of time, in the zones of Den Haag, Amsterdam and Rotterdam a growing group of migrant sex workers were soliciting and the zones became overcrowded. This led to pressure on the zones, the controlling police teams (who suspected the presence of victims of trafficking on the zones) and on the project workers in the living room, not only because the zones as well as the shelter were designed for a smaller group but also because of tension among the sex workers.[4] Critics of the zones accused city governments, who fund the rather expensive maintenance costs of zones, of running an open air brothel for illegals.

Van Doorninck (2004) argues that a shift in the political climate has contributed to the criticisms of the zones. There is also among the general public less sympathy for the policies of tolerance and on the whole less compassion for people who are surviving on the margins of society. Currently, the enforcement of law and order and policies of repression rather than regulated toleration are considered the best way to deal with societal problems. Of course this new attitude has its impact on how the zones are addressed.

Currently, debates are exploring a variety of ways forward. These include the closure of the zones. In 2002 Rotterdam city government decided to close its zone; it and its surroundings being perceived as a problem area. Although the majority of the council was in favour of the closure, several council members urged the city government to find alternative care projects for the women involved before the zone was to be closed. For this reason it was decided that the zone would keep functioning until 2005. In the meantime women who wanted to work in the zone needed a licence. For drug-using women a combination of drugs rehabilitation and exiting prostitution programmes were set up. This group were not considered to be voluntary sex workers so projects were focused on helping them out of prostitution (not necessarily to stop using) instead of supporting them while in sex work. The zone closed in September 2005.

In November 2003 the Amsterdam government also decided to close the zone in response to the presence of illegal sex workers and criminal activities following police raids. For a period the police were commissioned to make regular ID checks in the zone, and while the new law enforcement did result in a dramatic decline in the number of women in the zone and eliminated criminal activities, the council decided to close the zone anyway. The main reasons which the local councillors presented for this decision were that the original group, the drug-using women, never made use of the zone (because of its remote location and the absence of possibilities to buy drugs in the neighbourhood) and that a large number of women working in the zone were victims of trafficking. As the city's representatives, they did not want to be the facilitators of trafficking and criminal activities. The minority of councillors who objected to the closure of the zone (supported by resident groups, drug social work projects, sex workers rights organisations, anti-trafficking organisations) stressed that solutions to the problems that had occurred in the zone needed to be addressed instead of defining the (existence of the) zone itself as a problem. The Amsterdam zone was closed on 15 December 2003 without any alternative support arrangements for the women who had been working in the zone.

The city government of Den Haag (the Hague) closed its zone in March 2006. In council a motion was carried that before the proposed date of closure alternative projects for street sex workers had to be set up and functioning. Initially in October 2003 the opening hours were reduced from seven to three hours per night and the police had a high presence in the zone checking IDs and fining those working after two in the morning. By 2004 the majority of sex workers, drug users as well as migrants, were no longer working in the zone. The sex work support project began outreach for sex workers who had left the zone and were working in other parts of the city. The local prostitution project (SHOP) was commissioned to develop these projects. The fact that the zone was situated in the location for businesses and development projects was thought to be a reason for closure, as well as arguments about trafficking. Residents protested against the intended closure of the zone because they feared a return of the nuisance they had experienced before the zone was set up.

The second approach may be seen in Utrecht and Groningen. Women who solicit in the zone are obliged to carry with them their identity papers (including work permits), and police officers who regularly control the zones check the women for their papers. Utrecht has over the years been very transparent about, and defended, their policy and hosted many visitors since its opening (Muncipality of Utrecht 1999). The city government, the police and the sex work project of Utrecht have declared on several occasions that the zone is not a matter up for discussion.

The third approach is stricter regulation of the zones. This can include special streetwalking licences for sex workers. Such licences can be exclusive, for example for drug-using women or inhabitants of the municipality. In Heerlen, Arnhem and the zones are already exclusively for women with a licence. Utrecht has introduced a licence system but the licences are not restriced to drug using women habitants of Utrecht.

Van Doorninck (2004a, 2004b) is concerned that in some areas zones have been disqualified as solutions for the immense complex social problems concerning street prostitution. She reported that in discussions the aspect of the safety of women was no longer a key issue and little mention was made of the reduction in violence against street workers that had been achieved since the adoption of official zoning. Instead the emphasis was on the protection of public order and the regulation of sex work. Van Doorninck (2004a) stressed that sex work is not a static phenomenon – it reflects the changes in society. This is especially the case with street prostitution where major changes in society and patterns of social exclusion can be detected. Women, men and transgenders who do sex work on the street are predominantly people with less choices in life than others, often surviving on the margins of society. The better functioning zones, like that in Utrecht, are those that are less regulated – this has made them more able to adapt and incorporate societal changes. The more a zone is regulated, the less flexible it is in times of change. Originally the zones were meant to be a 'refuge' and a safe place for street sex workers. If zones are so regulated that they are only open for licensed sex workers they will lose their original and important function of providing a safe place for sex workers. Marginalised groups will either choose not to go there or will not be permitted to work there. The situation may then turn full circle with the creation of new unregulated beats manifesting all the problems for sex workers and communities that official zoning was developed to address.

Against this backdrop of closure and change a new zone opened in November 2003 in the city of Eindhoven. After many years of residents' protests and lobbying from social workers and health workers, an area was allocated as a temporary street walking zone. The brand new zone was set up for local drug-using women who have been soliciting for years in the town's small legal window prostitution area. In order to work in the zone women need a licence.

It is unclear if any more zones will close. Many politicians are aware that the advantages of having a zone outweigh the disadvantages. It seems likely there will probably be stronger regulation of the zones.

Some feminists point to the difficulties in some of the zones as evidence that zoning has failed to deliver the hoped for benefits (Bindel and Kelly 2004). Others stress that there are several official streetwalking zones that have successfully functioned over the past 20 years and continue to do so, with much lower levels of violence than identified in research studies in other European countries where street sex work is not regulated via zones and where street sex workers are criminalised (Van Doorninck 2004).

Pitcher *et al*. (2006) note that there has been little formal research into the feasibility and effectiveness of zones for street sex work. However, some research is available, such as the evaluation of the official street walking zone established in Cologne, Germany (Kerschl 2004).

Zoning in the UK

Over the last decade a number of local authorities in the UK have considered establishing some sort of official zone (Hubbard 1997). Often this has grown out of local research or consultation.

Perhaps the broadest consultation on zoning in a UK city took place in Liverpool and was commissioned by the City Council. Clark *et al*. (2004) concluded that there was broad support from all groups consulted – street sex workers, residents and businesses and the general public – for a managed zone in the city.

O'Neill and Campbell (2002) in a study in the West Midlands in which residents, sex workers and agencies were consulted found that the majority of residents, sex workers and agencies involved in the research supported the idea of a 'tolerance zone' of some kind. Most held the view that a pragmatic approach was needed and street zones offered the potential for 'managing' prostitution and improving the quality of residents' lives. Many residents felt existing approaches were not working and the street zone route should be explored. Some felt strongly that it was time to try more radical approaches to the regulation of street prostitution. Some residents pointed out that affected areas were by default 'tolerance zones' hence they wanted an actual zone in a non-residential area. Many saw it as an opportunity to improve the situation for all those involved, with a reduction in nuisance for residents and the improvement of working conditions for sex workers by removing arrest and 'turnstile justice' and providing health and welfare services on site. Representatives from the key support projects supported the idea in principle but also were concerned that the women's safety should be centrally considered. They also pointed out that sex workers would not go to an area that was unsafe and difficult to get to.

Pitcher *et al.* (2006) in a study of five towns in England and Scotland found that many residents and sex workers supported the concept of non-residential 'tolerance zones' or designated spaces for working, although few had a clear idea of how they might operate; the greatest consideration for sex workers was having a safer working environment. Many sex workers indicated that they would prefer not to work in a residential area if there were safer options elsewhere, particularly an area that was well-lit and with other women around. The safety elements were less frequently considered by residents. Of the study areas, only one had experience of a managed tolerance zone, which had been abandoned by the authorities in the light of changes to the socio-economic make-up of the area. Interviews with sex workers in this area suggested that they were not consulted on the abolition of the zone and it had forced them to relocate to new beats, provoking complaints from residential groups and creating problems for outreach services. When asked how their working conditions might be improved, the majority of sex workers in that area argued for the re-establishment of a managed zone.

In summary those in favour of zoning point to a range of advantages compared to the current situation.

- For many advocates improving the safety of sex workers is seen as very important. There have been no murders of women using the Dutch zones for both soliciting and providing sexual services and violence against sex workers using the zones is minimal. Kerschl *et al.* (2004) who evaluated the Cologne zone found that attacks against sex workers had reduced dramatically since the introduction of the zone.

- Zoning is also seen to provide a context in which health, social care, drugs and exit interventions could be more accessible and effectively delivered. Kerschl (2004) reported that following the introduction of a zone for one year a larger proportion of sex workers were accessing drugs, health, counselling and social care services. Services are directly on site offering direct harm reduction and support interventions, plus a gateway to a wide range of other services. This immediacy of services fast tracks the development of relationships between street sex workers and health and social care services (Kerschl 2004). Also sex workers are not 'criminals' in the area and hence are less likely to be wary of services. Kerschl reported that following the introduction of the zone a greater number of street sex workers were accessing services and that continuity of contact with the project allowed earlier availability and intervention possibilities for the drug treatment and other psycho-social care including exiting.

- The removal of street sex work from residential areas to an allocated non-residential area and hence the reduction of neighbourhood nuisance is seen as a major advantage. Experience from the Netherlands shows that when a suitable location is selected this can indeed be the case. Challenges to zones in the Netherlands have not been due to sex workers working outside of allocated areas. Kerschl (2004) found that in the city of Cologne in prohibited areas outside the zone nearly no prostitution activity had been found since the zone was operational.

- Zoning is seen as a possible way of reducing the vulnerability of sex workers to exploitation and enabling a more targeted approach to policing and prosecuting exploitation in street sex work, e.g. allowing a focus on coercers of children and adults. The Dutch police argue they can more effectively identify any children abused thorough prostitution who appear in the zone and focus their enforcement efforts on coercers.

Those opposed, or with an ambivalent view, have a range of concerns. These are expressed in local research and national debates. O'Neill and Campbell (2002) found several key reasons for opposition to zoning. These also appear at a national level.

- It is not possible to identify and agree a suitable area: those in favour respond that this has been possible, although not without problems, in a number of countries.

- Zones would be unsafe for sex workers who would be ghettoised in isolated and unsafe areas and sex workers would not use them. Those in favour argue this would not be the case if the model adopted was one in which the zone was policed for the safety of sex workers, with projects present in the zone during opening hours and places for exchanging sexual services as well as for soliciting were built in. (NB: Many murders and attacks on sex workers take place when the sex worker has gone alone with the man to perform sexual services.) As noted earlier attacks in managed areas in Netherlands and Cologne were very low and contrast with the high levels of violence reported among many street sex working communities in the UK (see Chapter 6). Kerschl (2004) reported a high level of acceptance of the zone in Cologne by street sex workers and nearly a total reduction of violence by clients and pimps in the area. The evaluation also found increasing acceptance and use of the competencies of the police and public security by the sex workers. It appears clear that zones would need to be developed with the safety of sex workers as central. In terms of sex workers using official street walking zones O'Neill and Campbell (2002) noted that while the majority of sex workers in their study supported the idea of a safe area where they could work without arrest, some were cynical about the possibility of them ever being 'left alone' by the police. Some women pointed out that they already purposefully work in non-residential areas and were still arrested; this made them cynical about the promise of zoning. Few women were aware of the organisation of zones in the Netherlands, where zones are policed for the safety of the women and health and welfare advice and support are available on site. Campbell (2004) argued that it is not surprising a section of sex workers consulted in various research studies may be sceptical about zoning, as it may be difficult for street sex workers to envisage a place where they would no longer be criminalised, where they would have a place to go, which would have services on site and would be policed for their safety, after a history of arrest and harassment. O'Neill and Campbell (2002) concluded that the views and perceptions of sex workers indicate that if such a policy were adopted further time would have to be spent building trust and communication between the police, other agencies and sex workers. Sex workers as well as residents and agencies would need to be involved in in-depth consultation and planning.

- More generally, zoning would compound the social marginalisation and stigmatisation of sex workers by confining them to specific areas. Hubbard (1997) expressed concern that the stigmatisation of sex workers had traditionally been reinforced by their spatial exclusion and there was therefore a danger that zoning would not challenge the marginal status of street sex workers. This is a danger if the only driver for zoning is to 'remove' sex workers from 'respectable' communities. Campbell (2004) has argued that for zoning to work and meet the needs of all stakeholders it should be developed within a framework of civic responsibility, with local authorities recognising their duty of care to all citizens. Hence the drivers informing the development of zones should balance both a concern to improve the safety and welfare of sex workers and improve the quality of life for communities.

- Men who pay for sex would not go to a zone for fear of being identified or arrested. Those in favour stress that while there may be some initial reluctance and sckepticism they point to the fact that men have used the zones where they exist. Kerschl (2004) reported that clients frequent and accept the place.

- If an area adopted a zone it would be a magnet for sex workers from other areas in the region. The Netherlands experience suggests that some sex workers are willing to travel to work in a zone but the much larger section of workers are resident in the municipality. Informal zones in the UK see sex workers who are predominantly resident in the city/town, with a smaller section who travel in. The majority of women who work beats in the UK have problematic drug misuse and have routines linked into local drugs markets. This means local working is more convenient and preferred (Campbell 2004).

- A zone would become a 'lawless' area with drug dealing, pimping and other crime thriving. In the Netherlands activity in the zone is tightly controlled by the police. Areas that have had informal zones in the UK point to reductions in criminality in the zones (Clark *et al*. 2004) where police are more able to control and manage activity. In Edinburgh, following the loss of the zone, increases in exploitation were reported (Morgan Thomas 2004), for example, with more identified cases of children abused through prostitution and more opportunities for 'pimps' to pressurise women. The pro zone argument is that in the zoned context potential exploiters would be aware that the authorities were closely managing the situation and supporting sex workers, plus incidents of exploitation and crime would be more easily observed and acted upon.

- The introduction of a zone would encourage and increase street sex work. Yet there has been no evidence of this in the Netherlands, Germany or in cities where informal zones have operated in the UK. The socio-economic drivers that lead people to street sex work remain.

- A zone would condone and normalise prostitution. For some this means condoning violence against and exploitation of women (Bindel and Kelly 2004). This is an ideological position which is held by some policy-makers and feminist activists and theorists (see O'Neill 2001). Other feminist activists and sex worker activists have challenged the notion that sex work itself is violence (O'Connell Davidson 1998; Nagel 1998; see also Chapter 6) and propose that the policy focus should be on preventing forms of exploitation and violence that can occur within sex work and improving the rights of sex workers.

- Police would be unable to cooperate due to legal responsibilities. At the national Vice Conference 2004 the Association of Chief Police Officers (ACPO) lead on vice launching the ACPO strategy made it clear ACPO did not support zoning. Despite this police in a number of cities in the UK are involved in 'de facto' zoning or are developing policies of strategic enforcement. O'Neill and Campbell found that police in the local area where they carried out their research were guided by ACPO and wider force policies, which at the time of the study did not support zones. Yet the majority of officers made it clear that if politicians took the lead or there were changes in the law that enabled zones they would have no opposition to being involved in policing and managing such zones with other agencies. Many advocating for zones have argued for the need for changes in the legislative framework to enable zoning to happen 'formally' within the law so that the police and local authorities would not be compromised, e.g. the Prostitution Tolerance Zones (Scotland) Bill (SP Bill 67).
- Zoning in other areas and countries has failed on a number of fronts (Golding 1994; Benson and Matthews 1995; Bindel and Kelly 2004). Others in support of zoning would acknowledge the difficulties for some zones in other countries but point to the sustained benefits of other zones (Van Doorninck 2004), especially compared to unmanaged street sex work in the UK (Campbell 2003).

O'Neill *et al.* (2004) noted that many of these concerns were acknowledged by those in favour of zones who felt such concerns could be overcome through consultation, inclusive partnership working and environmental planning, particularly in relation to where the zone was sited and how it was organised, policed, managed and supported. The evidence from the Netherlands and Cologne is that many of these concerns could be overcome in practice, although new challenges will often arise.

In Liverpool, following the murder of two street sex workers in July 2003 and continued complaints from a number of residential communities, the city council carried a vote to commission a consultation on 'managed areas', looking to the Utrecht official street walking zone model. Sex workers, businesses and residents were consulted. Eighty-five per cent of respondents agreed in principle to a managed zone where sex trade workers could work without fear of arrest and 83 per cent were in favour of a managed zone in Liverpool. The main characteristic that respondents felt should be taken into account was that it should be away from a residential area (91 per cent). Of the 50 street sex workers consulted 96 per cent (n = 48) agreed with the principle of a managed zone and 96 per cent said they would work in a managed area, the main reason being added safety. Among the 98 per cent of those supporting zoning, no risk of arrest was seen as an incentive (88 per cent), while 72 per cent said that having restricted hours in which they could work would not deter them from working in a zone (Clark *et al.* 2004). The consultation concluded that there was broad support from all groups for a managed zone in the city. Liverpool was open and high-profile about the 'managed area', engaging with the media and also seeking discussion with and support from government. Liverpool, alongside a number of other authorities, called for the Home Office to consider permitting the piloting of a 'managed area' as part of the 'Paying the Price' consultation. Representatives from the council, while waiting for the government response, have stated that they would require a change in primary legislation before piloting a zone (Clucas 2005).

This high-profile approach in Liverpool contrasted with other areas. Hubbard (1999) points out that several local authorities have 'flirted' with the notion of establishing a designated zone. However, he notes that such discussions have been kept very low profile and not 'always widely publicised for fear of attracting negative and sensationalist media headlines that might suggest that a particular city is thinking of "legalising prostitution" because it is considering a toleration zone'. An example of the adverse effects of media attention is Sheffield which was attempting a planned and careful approach. Sheffield Prostitution Forum in the late 1990s, after community consultation, agreed to adopt a policy of geographical relocation. The forum wanted to move street prostitution from the traditional soliciting area that was predominately residential and identified twelve possible sites. One site which was mainly non-residential was selected and the authorities were ready to go ahead when media coverage created problems. A map of the area was leaked and published in the local press, which led to some complaints from local people and high-profile opposition from a large banking company which was located within the zone.

This demonstrates the need for thorough and wide-ranging consultation at all stages. Street zoning did not go ahead in Sheffield. As Hubbard points out: 'In the light of this it is not surprising that other cities considering creation of an official red light district have sought not to publicise their plans.' While this 'silence' and ambiguity still surrounds discussion about street zones a number of areas have developed what Hubbard (1999) calls 'de facto' zones. Pitcher *et al.* (2006) describe such zones as areas where the police ignore solicitation, but use laws relating to exploitation, under-age working, procuring and other criminal activities. They argue that such areas are best described as areas of selective decriminalisation rather than tolerance per se (Clark *et al.* 2004).

From the early 1980s to December 2002 in Edinburgh there was a 'non-harassment zone', located in an area of the city where street prostitution has historically taken place. In a small area a specified maximum number of women could solicit during permitted hours. No provision was made for a place for sexual services. Enforcement of soliciting legislation still occurred when women worked outside the specified area, but efforts were made to relay complaints from residents to sex workers via the police Prostitution Liaison Officer and the sex worker project. The zone was lost in December 2002.

The sex work project which had been in place during this period reported a range of detrimental impacts including: an increase in attacks against street sex workers; a reduction in reporting to the police; erosion of the degree of solidarity between sex workers; street prostitution becoming dispersed over a larger area; increased community complaints and direct action from residents; the police having less intelligence and control over the situation; projects finding it more difficult to contact clients; a decreased attendance at drop-in; increased occurrence of pimping; and an increase in under 18s working in the zone. Morgan Thomas (2004) reported that from the monitoring data of the outreach project women became dispersed across the area in attempts to avoid police attention, working over a three square mile area. There was an increase in 'Ugly Mugs' reported to the sex work support project. In 2001 there were 11 Ugly Mug incidents reported by street-based sex workers. In 2002 there were 31, a 300 per cent increase since the loss of the designated area. In 2003 there were 111, a 1,000 per cent increase since the loss of the designated area (Morgan Thomas 2004). The loss of the zone had a detrimental impact on sex worker/police relationships with cooperation and trust, established during the operation of a designated area, between the women and the police having deteriorated, as the police were now their persecutors rather than their protectors. It was difficult though to find a formal policy document outlining this approach which Hubbard (1999) referred to as an 'unofficial zone'. This model contrasted with the Dutch model of an 'official street walking zone' primarily because it was not 'formally' established under local bye-laws, and in addition it did not have an area for sexual services.

The lack of formality, however, did make it vulnerable to sudden 'closure'. Even in those cases in the Netherlands where zones have been closed, prior to closure there has had to be discussion and forward planning. The case of Edinburgh with the changes after the loss of the zone suggests there are some real advantages to zoning.

Since 2001 Aberdeen has had an area, located near the harbour, where street sex workers can work with less chance of being arrested for soliciting, and the majority of street sex workers will work within this area. Outreach is carried out by the drug action team a couple of evenings per week. There is a police Prostitution Liaison Officer. The council has reported improved safety for sex workers and lower levels of crime due to cooperation with the police.

Aberdeen council provided evidence which supported the Prostitution Tolerance Zones (Scotland) Bill (SP Bill 7) introduced to the Scottish Parliament by Margo McDonald MSP in October 2002, following the debate about the zone in Edinburgh. A section of residents had threatened to take the police and council to court for failing to enforce the law. This bill was an attempt to create a legislative framework which would enable formal zoning in those areas which wished to pursue such an approach. The objective of the bill was to enable local authorities to designate areas as 'prostitution tolerance zones'. It proposed an amendment to section 46 of the

Civil Government (Scotland) Act 1982 to make soliciting, loitering or importuning by sex workers in such zones not illegal.

The policy memorandum for the bill made it clear that this was not legalisation of prostitution across the board, and apart from the proposed change to allow local authorities to designate an area and for soliciting to fall outside the criminal law, the law would remain the same (Scottish Parliament 2002). The bill obligated local authorities to carry out consultation with local interests and did not propose a uniform of policy for managing street sex work for local authorities, but enshrined the principal that local areas should be able to choose the model most suitable for them. The bill was not successful. The Scottish Executive set up an Expert Group to review street prostitution in Scotland, which reported and made recommendations in December 2004 (Scottish Executive 2004). One recommendation was to replace the law criminalising soliciting specifically and creating a more general offence focusing on offensive behaviour or conduct arising from a prostitution-related sexual transaction caused by either the purchaser or seller. The expert group noted that this would

> amend the case for 'management zones' as a possible useful local strategy for focusing service delivery and managing nuisance arising from street prostitution. This would change from a case based on discretionary suspension of the criminal law to one which is within the law and can be considered and used in the right circumstances as part of the agreed strategy. (Scottish Executive 2004: 3)

A number of areas have had periods when they stress that they do not have policies of 'tolerance' zones but, for reasons of sex worker safety and also to minimise residential impact, utilise enforcement in a strategic manner. They have not adopted policies which declare that the law will not be enforced in certain areas but will utilise enforcement in some geographical areas strategically, i.e. in a manner which fosters strategic aims such as reducing street crime, improving sex worker safety or minimising nuisance to residents (O'Neill and Campbell 2002). In 2005 Northampton had a small area within a industrial estate where the police and local support project communicate to women that they can solicit there without arrest between certain times. No provision is made for an area for sexual services. Outreach work is carried out in the area. If women work outside this area they risk arrest and possibly an Anti-Social Behaviour Order. In this model the men who pay for sex are not given any amnesty and could be cautioned or arrested in the area.

Pitcher *et al.* (2005) described one of their study areas, a large Northern city where in its largest beat strategic enforcement takes place. Sex workers are directed to work in a predominantly industrial area where they are less likely to be arrested. The mobile sex worker outreach van parks in the area two evenings per week in this area of lesser complaint and car outreach is carried out in the area. A Prostitution Police Liaison Officer monitors the area, deals with any complaint, initially via mediation, and encourages the reporting of violence against sex workers. While this policy of an 'area of lesser complaints' was not official it was negotiated via the well established multi-agency prostitution forum.

This approach is not taking place in isolation but is part of a city-wide strategy developed by the multi-agency forum involving a number of initiatives aimed at reducing prostitution, reducing the impact on local communities and improving the health and safety of sex workers.

Concluding comments

Whatever the future holds in the UK and the Netherlands lessons can be learned from the successes and difficulties in the Netherlands over the last 20 years, the development of zones in other countries such as Germany and areas in the UK that have had informal zones. There is evidence that public order and the safety and health of street workers can benefit from zoning. The installation of a zone is the result of a complicated, sensitive and sometimes long process and requires a precarious balance of enough regulation to secure a legal and safe area for sex workers to work, but not too much regulation that will create a static, monolithic zone that cannot adapt to societal changes and will scare off marginalised groups. Location should be far enough away from residential areas to safeguard residents from the nuisances associated with street prostitution, but close enough to town/city centres to make sure sex workers have safe and easy access to the zone.

The establishment and management of a zone is always a compromise between the interests of all the different parties involved in street prostitution: local government, police, sex workers, neighbours, health, drug and social care services – all of whom have their own interests. Therefore it is vitally important there is direct and ongoing communication among all the parties involved. The balance between the different interests can change at times but should not permanently be disturbed. This will affect the functioning of the zone. Ongoing involvement and commitment, not only from the local government but from all parties, is necessary to have and maintain a good functioning zone. Careful ongoing planning, consultation and management is needed to establish an official street walking zone. This can also overcome the practical challenges. Political involvement and commitment is necessary for both establishing and sustaining a zone. Social economic changes in society will have immediate and sometimes drastic effects on street prostitution and the zones should be in a position to respond to these changes. The zones in the Netherlands were adopted with clear objectives, i.e. reducing community impact and improving the safety of sex workers. What we have learnt is that social and political conditions change and impact on street sex work policy, hence policy-makers have to try and think ahead and have structures for ongoing management, close monitoring and inclusive consultation. Zones are part of a changing society and should never be regarded as a static response to the management of street sex work.

Zoning is not an 'easy', 'ideal' or laissez faire 'solution' but involves a considerable degree of ongoing management and regulation and demands a high degree of joint inter-agency working. Zoning should not, and rarely has, taken place in a policy vacuum and if adopted needs to be a part of a multi-layered coordinate strategy which proactively addresses issues including the prevention of the commercial sexual exploitation of children, broader policies to prevent social exclusion, the creation of equal opportunities, the prevention of childhood sexual abuse, interventions to address coercion in sex work, the provision of holistic accessible health, drugs and, social care interventions which deliver both harm reduction and exit support services, and policies to improve the labour and human rights of sex workers.

Pitcher *et al.* (1996) recommend that national policy needs to accommodate local negotiation and exploration within each locality of a range of options for managing street sex work. This would include 'managed areas' for those areas where there was a consensus to develop them. They advocate a framework of 'citizenship and safer space for both residents and sex workers', which recognises differences in local conditions and views and hence allows for exploration of a range of options for the management of street sex work in local areas which permits zoning as one option.

Creating a safe space for dialogue might be seen as a necessary step before considering safe physical space, to encourage greater tolerance and joint exploration of viable practical outcomes. In some areas of modest to proactive tolerance these may include the potential for coexistence and the revitalising of shared public spaces. In others the polarisation between some groups of residents and sex workers may be too entrenched to allow initially for constructive discussions concerning the sharing of space. It may be pertinent to consider a framework which allows for the exploration of alternative designated spaces among a range of potential options, to work towards area-specific solutions that best suit shared interests. (Pitcher *et al.* 2006: 46)

In 2001 *The Economist* noted:

In dealing with prostitution, the government and the councils that run Britain's cities are pulling in different directions. (*The Economist* 2001)

This certainly still seems to be the case with regard to official street walking zones. There are few signs from government that they will consider initiatives or changes in the law which would give local authorities such as police, councils and health authorities more confidence and scope to trial zoning. Government statements do not support approaches which they class as involving the 'liberalisation' of prostitution (*The Economist* 2000). The Home Office consultation document *Paying the Price* acknowledges that areas such as Liverpool and Doncaster are considering 'managed areas' and focus on the recent challenges for zones in the Netherlands, the closures and the challenges of siting a zone. It indicates a disapproval of zones referring to them as 'problematic' and as an approach that is accepting of street sex work:

We need to consider how flexible communities are prepared to be and to hear strong and convincing arguments of the workability and benefits of managed areas before setting off down a road towards what has so far proved to be a problematic measure. Such a move normalises the concept of street prostitution and pre-supposes its continuing existence, and these are assumptions we need to challenge strongly. (Home Office 2004: 84)

Hubbard's (1999) analysis offered a modicum of hope for those who wish to trial street zoning:

> The Edinburgh approach has also not been greeted with enthusiasm by the Home Office, but the idea of geographically-selective decriminalisation remains a distinct possibility in Britain and elsewhere as principles of subsidiary and local accountability head towards the top of the political agenda. (p. 144)

Whether there will be scope for such local autonomy within the national strategy is unclear. In the UK, where present policies for dealing with street sex work seem to fail all groups, there is a great appetite for more effective policies. For some, official zoning has been seen as a pragmatic approach which could address in a more effective manner some of the problems which have been associated with street sex work. People want to see a reduction in sex workers attacked and murdered, a more conducive environment for providing accessing to support projects for sex workers, a notion of civic responsibility among all citizens for a safe working environment and a reduction in the impacts on communities.

Official zoning should be given a chance and the barometer on which zones should be judged should be evidence-based assessments of whether they improve the safety, welfare and rights of street sex workers, reduce the impact on communities, increase accessibility to services and enable more targeted and effective action on crime. The current reviews do not give the go ahead for a formal framework to enable zoning (in those areas that wish to develop them); it is likely that in the UK we will continue to have unofficial arrangements in some areas. Unless alternative approaches recommended by the government in its strategy bring improvements over the next couple of years then official street walking zones are likely to be back on the agenda.

Notes

1 From 1998 in several Dutch cities special 'tolerance places' have been established for drug users. The idea behind such places is that drug use in the street is very confronting for the public. Repression of drug use often leads to unsafe use, aggression among users, and between users and the public and the police. In these 'tolerance places' people can use and enjoy their drugs in a quiet environment. There are special rooms

for shooters and smokers. People are only allowed to stay a limited time in the using rooms. The 'tolerance places' are part of the Dutch 'harm reduction' approach towards drug use.

2 M. Barth and T. Apostolou (2001) 'Tippelzones horen niet in een beschaafde samenleving', *De Volkskrant*, 24 August 2001. This discussion is on and off in the Netherlands. Two Labour MPs launched the discussion, not for the first time, in the daily newspapers, pleading for a change in drugs policies as a solution.

3 From October 2000 the Dutch Penal Code no longer treats organising the prostitution of an adult female or male person as a crime provided this is done with the consent of the prostitute. However, any form of forced prostitution, pimping or trafficking remains in the Penal Code, with the maximum penalty of six years' imprisonment. In short, the exploitation of voluntary prostitution is legalised, while the exploitation of involuntary prostitution is punished more severely.

4 The policy of most of the living rooms has always been to create solidarity among the different groups of women and transgenders who work in the zone in order to increase their safety.

References

Aids Council of New South Wales (ACON) and Sex Workers Outreach Project (SWOP) (2000) *Unfinished Business*. ACON/SWOP.

Benson, C. and Matthews, R. (1995) 'Street prostitution: ten facts in search of a policy', *International Journal of the Sociology of Law*, 23: 395–415.

Bindel, J. and Kelly, L. (2004) *A Critical Examination of Responses to Prostitution in Four Countries: Victoria, Australia, Ireland, the Netherlands and Sweden*. Child and Woman Abuse Studies Unit, London Metropolitan University.

Bovenkerk, F. (1993) *Een veilige plek, 'huiskamers' voor straatprostituées*. Werkgroep Vraag en Aanbod: 's Hertogenbosch.

Campbell, R. (2002) *Towards Inclusive Multi Agency Responses to Sex Work*. Paper presented at: 'What Future Sex Workers? Reducing the Impact on the Community Through a Multi-Agency Approach', Barbican Centre, Silk Street, Tuesday, 28 May.

Campbell, R. (2003) *'Un-Managed' Street Prostitution in the UK*. Paper presented at Working Conference: 'The Future of Street Prostitution in the Netherlands', Parliament Building, The Hague, Netherlands, 29 September.

Campbell, R. (2004a) *Supporting Managed Areas: As Part of a Co-ordinated Multi-Agency Strategy on Sex Work*. Paper presented at: 'Duncan Society Debate on Zoning of Street Prostitution', Blackburne House, Liverpool, 20 October.

Campbell, R. (2004b) *Celebrating the Work of Sex Work Projects*. Paper presented at Manchester Prostitution Forum Conference, Manchester Town Hall, 14 November.

Campbell, R. (2006) *Creating Choices: Exit Support for Sex Workers in Walsall Good Practice Review and Gap Analysis.* Walsall South Health Action Zone.

Campbell, R. and O'Neill, M. (2001) *Working Together to Create Change: Consulting Communities Affected by and Involved in Prostitution.* Paper presented at: 'The National Vice Conference: Enforcement and Protection', Avon and Somerset Constabulary Headquarters, Portishead, 25–27 June.

Campbell, R., Coleman, S. and Torkington, P. (1996) *Street Prostitution in Inner City Liverpool.* Liverpool City Council.

Clark, P., Bellis, M., Cook, P. and Tocque, K. (2004) *Consultation on a Managed Zone For Sex Trade Workers in Liverpool.* Centre for Public Health, Liverpool John Moores University, Liverpool.

Clucas, F. (2005) 'Welcome from Liverpool City Council', Working with Diverstiy in Sex Work: UK Network of Sex Work Projects National Conference, 25th February, Britannia Adelphi Hotel, Liverpool.

Economist, The (2001) 'Mean Streets', 6 January, p. 25.

Golding, R. (1994) 'Prostitution in Holland', *Police Review*, 10, Spring, 48–57.

Hester, M. and Westmarland, N. (2004) *Tackling Street Prostitution: Towards a Holistic Approach*, Home Office Research Study 279. London: Home Office Development and Statistics Directorate.

Home Office (2004) *Paying the Price: A Consultation Paper in Prostitution.* London: Home Office.

Hubbard, P. (1997) 'Red light districts and toleration zones: geographies of female street prostitution in England and Wales', *Area*, 29 (2): 129–40.

Hubbard, P. (1998) 'Sexuality, immorality and the city: red-light districts and the marginalisation of female street prostitutes', *Gender, Place and Culture*, 5 (1): 55–72.

Hubbard, P. (1999) *Sex and the City: Geographies of Prostitution in the Urban West.* Aldershot: Ashgate.

Kerschl, A. V. (2004) *The Dislocation Process of the Illegal Street Prostitution Scene in Cologne: Results of the Scientific Evaluation of the Pilot Project.* Paper presented at 'Drugs and Mobility in Europe AMOC Conference', Prague, 3–5 June.

Lamboo, T. (1995) *Straatprostitutie in Nederland. Een analyse en overzicht van het erschijnsel, beleid en tippelzones.* Thesis, University of Amsterdam.

Matthews, R. and Benson, R. (1996) *Report of the Parliamentary Group on Prostitution.* London: Middlesex University.

Morgan Thomas, R. (2004) *SCOT-PEP – The Edinburgh Zone and ASBO Experience.* Paper presented at: Manchester Prostitution Forum Conference, Manchester Town Hall, 14 October.

Municipality of Utrecht (1999) 'Police, Drop-in Living Room for Prostitutes', De Baan. Street Prostitution in Utrecht, Municipality of Utrecht.

Nagel, J. (1997) *Whores and Other Feminists.* London: Routledge.

O'Connell Davidson, J. (1998) *Prostitution, Power and Freedom.* Cambridge: Polity Press.

O'Neill, M. (2001) *Prostitution and Feminism*. Cambridge: Polity Press.

O'Neill, M. and Campbell, R. (2002) *Working Together To Create Change: Walsall Prostitution Consultation Research*. Walsall South Health Action Zone/Staffordshire University/Liverpool Hope University.

O'Neill, M. and Campbell, R. (2003) *Participatory Action Research With Sex Workers and Communities Affected by Street Prostitution: Working Together to Create Change, One Step Forward, One Step Back*. Paper presented at: 'Safer Sex and the City: International Conference on Street Prostitution, Research, Policy and Practice', University of Liverpool, 11 September.

O'Neill, M., Campbell, R., James, A., Webster, M., Green, K., Patel, J., Akhtar, N. and Saleem, W. (2004) 'Red lights and safety zones', in D. Bell and M. Jayne (eds), *City of Quarters: Urban Villages in the Contemporary City*. Aldershot: Ashgate.

Penfold, C., Hunter, G., May, T., Campbell, R. and Barham, L. (2004) 'Tackling client violence in female street prostitution: inter-agency working between outreach projects and the police', *Policing and Society*, 14 (4): 365–79.

Pitcher, J. E., O'Neill, M., Scoular, J., Hubbard, P. J and Campbell, R. (2006) *From Conflict to Coexistence: Living and Working in Areas of Street Sex Work*. York: Joseph Rowntree Foundation.

Scottish Executive (2004) *Being Outside, Constructing a Response to Street Prostiution: A Report of the Expert Group on Prostiution in Scotland*. Edinburgh: Scottish Executive.

Scottish Parliament (2002) *Prostitution Tolerance Zones (Scotland) Bill: Policy Memorandum*. Edinburgh: Stationary Office.

Ten Dan, C., Bieleman, B., Biesma, S., Goeree, P., Meijer, G. and Snippe, J. (1999) *Evaluatie Tippelzone*. Netherlands: Groningen.

UK Network of Sex Work Projects (2004) *United Kingdom Network of Sex Work Projects: Response to 'Paying the Price'*. Manchester: UK Network of Sex Work Projects.

Van Doorninck, M. (2003) *Streetwalking Zones: The Amsterdam Experience*. Paper presented at: 'Prostitution in the 21st Century: Pulling Apart the Myths', Joint Conference of UK Network of Sex Work Projects and Mainliners, Paragon Hotel, Birmingham, 5 December.

Van Doorninck, M. (2004) *Trial and Error: Some Lessons Learned from the Dutch Experiences of Zoning*. Paper presented at Manchester Prostitution Forum Conference, Manchester Town Hall, 14 October.

Viet, N. (1996) *Straatprostitutie in Nederland, problematiek en maatregelen*. Netherlands: University of Groningen.

Visser, J. (1997) *The Dutch Law Proposal on Prostitution: Text and Explanation*. Mr A. De Graaf Foundation, Institute for Prostitution Issues, Amsterdam, Netherlands.

Visser, J. (1998) *Selling Private Sex in Public Places: Managing Street Prostitution in the Netherlands*. Paper presented at: 'Changing Perspectives on Female Prostitution: A Regional Conference', Greenbank Hall, Liverpool University, 6 February.

Chapter 4

Behind the personal ads: the indoor sex markets in Britain

Teela Sanders

In what has been described as an 'unbridled ethic of sexual consumption' (Bernstein 2001), the USA and Western Europe has experienced a growth in all areas of the sex industry. Contrary to what Ryder (2004: 1659) documents as a 'spectacular decline of traditional adult entertainment districts' in the USA, in Britain, lap-dancing bars and strip joints are no longer consigned to the back alleys of Soho but are an expected and accepted part of the high-street entertainment zone. Pornography is increasingly available in a wide range of outlets and accessible through the Internet and mail-order stores and X-rated material is broadcast on terrestrial television. Sex tourism in palm-lined beach resorts has increased as Western men (O'Connell Davidson 2002) and, to a lesser extent, women (Sanchez Taylor 2001) seek commercial sex in the sun. With the popularity of Ann Summers parties, and now shops (Storr 2003), some forms of sexual consumption are overtly available for women as purchasers in their own right.

This growth in sexual commercialisation has not escaped the direct sexual services industry. Largely the responsibility of the Internet and computer-mediated communication (hereafter CMC), including mobile telephones, prostitution can only be described as booming in Britain. Similar to the expansion of massage parlours in Oslo during the 1990s (Skilbrei 2001), it is the indoor markets where supply has increased to match the demand. Contrary to the familiar newspaper image of the stiletto-clad woman leaning into the window of a car, it is in the indoor arenas that the majority of commercial sex is exchanged. The increase in indoor sex establishments can be attributed, among other factors, to harsh zero tolerance policies, particularly in London, that have encouraged women to work inside while street prostitution has seen a steady decline (Matthews 1997).

This chapter concentrates on the organisation of sex that is sold through escort agencies; brothels and working premises where women congregate to work collectively in pairs or larger groups; independent entrepreneurs who work alone, offering 'outcalls' to meet a client at a location of his choice; and premises that are legitimately licensed by local councils and magistrates as massage parlours but in fact offer direct sexual services.

The rise of direct and indirect sexual services is an indication of wider changing social relationships, structures and attitudes. As Agustín describes in this collection (Chapter 5), the movement of female economic labour is responsible for the growth in sexual, emotional and domestic labour performed by women. What is also relevant, as Jackson and Scott (2004) argue, is the change in mores relating to sexual behaviour and sexuality in late modern societies. The tolerance of pre-marital and, to some extent, extra-marital sex coexists with the inclusion of celebrated homosexuality in the form of popular entertainment venues such as the 'gay village' (Collins 2004). This suggests some sexual liberal progress and perhaps the beginnings of a shift away from 'compulsory heterosexuality'. Logically, this moral shift should extend to tolerating commercial sex that is consensual and harmless. But in the legal sphere and increasingly among the moral police, prostitution continues to cause anxiety and is framed as a social problem and a nuisance to communities, with a concentration on punishing and excluding mainly the women who take part. While sex workers continue to bear the brunt of discourses of disease and criminalisation (Lerum 1998), the demand side of prostitution has recently been at the front of public and private disapproval as laws increasingly problematise male sexuality (Brookes-Gordon and Gelsthorpe 2003), driven by a distinct public nuisance discourse aimed at 'kerb-crawlers' (Kantola and Squires 2004).

This chapter will draw on the small number of empirical studies that have been conducted on the indoor prostitution markets in Britain. Although it has been recognised that prostitution is a hard-to-access activity (Faugier and Sargeant 1997; Pyett 1998b), the indoor markets involve particular methodological problems because they are literally hidden from view, posing barriers to access and negotiation for the researcher (Lever and Kanouse 1998; Sanders 2005b). The lack of attention from researchers on the indoor markets is also political: most of the empirical data collected in prostitution studies focuses on the visible nature of the street markets that signals the overt face of prostitution. Generated by the discourse that problematises all prostitution as an illicit, diseased activity that is a blight on civility, much of the research that is commissioned on prostitution concentrates on the extreme end: drug use, sexual abuse, exploitation and establishing links between street markets, trafficking and organised crime. On the whole, the concentration on the street markets, which is the smallest arena in which commercial sex is sold in Britain, exonerates only the harsh end of a wide spectrum of the sex industry, presenting an unbalanced and unrealistic picture of prostitution. This results in the ordinary, non-violent and consensual sexual exchanges that constitute the majority of commercial sex between men and women being left out of the policy-making and decision-making process.

This chapter attempts to draw together empirical findings that highlight what Scambler (1997: 112) has described as the mundane aspects of commercial sex. The conviction with which I write stems from an ethnographic study in 2000–01, in a large English city, where I had the opportunity to speak with women who worked in prostitution and spent many hours in their various places of work. This year-long project brought me into contact with over three hundred sex workers (most of whom worked independently and indoors), resulting in 55 formal taped interviews. I also spoke with female owners of establishments, managers and receptionists and others who worked on the periphery of the industry such as doormen, drivers and web designers. Alongside this study, I conducted a virtual ethnography of one particular website designed for sellers and purchasers of sex in Britain (Sanders 2005a). Much of these findings are reported in a monograph *Sex Work: A Risky Business* (Sanders 2005c), and various data collected during this study will be referenced in this chapter.

This chapter is divided into four main parts. First, the current legislative framework relating to the indoor markets is ironed out with some reflections on possible changes to the law in England and Wales. Second, the landscape of the markets is explored to convey the characteristics of what has often been portrayed as an elusive economy. Third, the role of the Internet in the indoor markets is examined as a distinct change in the social organisation of prostitution. Fourth, relying on my own findings of what I argue is an 'occupational culture', I describe how the ordinary and mundane nature of the indoor sex markets are effectively regulated and managed by all involved.

The legal landscape

Going back to at least 1161 under Henry II, Sharp (1998: 190) documents how women involved in prostitution have been the subject of regulation, rehabilitation and repression. Historically in Britain, throughout the reign of various monarchs, brothels have been closed, opened, reopened and sanctioned by the Crown, while at the same time the women who have worked in them have been punished, sometimes by public execution. During the sixteenth and seventeenth centuries brothels and bathhouses flourished, although women were persistently excluded and shamed. During the nineteenth century in Victorian Britain, existing vagrancy laws regulated prostitution while the narrative that justified the confinement of prostitutes was gathering pace (see Finnegan 1979; Walkowitz 1980). Led by medical discourses to disguise the moral reproach of 'fallen women' (Spongberg 1997), the 1860s was a significant period when the Contagious Diseases Acts focused on controlling women in prostitution because of a national concern about public sexual health. This took place at a time when 'bawdy' houses were commonplace, especially in garrison towns and ports; in 1859, police records show there were some 2,828 brothels in London, with as many as 80,000 women working in them (Porter 1994).

Contemporary prostitution is still subject to laws made over fifty years ago, although there are moves by the government to make imminent changes (Home Office 2004). The law has not taken a strict abolitionist stance and outlawed the exchange of sex for money as it has done in the USA, but instead criminalises the relationships that surround prostitution. The Sexual Offences Act 1956 made it an offence to procure (encourage) a woman into prostitution, for a man to live off the immoral earnings of a woman or a woman to control another woman's activities. This Act made a specific offence of brothel-keeping which implicated landlords who knowingly rented premises for this purpose.

It is commonly accepted that this legislation concentrated on criminalising relationships between workers and those involved in organising the sale of sex. The reaction to this law saw women take to the streets while the preceding Street Offences Act 1959 criminalised loitering and soliciting in a public place, 'sweeping women off the streets and into call-girl flats' (Self 2003: 8). Today, what is significant for women who work indoors is that the law prevents two or three women working together legitimately, effectively discouraging safe working conditions and collective business relationships (Kennedy

1993: 148). What the law fails to do is make any distinctions between coercive procuring as opposed to consensual working partnership between organisers and workers. The failure to recognise the spectrum of consensus and coercion that is apparent in prostitution could theoretically result in those involved in effectively assisting women to work safely receiving custodial sentences. This confusion continues under the recent Sexual Offences Act 2003 which introduced a new penalty: that of keeping a brothel used for prostitution, with a sentence of up to seven years in prison.

Phoenix (1999: 20) summarises: 'In practice, then, the only way that prostitution can be practised without committing a criminal offence is as a one-to-one arrangement between two consenting adults in private.' Day (1996) reflects from extensive contact with sex workers in London how women respond to the ambiguities of the law by working flexibly in an informal economy. However, these accounts highlight sex workers' complaints of arbitrary policing and the pressure to work in extreme isolation because of the legal constraints.

In reality, those who work in the indoor markets are rarely subject to police intervention. As a Home Office reports notes:

> Although it is illegal for such premises to offer sexual services, police regulation is generally minimal and intervention will occur only in response to a police complaint ... there was an 'unwritten rule' that parlours would only be prosecuted if a complaint had been made against them – leading to a reasonable expectation that a well-run operation would not attract police attention. (May, Harocopos and Hough 2000: 9)

Benson and Matthews (1995) conducted a survey of vice squads in Britain and found that although some forces employed surveillance tactics on indoor premises, this practice varied considerably. In some areas the police were reluctant to get involved in the indoor markets, so operated an informal policy of toleration. There is also evidence that brothel owners and independent workers strike up informal relationships with local police officers on the basis of an exchange of information relating to other crimes if businesses are left alone to ply their trade (see Nemitz 2001; Sanders 2005c). The limited use of brothel-keeping laws is demonstrated in the crime statistics. Over the past twenty years the peak of convictions occurred in 1990 when 141 persons were found guilty of brothel-keeping offences, while in 2002 this had declined to only eight convictions (Home Office 2004: 93).

Yet, it has been documented that indoor workers have been subject to underhand methods of control. Hubbard (2004: 1687) reports on the, what he calls, 'spatial cleansing' of prostitution through brutal strategies to displace establishments. For example, Westminster Council applied a policy of the compulsory purchase of properties that the council claimed were used for 'immoral purposes', resulting in some women being evicted from their homes. The relaxed attitude that has traditionally been shown by the police may be changing, as aggressive and authoritarian styles of policing become apparent. In recent years there have been various raids on indoor premises across the UK, usually a combined investigation from immigration services and international police operations concerned with trafficking and illegal migrants (Dickson 2004: 91). These operations have been made possible by a welcomed strengthening of the law through the Sexual Offences Act 2003 that made a new offence of the trafficking of people for sexual exploitation. This has led to women being arrested, detained and in some cases deported into what would most probably be dangerous situations in their home country.

The 2003 Act further outlaws third-party involvement in 'controlling prostitution for gain' (Section 58) without making any specific definitions regarding coercion or deception. Therefore a person running a brothel or escort agency could be charged with committing an offence when no harm is caused. Without stating the nature of the relationship in the law, this leaves open the possibility that romantic partners who are involved in organising escort agencies, or who act as drivers for women, could be charged when no harm is apparent.

Aside from controlling prostitution through legislation, the indoor markets are also subject to community resistance and public outrage. Individual women who have been found to be working from home or a rented apartment in the suburbs are often the subject of aggressive hate campaigns (Hubbard 1998). In my own research women reported that they experienced verbal and physical harassment from residents and 'name and shame' campaigns which often included media attention and front-page exposures, as well as letters and photographs sent to their family who usually were not aware of their money-making activities (Sanders 2005c: chapter 6).

The Home Office Report *Paying the Price: A Consultation Paper on Prostitution* offers a welcomed opportunity to change what the Home Secretary describes as laws that are 'outdated, confusing and ineffective' (2004: 5). There is a decisive shift in the tone of the review that reflects a recent trend to concentrate on those who are abused through prostitution, either because they are minors (see Pearce, this volume) or because they are migrant women who are trafficked from predominantly Eastern European countries. As Kantola and Squires (2004) document, the international and European legal frameworks have largely influenced recent policy directions in Britain, in particular the United Nations Convention against Transnational Organised Crime adopted in November 2000. This Convention includes a pledge to combat the buying and selling of women and children for sexual exploitation. Addressing the issues of sexual exploitation and trafficking set out in this agenda, together with the discourse of public nuisance that has been aired closer to home in local communities, has influenced current parliamentary debates. The Home Office review states clearly that their focus is on preventing young people from being coerced into prostitution, protecting and supporting adults involved with a specific aim to provide pathways out of prostitution, and bringing pimps and traffickers to justice (2004: 7). From the outset there appears to be little intention to address prostitution as an activity that women, free from coercion, can choose to engage in as a rational way of earning money. Instead, the public protection agenda is concerned largely with the extreme end of exploitation, the role of the police in transnational organised crimes and the visible effect on communities. This places the complex world of escorts, domination services and massage parlours at the margins of policy and legislative change, possibly because these markets remain out of sight.

The consultation paper acknowledges that street-based prostitution is characterised differently from indoor prostitution and that alternative measures are necessary to regulate this part of the industry. Although the research conducted in this country has not been utilised, the report highlights that 'drug use, sexually and drug transmitted infections, nuisance behaviour and other issues common on the street are less prevalent' in the indoor markets (p. 84). In turn, the paper goes on to recognise that the vague definitions of a brothel prevent two or more individuals working together and for the sake of safe working conditions this may be amended (p. 84). Despite a lack of empirical research summarised in the Home Office consultation, there are suggestions that there will be legislative reform that will affect the organisation of the indoor markets and the way sex is sold and purchased.

What the review does not offer is a debate on the place of commercial sex in contemporary society, where sexuality has been removed from the shackles of religion, gender oppression and biological determination. What is missing from the review is any notion that some women can be involved in prostitution by an informed choice made by a rational decision-making process. This has been argued by McLeod (1982) and O'Neill (1997) who have met many sex workers in Britain who would describe themselves as working in prostitution through choice. The dichotomy of victim/ agent is the precise dilemma that feminists and scholars have debated for several decades (see O'Connell Davidson 1995; Kesler 2002). The United Nations are consistent in differentiating prostitution as choice and that which is imposed on individuals because they do not define consensual prostitution as a human wrong but a human right (Raymond 1999). This is not acknowledged in the Home Office consultation paper but instead continues with the moral order discourse of women who either need 'protection' or those who are a public nuisance worthy of control.

The consultation document offers a review of the licensing system for brothels in Victoria and New South Wales in Australia, Austria and the Netherlands, highlighting the pros and cons of each system. All of these places operate a system of licensed brothels yet still criminalise prostitution that spills out from the regulated properties. Taking stock of these regimes in more progressive systems, the coming months may see changes to the indoor markets in England and Wales. This could take the form of an interventionist strategy consisting of a licensing system, with potentially a health registration scheme, to replace the informal system that currently exists.

However, it is also a possibility that the abolitionist movement currently strong in Europe (for instance, in Sweden, since 1999, there has been a law against the purchasing of sexual services, criminalising the demand side (see Ostergren 2004)) will reframe the solutions to what have been painted as problems, rather than concentrate on facilitating safe commercial exchanges. The tone of the Home Office consultation paper already echoes that of the Wolfenden Report that was concerned either with 'public decency' or with the exploitation of women rather than the place of prostitution in contemporary society. Therefore there is the possibility that the laws first introduced in the 1985 Sexual Offences Act could further criminalise those who seek to buy commercial sex by soliciting on the street. The discourse surrounding men who buy sex as a public nuisance (Kantola and Squires 2004) or that of abusers of women (Raymond 2004) is a rhetoric that has gained strength over the past two decades in Britain and could be seized upon by policy-makers.

Mapping out the markets

The markets

There can be no useful typologies of women who become involved in prostitution or typical profiles of how women enter into prostitution (O'Neill 2001: 75), despite evidence of a high degree of sexual abuse in childhood among those involved in prostitution (Cusick 2002). As O'Connell Davidson (1998: 99) states: 'people come to prostitution as individuals with particular personal histories and subjective beliefs, and some people's psycho-biographies and attitudes leave them far more open to abuse and exploitation than others.' Indeed, the variety of women that are involved in the indoor markets is highlighted by Day (1996: 78) who presents individual case studies to show how prostitution is defined by 'radical individualism'. Day argues that all women involved in prostitution are driven by 'the idea of business' that accumulates in a process of 'spending, saving and investing money'. Women who work indoors tend to be older than those on the street, with a longer work history in the mainstream labour market. As Rickard (2001) describes through the curriculum vitaes of five sex workers, women have often worked in various mainstream jobs before entering prostitution. In my own study, all of the 55 women who were interviewed had worked in the official labour market: 11 women had college qualifications, 5 others had trained and practised as a nurse, while three were studying for a degree at university (Sanders 2005: chapter 3).

Often women who enter the indoor sex markets have also been involved in other parts of the sex industry. Whittaker and Hart (1996) report from their study in London that most women who work in flats had also worked on the street, in saunas and as escorts. In my own study, only seven of the 55 women interviewed had only worked in one market, and 16 women had previously worked on the street. There is also a high degree of geographical mobility among sex workers as they work 'away days' in other cities and towns, often to preserve anonymity.

Indoor sex markets can be characterised in different ways. May, Edmunds and Hough (1999: 3) describe how the markets in Britain differ on three dimensions: first, there is the contractual nature of the sexual relationship where money is exchanged; second, the market is determined by the method of contact between the buyer and the seller; third, the organisation and management of the market ranges from coercive pimping, to an employee relationship and to women who are autonomous, self-employed workers. Phoenix (1995) also determines the difference between the street and parlour work in Britain by the place of work, the mode of client contact, the employment status of the woman, the financial exchange practices and the risks they face.

A recent headline in a broadsheet declared 'Sex comes out of the city into middle England' (*The Observer* 18 April 2004). Working premises are increasingly found in quiet suburbs, sometimes disguised by legitimate businesses such as hairdressers. Larger massage parlours or licensed saunas are often closer to main streets in towns and cities, identifiable by neon signs or metal shutters. Escort agencies, many of which are now online, make up one section of the indoor markets (Soothill 2004). The agency charges the client an introduction fee while the escort negotiates her own fee with the client. The escort pays a fee to the agency for advertising costs as they take the burden for attracting clients.

Based in a middle England town, O'Connell Davidson (1998: 21–2) describes 'Stephanie's' as a typical sauna that involves a complex financial system of fees. Owners receive a 'shift fee' as rent from each worker plus a 'punter fee' from the worker for each client that purchases a service. In addition, a 'receptionist fee' is also paid by the workers to cover the managerial overheads. The owner also receives a 'massage fee' directly from each client who enters the building.

Whittaker and Hart (1996) were among the first to present findings that describe the indoor sex scene in England. With the intention of exploring how sex workers develop strategies for managing risk in relation to occupational health, they report on the social organisation and conditions of work among 'flat-working women'. The study involved 14 interviews with sex workers and six lengthy visits to 59 flats in the heart of the 'erotic entertainment' district in London. Some of the flats were seen to be in dilapidated conditions with basic washing facilities, often without hot water. There was often only one woman working at any one time in order to stay within the law. However, Whittaker and Hart highlight the importance of the 'maid': a receptionist who co-works with the sex worker and is involved in the daily operations by checking the clients as they arrive and during the transaction. The maid is essential in terms of protective strategies and monitoring client interactions and this was the most popular method of working in flats.

Increasingly women are working independently, either seeing clients at their home or visiting them in hotels. Independent workers also rent out premises where they work alone or with another colleague.

Those who work alone from their own property operate a legal activity because there is no third party or brothel-keeping involved. O'Connell Davidson (1998: 88–90) describes 'entrepreneurial' prostitution using the example of 'Desiree', a self-employed independent worker who owns a separate property for business. She is highly successful, earning between £1,000 and £2,000 each week, owns two properties and a top-of-the-range car. O'Connell Davidson (1996) describes how Desiree keeps control of her interactions with clients in such a way that she has never come to any harm.

Women who work independently offer an extensive range of sexual services including domination services (with facilities such as dungeon rooms) and various other role play and fantasies. Sex workers also offer other services such as tantric massage, destressing services, socialising and holidays with clients. There have been several anecdotal accounts from sex workers regarding their role as sex educators, counsellors and assisting men to address their sexual dysfunctions (Delacoste and Alexander 1988; Sanders 2004b).

Advertising

In any economic transaction where a buyer and a seller is integral to the commodity, a signalling process is needed to indicate what is available and how it is purchasable. In an illicit economy where the goods on offer are shrouded in taboo, stigma and secrecy, this signalling relationship takes on specific dynamics. On the street, the availability of women for hire takes place through the physical presence of women in certain areas known as 'red light districts', or through workers directly asking if a man is 'looking for business'. In the indoor markets, advertising is a considerable drain on the profits of workers and requires a considerable outlay in resources (Phoenix 1995). Although advertising prostitution services is illegal, long gone are the play on words such as 'French Polishing a Speciality' and 'Large Chest for Sale' that appealed to those with an imagination during the 1970s.

To manoeuvre around the legal hitches, legitimate businesses are organised as a disguise or, more traditionally, the classified and personal columns of local newspapers offer individual telephone numbers at a considerable weekly fee. More recently, there has been a major shift in advertising as many entrepreneurs use online facilities (see below). This has not reduced the number of specialist contact magazines that often show a gallery of photographs of women offering domination and fantasy services as well as basic sexual services.

In the capital calling cards found in telephone booths have been one of the few visible signs of a prolific indoor sex market (Swirsky and Jenkins 2000). This method has recently been the subject of legislative change sparked by the 1999 Home Office consultation paper, *New Measures to Control Prostitutes' Cards in Phone Boxes.* The government described calling cards as undesirable and offensive to the community not only because they give tourists a poor impression of the country but because it reduced the profits of telecommunication companies. During the 1990s much of the capital's indoor establishments advertised by using 'card boys' (who were paid approximately £100 per day) to replace up to 170,000 cards each week that were removed by cleaning companies hired by the local authority. In addition, telecommunication companies barred the telephone numbers advertised on the cards, which consequently left some women without access to help if needed. This cat-and-mouse game was dramatically reduced by the introduction of a specific offence relating to advertising prostitution in the Criminal Justice and Police Act 2001, which has reduced the number of cards visible in the public domain.

The routine

In the exchange of money for sex, a whole host of activities take place including soliciting for custom, negotiating contracts, providing a setting for executing business and managing the throughput of clients. In the indoor markets, where the quality of a service can mean a client is present for hours rather than minutes, sex workers concentrate on a set routine. Desiree, an entrepreneurial sex worker, describes the five-stage process she goes through with each customer as 'settling him in', 'getting him going', 'getting him to shoot his load', 'reassuring him' and 'normalising and getting him out' (O'Connell Davidson 1996: 184–5). Sex workers I spoke with described how their services also included health education for men about sexually transmitted diseases and their own bodies, sexual functioning and sex therapy as well as a counselling relationship. Plumridge *et al.* (1997) interviewed male clients who also said that commercial sex was attractive because of the emotional exchange as well as the physical/sexual relationship. It could be suggested that the service offered indoors is different to that available on the streets where sexual services are basic in terms of shorter interactions and only one sexual service agreed upon for a stated price.

The working environment and characteristics in which sex is

Sex Work Now

sold in the indoor markets is not unlike that of other mainstream professional jobs that deal with emotions and bodies. There are similar processes for training novice workers and 'house rules' to pass on strict standards of behaviour. May, Harocopos and Hough (2000: 26) interviewed ten managers who established a list of common rules: 'Never employ juveniles, no anal sex, condoms always to be used, no partners allowed in the workplace, no overcharging, no rudeness or unpunctuality, no drunkenness and no clients under the age of 18.' As Jaget (1980: 148) describes from a personal account, indoor workers usually go through some form of 'sexual apprenticeship' from experienced workers who introduce the house rules as well as the routines in the bedroom. As O'Connell Davidson (1996) notes from her observations of entrepreneurs at work, humour, role-play and thespian skills are as important as sexual skills. Humour is an integral organising feature of the industry; women use jesting and joking to manage their own emotions and that of their colleagues and clients (Sanders 2004a).

Indeed, the role of the sex worker has been likened to performing 'emotional labour' on herself and her clients. O'Neill (2001: 89) argues that 'emotional labour is a central aspect of the women's relationship with the client and involves them in manipulating, suppressing and falsifying their own feeling life in order to do the intimate work'. Kempadoo and Doezema (1999) and Chapkis (1997) have already argued that when women engage in sexual or erotic activities in prostitution it should be understood as selling a form of emotional labour. The nature of this labour has been recognised: 'Prostitution is extraordinarily stressful work ... it calls for emotional labour of a type and on a scale which is probably unparalleled in any other job ... the self-employed prostitute must keep herself in a constant state of readiness for tasks that are emotionally demanding and intrusive' (O'Connell Davidson 1995: 4). Some women speak of their job satisfaction in sauna work (see O'Neill 2001: 86) and their economic earning power by capitalising on expected notions of feminine sexuality. The relationship between sexual labour through prostitution has been compared to other forms of feminised labour where women consciously engage in the commodification of femininity as a profit-making enterprise (see Sanders forthcoming).

Drugs, condoms and violence

Contrary to what has been established in relation to the links between street prostitution and the drug markets, evidence suggests there is

104

limited use of illegal drugs in off-street prostitution. A study conducted for an outreach project in Streatham, London notes 'the split between users and non-users was divided almost exactly between flat workers and street workers' (Taylor 2003: 7). This has been substantiated in other parts of the country: Morgan Thomas *et al.* (1989) interviewed parlour workers in Edinburgh of whom only one reported injecting drugs. From a sample of 55 sauna workers, McCullagh *et al.* (1998) found only five reported ever injecting. Brewis and Linstead (2000: 87) highlight how sophisticated parlours do not accept women who use drugs because organisational rules within off-street prostitution prohibit substance use.

A comprehensive survey among 240 workers across the sex industry in Leeds, Edinburgh and Glasgow found a lower level of drug consumption indoors compared to on the street (Church *et al.* 2001). A closer analysis of the results confirms that the type of drug differs between street and indoor workers: 78 per cent (90) of women who worked outside had used cocaine while only 5 per cent (6) of indoor workers reported using this drug. Interestingly, the use of tranquillisers was common practice among the indoor workers (79 per cent, 99) compared to street workers (43 per cent, 37). This evidence and my own observations suggest that addictive opiate use is common among street workers while indoor workers prefer recreational drugs. This may reflect wider use of drugs by women in the general population or trends among young people to take recreational drugs (Malbon 1999). Yet, evidence from a Scottish study (Cusick 1999) highlights that there may be geographical differences in the use of drugs in the indoor markets, as the traditional demarcations between street drug users and those non-drug users who work indoors have reduced in Glasgow over recent years.

The use of condoms also appears to be prolific in the indoor markets, reflecting wider trends among sex workers who work on the street (Ward *et al.* 1999). In London, Whittaker and Hart (1996: 405) found among flat workers that all women spoke of their persistent condom use, even for oral sex, despite frequent requests from clients and offers of extra cash to forfeit safe sex. Sanders (2004b) notes how indoor sex workers described two key health risks related to their work: clients forcing unprotected sex or condoms breaking, leaking or coming off, all of which could cause sexually transmitted infections and HIV. However, these were relatively isolated incidents and because of the medical and health protection advice the women regularly used, they felt that health risks were one aspect of occupational hazards that they could control. Comprehensive awareness of health issues can be

105

explained by the intense health promotion work that has taken place with sex workers over the past decade that continues through over ninety projects in Britain (see Cooper *et al.* 2001).

Non-condom use is normally related to drug use, chaotic behaviour and male coercion: the type of characteristics that are more prominent on the streets compared to the relatively ordered nature of the indoor markets. Of the 240 women surveyed across three cities in Britain, although 63 per cent (151) had experienced client violence in their lifetime there were differences between the markets (Church *et al.* 2001). Reports from the same survey show significant differences in the extent of violence: 81 per cent (93) of street workers had experienced violence from clients, compared to 48 per cent (60) who worked indoors.

Whittaker and Hart (1996: 406) note that flat workers describe safety in terms of a guaranteed payment, sex with a condom and a reduction in the potential for client violence. Although women they spoke with had experienced violence indoors, there were two characteristics that made the indoor market safer. First, indoor space was the woman's own territory – it was safe and contained. Second, the presence of another person in the role of a maid provided extra security and assistance in the eventuality that a client should act aggressively. Sex workers revealed to me how they adopt a host of precautionary mechanisms before they meet the client (such as not wearing jewellery, keeping on shoes, taking control of the sexual position, using various forms of contraception, telling someone where they are), which are backed up by deterrents and remedial protection (Sanders 2005c: chapter 5). If sex workers visit men in hotels or somewhere else in private, then various monitoring systems are in place and often drivers take and wait for women to complete the service. As research shows in New Zealand and the USA, the likelihood of violence in prostitution is variable depending on the market because the indoor sectors have safer working conditions and access to checking systems (Pyett and Warr 1997: 544; Raphael and Shapiro 2004).

Risks to health cannot be considered in isolation but must be contextualised as one hazard on a continuum of risks that sex workers engage in and are exposed to. Sex workers consider the emotional and psychological consequences of selling sex as a hazard equal to that of physical violence and health-related concerns. One reason for this is that unlike physical harm, the emotional consequences of selling sex do not stop when a woman leaves the sauna or street. If a woman is found out as working in prostitution, this could mean irreparable consequences for her personal relationships, reputation and status as a mother. Emotional risks are not confined to the place or hours of work, but are to be guarded against always – at home, in private and even when women are no longer involved in prostitution.

Online offers

In pondering the social meaning of electronic erotica as an outlet for carnal thoughts and an exchange of sexual information, advice and ideas, Durkin and Bryant (1995) note how computer communication has established a new normative pattern for sexual behaviour. The Internet acts as a 'social consolidation mechanism' that aggregates large numbers of like-minded people providing easy identification of sexual services and a platform where sex workers and customers can negotiate business. As Sharp and Earle (2003: 37) conclude from their study of a prominent website in the UK, 'social relationships involved in paying for sex are being transformed by the Internet'.

The Internet enables women to control their own businesses by marketing their service on websites and negotiating by e-mail. Using CMC is considered more effective because women are no longer restricted by the telephone but instead check e-mails when it suits. O'Neill (2001: 150) surmises 'prostitutes can tempt their customers much more effectively in cyberspace than by paying for advertising space in small ads, telephone cards and contact magazines'. The cost of web-based advertising is also cheaper than the traditional newspaper method. The visual capacities of the Web mean that various photo galleries can be included as well as more textual descriptions than the ordinary adverts. Independent sex workers who use the Web also market their services for a higher paying customer than the other markets: women charge from approximately £100 per hour up to a minimum of £750 for an overnight stay.

The Internet is an arena where purchasers and providers can meet to discuss their activities, negotiate business and learn from each other how the industry works. In the virtual ethnography that I conducted of a popular website used by patrons of the sex industry in the UK, a vibrant virtual sex work community was evident (Sanders 2005a). This asynchronous arena enables sellers, buyers and organisers to congregate through message boards, lively chat rooms and various facilities that are promoted to match people with similar interests. The website provides the facility for men who describe their sexual encounters ('field reports') and make recommendations to fellow hobbyists (see Sharp and Earle 2003). The site also offers an 'announcements board' where women can advertise recent changes to their services as well as a comprehensive service providers database that hosts adverts for independent workers and escort agencies in the UK. There is also a 'Beginners Guide to Saunas and Massage Parlours' with all the information a new customer needs to know from 'how to find one' to explaining the 'communal lounge' and 'what happens in the room'.

An analysis of this website also shows a glimpse of the moral codes of the indoor sex industry. This site explicitly rejects child prostitution asking 'Have you been offered an underage girl? Report child prostitution – ring *Crimestoppers* on 0800 555 111'. On the message board there is a strict set of rules that determines what topics are acceptable, rejecting derogatory talk about sex workers or distasteful sexual activities. There are also board moderators who quickly delete messages that are inflammatory and it has been known for contributors to be banned from the board for not sticking to the rules.

Soothill (2004) explores an Internet forum in the North West of England for those who pay for sex and acknowledges the 'latent function' in the maintenance of order in the commercial exchange. In his analysis of 623 message board replies, Soothill presents a preview of the social organisation of parlours in this locality. What is interesting from this rare exposure of the role of the Internet in the sex industry is how clients, organisers and sex workers who contribute to the site strive to maintain a stable situation. One example that Soothill provides is that of underage girls working in the industry, noting the conflict this topic creates as most respondents are concerned with abiding by the age of sexual consent in their transactions. Soothill concludes that 'an Internet site that is developed responsibly can help to ensure that the parlour game can continue without necessary conflict' (p. 53).

The Internet also provides a space for sex workers, who are located all over the country, to pass on information, support and details relating to their own working practices. For instance, a group of independent escorts have created an Internet based resource, 'Support and Advice for Escorts' (www.saafe.co.uk) that provides information to colleagues. The website includes extensive tips and case studies on topics such as 'paying tax', 'ways of working' and 'difficult clients', offering a shortcut to 'the learning process in a business where experience really does count'. Another popular website for independent workers, Escortwatch, provides a message board where sex workers can post recent incidents, scams or untrustworthy men who have posed as genuine customers.

An occupational culture

Probing the types of risks that sex workers experience highlights that there is a crucial need for methodical routines and rituals that govern all aspects of the commercial sexual exchange. From my own observations of the indoor sex industry, regularity was essential in both the practice of individuals' routines and the operation of a sauna or escort agency because of the high likelihood of choosing a customer who would not pay or indeed act violently. In my study, sex workers regularised their interactions with clients in two ways.

First, findings from the study suggest that there is not a random mismatch between the client and the sex worker, but in fact sex workers exercise a strict screening strategy which involves assessing potential customers and making judgments on who will pay the agreed amount and perform the transaction without incident (Sanders 2005c: chapter 4). Screening strategies take place through all kinds of mediums: face-to-face assessment is the most popular, but also through CCTV cameras, the Internet and over the telephone. The type of signals that are assessed range from age (young men are considered to be less trustworthy that older men), ethnicity (a general strategy was the rejection of black men, in particular Caribbean men), behaviour and demeanour (signs of wealth and cultural consumption are preferred) and attitude to the commercial transaction (how they negotiate the service). Some workers gave greater priority to certain signals (such as ethnicity) whereas others are more flexible and look for several signals of trustworthiness rather than just one. Screening strategies were found in all of the indoor markets and were often determined by managers and owners as part of the 'house rules'. There was a common set of assumptions regarding the types of clients that would be genuine and these informed sex workers judgments during the selection process. It has been documented how this screening system is made much more difficult on the street because of the pressure to get off the street (McKeganey and Barnard 1996; Hart and Barnard 2003).

The second significant regularisation of the behaviour of sex workers was in relation to minimising the likelihood of violence. The extent of violence is well established in the literature (see Barnard 1993; Church *et al.* 2001). However, sex workers guard against the prevalence of violence by a complex set of precautionary working rules, deterrents and remedial protection strategies. These were found in various combinations in the sex markets. Most notably, precautionary rules included taking the money first, spatial controls in terms of only allowing clients to enter certain rooms, sticking stringently to the time the client had paid for and deciding the type of clothing they wore. All these strategies reinforced the routinisation of the commercial transaction with the ultimate aim of controlling the encounter. These two examples of standardising practice were important in prostitution because of the risk of violence and, although many workers remained violence-free, these strategies minimised the chances of choosing a bad customer or an opportunist attacker.

A set of competencies and work-based expectations have been identified that form a 'social code' (Sharpe 1998: 80) accompanied by 'etiquette and rules' (Hart and Barnard 2003: 36). The norms among sex workers are social rather than individual norms because they do not always maximise individual advantage but they are designed to foster collective interest. Using condoms in the sexual service and a fixed price code are good examples of social norms. In Hoigard and Finstad's (1992) study in Norway, the women displayed internal solidarity in terms of agreeing and complying with the minimum fee in the same way that workers do in other professions. If one prostitute begins to undercut the price code then everyone is affected because all prices eventually plummet. Whittaker and Hart (1996: 405) note that flat workers distinguished themselves as 'professionals' with a specific code of conduct which differentiated themselves from those who worked dangerously and irresponsibly by not using condoms, for instance. This supports the idea that there is a shared sense of professional practice among sex workers who take an occupational approach to their business. There is also a strong sexual code in terms of what behaviours are acceptable and what are not. McLeod (1982: 40) interviewed sex workers in Birmingham in the 1970s and found a similar pattern of unacceptable sexual behaviour where anal sex and kissing were generally frowned upon.

The regulation of the indoor markets reflects the relationships of trust that often characterises colleague relations. Brewis and Linstead (2000: 264) suggest street prostitution breeds low-trusting relationships because of pimps, drug use and sporadic customers, while indoor markets attract high-trusting relationships where workers support each other. The mobility between markets in towns and cities, as well as the virtual community, means that the sex industry is a small world and often tightly-knit work-based relations are formed.

In conclusion, there appears to be evidence of an occupational culture in the indoor sex markets where coercion and exploitation are minimal, replaced by a professional business ethic, routines and regulation. The Internet has provided the opportunity for structure where a community did not exist before because it was shrouded in secrecy by the very nature of the activity. Through the Internet the social organisation of prostitution has been operationalised and effectively implemented in asynchronous time. The Internet provides a view of the behaviour of clients and their patterns of behaviour that determine the demand side of prostitution. However, it is not only the market forces that affect the organisation of prostitution but the range of economic, social, legal, political and ideological forces that determine how, when and where indoor prostitution takes place.

While there are changes in the social organisation of the indoor markets in terms of increasing orderliness and regulation, what is worrying is the unknown extent of women who are confined and coerced into prostitution through trafficking. The relationship, nature and extent of prostitution indoors in Britain in the twenty-first century is growing increasingly complex as the industry accommodates different types of markets and demands that range from women as active agents who set themselves up as entrepreneurs to those who are trafficked or falsely imprisoned and coerced into selling sex. If the current review of prostitution laws and future legal and policy reviews ignore the complexities of the relationships and organisational features that make up the indoor prostitution markets, then there is a risk that legislative change will only continue the legal injustices and confusions, rather than respect individuals' will to make choices. Of great concern is the unwillingness for the government to accept the 'sex work discourse' that promotes the safe working conditions and employment rights of individual women. Relying on the rhetoric of a moral order and public nuisance that frames women *either* as nefarious outcasts that need containing or innocent victims that need protection and relocation is a dated and unrealistic reflection of the majority of women who sell sex in Britain.

References

Barnard, M. (1993) 'Violence and vulnerability: conditions of work for street working prostitutes', *Sociology of Health and Illness*, 15: 5–14.

Benson, C. and Matthews, R. (1995) *National Vice Squad Survey*, School of Sociology and Social Policy, Middlesex University.

Bernstein, E. (2001) 'The meaning of the purchase: desire, demand and the commerce of sex', *Ethnography*, 2 (3): 389–420.

Brewis, J. and Linstead, S. (2000). *Sex, Work and Sex Work*. London: Routledge.

Brooks-Gordon, B. and Gelsthorpe, L. (2003) 'Prostitutes' clients, Ken Livingstone and a new Trojan Horse', *The Howard Journal*, 42 (5): 437–451.

Chapkis, W. (1997) *Live Sex Acts: Women Performing Erotic Labour*. New York: Routledge.

Church, S., Henderson, M. *et al*. (2001) 'Violence by clients towards female prostitutes in different work settings: questionnaire survey', *British Medical Journal*, 322: 524–5.

Collins, A. (2004) 'Sexuality and sexual services in the urban economy and socialscape: an overview', *Urban Studies*, 41 (9): 1631–42.

Cooper, K., Kilvington, J. *et al*. (2001) 'HIV prevention and sexual health services for sex workers in the UK', *Health Education Journal*, 60 (1): 26–34.

Cusick, L. (1999) *Social and Commercial Experiences of Glasgow Prostitutes Working in Different Sectors*. PhD thesis, University of London.

Cusick, L. (2002) 'Youth prostitution: a literature review', *Child Abuse Review*, 11 (4): 230–51.

Day, S. (1996) 'The law and the market, in O. Harris (ed.), *Inside and Outside the Law*. London: Routledge, pp. 75–98.

Delacoste, F. and Alexander, P. (1988) *Sex Work: Writings by Women in the Sex Industry.* London: Virago.

Dickson, S. (2004) *Sex in the City.* London: Poppy Project.

Durkin, K. and Bryant, C. (1995) ' "Log on to sex": some notes on the carnal computer and erotic cyberspace as an emerging research frontier', *Deviant Behaviour*, 16: 179–200.

Faugier, J. and Sargeant, M. (1997) 'Sampling hard to reach populations', *Journal of Advanced Nursing*, 26: 790–7.

Finnegan, F. (1979) *Poverty and Prostitution: A Study of Victorian Prostitutes in York*. Cambridge: Cambridge University Press.

Hart, G. and Barnard, M. (2003) ' "Jump on top, get the job done": strategies employed by female prostitutes to reduce the risk of client violence', in E.A. Stanko (ed.), *The Meanings of Violence*. London: Routledge, pp. 32–48.

Hoigard, C. and Finstad, L. (1992) *Backstreets: Prostitution, Money and Love.* Cambridge: Polity.

Home Office (1999) *New Measures to Control Prostitutes' Cards in Phone Boxes.* London: HMSO.

Home Office (2004) *Paying the Price: A Consultation Paper on Prostitution.* London: HMSO.

Hubbard, P. (1998) 'Community action and the displacement of street prostitution: evidence from British cities', *Geoforum*, 29 (3): 269–86.

Hubbard, P. (2004) 'Cleansing the metropolis: sex work and the politics of zero tolerance', *Urban Studies*, 41 (9): 1687–702.

Jackson, S. and Scott, S. (2004) 'Sexual antinomies in late modernity', *Sexualities*, 7 (2): 233–48.

Jaget, C. (1980) *Prostitutes: Our Life*. London: Falling Wall Press.

Kantola, J. and Squires, J. (2004) 'Discourses surrounding prostitution policies in the UK', *European Journal of Women's Studies*, 11 (1): 77–101.

Kempadoo, K. and Doezema, J. (1999) *Global Sex Workers*. London: Routledge.

Kennedy, H. (1993) *Eve was Framed: Women and British Justice*. London: Vintage.

Kesler, K. (2002) "Is a feminist stance in support of prostitution possible? An exploration of current trends', *Sexualities*, 5 (2): 219–35.

Lerum, K. (1998) 'Twelve-step feminism makes sex workers sick: how the state and the recovery movement turn radical women into "useless citizens" ', *Sexuality and Culture*, 2 (Special Issue): 7–36.

Lever, J. and Dolnick, D. (2000) 'Clients and call girls: seeking sex and intimacy', in R. Weitzer (eds.), *Sex for Sale*. London: Routledge, pp. 85–100.

Lever, J. and Kanouse, K. (1998) 'Using qualitative methods to study the hidden world of offstreet prostitution in Los Angeles County,' in J. Elias, V. Bullough, V. Elias and G. Brewer (eds), *Prostitution. On Whores, Hustlers and Johns*. New York: Prometheus Books, pp. 396–406.

Malbon, B. (1999) *Clubbing: Dancing, Ecstasy and Vitality*. London: Routledge.

Matthews, R. (1997) *Prostitution in London: An Audit*. London: Department of Social Sciences, Middlesex University.

May, T., Edmunds, M. *et al.* (1999) *Street Business: The Links between Sex and Drug Markets*. Police Research Series Paper 118. London: Home Office Policing and Reducing Crime Unit.

May, T., Harocopos, A. and Hough, M. (2000) *For Love or Money: Pimps and the Management of Sex Work*. Police Research Series Paper 134. London: Home Office Policing and Reducing Crime Unit.

McCullagh, J., Syed, Q. *et al.* (1998) *Female Prostitution and Associated Drug Use in the North West of England*. Liverpool: Sexual Health and Environmental Epidemiology Unit, Liverpool University.

McKeganey, N. and Barnard, M. (1996) *Sex Work on the Streets*. Buckingham: Open University Press.

McLeod, E. (1982) *Working Women: Prostitution Now*. London: Croom Helm.

Morgan Thomas, R., Plant, M.A. *et al.* (1989). 'Risks of AIDS among workers in the "sex industry": some initial results from a Scottish study', *British Medical Journal*, 299: 148–9.

Nemitz, T. (2001) 'Gender issues in informer handling', in R. Billingsley, T. Nemitz and P. Bean, *Informers: Policing Policy and Practice*. Portland, OR: Willian Publishing: 98–109.

O'Connell Davidson, J. (1995) 'The anatomy of "Free choice" prostitution', *Gender, Work and Organization*, 2 (1): 1–10.

O'Connell Davidson, J. (1996) 'Prostitution and the contours of control', in J. Weeks and J. Holland (eds.), *Sexual Cultures*. London: Macmillan, pp. 180–98.

O'Connell Davidson, J. (1998) *Prostitution, Power and Freedom*. London: Polity.

O'Connell Davidson, J. (2001) 'The sex tourist, the expatriate, his ex-wife and her "Other": the politics of loss, difference and desire', *Sexualities*, 4 (1): 5–24.

O'Connell Davidson, J. (2002) 'The rights and wrongs of prostitution', *Hypatia*, 17 (2): 84–98.

O'Connell Davidson, J. and Sanchez Taylor, J. (1999) 'Fantasy islands: exploring the demand for sex tourism', in K. Kempadoo (ed.), *Sun, Sex and Gold: Tourism and Sex Work in the Carribbean*. Oxford: Rowman & Littlefield.

O'Neill, M. (1997) 'Prostitute women now', in G. Scambler and A. Scambler (eds), *Rethinking Prostitution: Purchasing Sex in the 1990s*. London: Routledge, pp. 3–28.

O'Neill, M. (2001) *Prostitution and Feminism*. London: Polity Press.

Ostergren, P. (2004) *Sexworkers Critique of Swedish Prostitution Policy*. Available online at: www.petraostergren.com. March.

Phoenix, J. (1995) 'Prostitution: problematizing the definition', in M. Maynard and J. Purvis (eds), *Heterosexual Politics*. London: Taylor & Francis, pp. 65–77.

Phoenix, J. (1999) *Making Sense of Prostitution*. London: Macmillan.

Plumridge, E., Chetwynd, S. J. *et al.* (1997) 'Control and condoms in commercial sex: client perspectives', *Sociology of Health and Illness*, 19 (2): 228–43.

Porter, R. (1994) *London – A Social History*. Oxford: Basil Blackwell.

Pyett, P. (1998a) 'Researching with sex workers: a privilege and a challenge,' in J. Elias, V. Bullough, V. Elias and G. Brewer (eds), *Prostitution. On Whores, Hustlers and Johns*. New York: Prometheus Books, pp. 368–75.

Pyett, P. (1998b) 'Doing it together: sex workers and researchers', *Research for Sex Work*, 1 (http://www.nswp.org/r4sw – retrieved 2003).

Pyett, P. and Warr, D. (1997) 'Vulnerability on the streets: female sex workers and HIV risk', *AIDS Care*, 9 (5): 539–47.

Raphael, J. and Shapiro, D. (2004) "Violence in indoor and outdoor prostitution venues', *Violence Against Women*, 10 (2): 126–39.

Raymond, J. G. (1999) 'Prostitution as violence against women', *Women's International Forum*, 21 (1): 1–9.

Raymond, J. (2004) 'Prostitution on demand.' *Violence Against Women*, 10 (10): 1156–86.

Rickard, W. (2001) ' "Been there, seen it, done it, I've got the T-shirt": British sex workers reflect on jobs', *Feminist Review*, 67 (Spring): 111–32.

Ryder, A. (2004) 'The changing nature of adult entertainment districts: between a rock and hard place or going from strength to strength?', *Urban Studies*, 41 (9): 1659–86.

Sanchez Taylor, J. (2001) 'Dollars are a girl's best friend? Female tourists' sexual behaviour in the Caribbean', *Sociology*, 35: 749–64.

Sanders, T. (2004a) 'Controllable laughter: managing sex work through humour', *Sociology*, 38 (2): 273–91.

Sanders, T. (2004b) 'A continuum of risk? The management of health, physical and emotional risks by female sex workers', *Sociology of Health and Illness*, 26: 1–18.

Sanders, T. (2005a) 'Researching the Online Sex Work Community', in C. Hine (ed.) *Virtual Methods in Social Research on the Internet*. Oxford: Berg.

Sanders, T. (2005b) 'Researching Sex Work: Dynamics, Difficulties and Decisions', in D. Hobbs and R. Wright (eds), *A Handbook of Fieldwork*. London: Sage.

Sanders, T. (2005c) *Sex Work. A Risky Business*. Cullompton: Willan.

Sanders, T. (forthcoming) 'It's just acting: sex workers' strategies for capitalising on sexuality', *Gender, Work and Organization*.

Scambler, G. (1997) 'Conspicuous and inconspicuous sex work. Neglect of the ordinary and mundane', in G. Scambler and A. Scambler (eds), *Rethinking Prostitution. Purchasing Sex in the 1990s.* London: Routledge, pp. 105–20.

Self, H. (2003) *Prostitution, Women and Misuse of the Law*. London: Frank Cass.

Sharp, K. and Earle. S. (2003) 'Cyberpunters and cyberwhores: prostitution on the Internet', in Y. Jewkes (ed.), *Dot Cons. Crime, Deviance and Identity on the Internet.* Cullompton: Willan, pp. 36–52.

Sharp, K. (1998) *Red Light, Blue Light: Prostitutes, Punters and the Police.* Aldershot: Ashgate.

Skilbrei, M. (2001) 'The rise and fall of the Norwegian massage parlour: changes in the Norwegian prostitution setting in the 1990s', *Feminist Review*, 67 (Spring): 63–77.

Soothill, K. (2004) 'Parlour games: the value of an internet site providing punters' views of massage parlours', *Police Journal*, 77 (1): 43–53.

Spongberg, M. (1997) *Feminizing Veneral Disease: The Body of the Prostitute in Nineteenth Century Medical Discourse.* Basingstoke: Macmillan.

Storr, M. (2003) *Latex and Lingerie: The Sexual Dynamics of Ann Summers Parties.* Oxford: Berg.

Swirsky, R. and Jenkins. C. (2000) 'Prostitution, pornography and telephone boxes', in J. Radford, M. Friedberg and L. Harne (eds), *Women, Violence and Strategies for Action.* Buckingham: Open University Press, pp. 57–71.

Taylor, D. (2003) *Sex for Sale: New Challenges And New Dangers for Women Working On and Off the Streets.* London: Mainliners.

Walkowitz, J. (1980) *Prostitution and Victorian Society: Women, Class, and the State.* Cambridge: Cambridge University Press.

Ward, H., Day, S. *et al.* (1999) 'Risky business: health and safety in the sex industry over a 9-year period', *Sexually Transmitted Infections*, 75 (5): 340–3.

Whittaker, D. and Hart, G. (1996) 'Research note: managing risks: the social organisation of indoor sex work', *Sociology of Health and Illness*, 18 (3): 399–413.

In Campbell, R. + O'Neil, M (eds) Sex Work Now 2006

Chapter 5

The conundrum of women's agency: migrations and the sex industry

Laura María Agustín

In this article I begin with an overview of migration theory as it relates to those selling sex, including two key concepts: the feminisation of migration and labour migration. I then explore the interest that has arisen regarding the ways people leave their countries and arrive in others in general, and then the particular concern for those who sell sex after arrival in Europe. I describe the ideas involved in the 'trafficking' discourse, the conflicts associated with efforts to define the crimes involved, the role played by the 'violence against women' discourse and the subtleties encountered in migrants' own testimonies that destabilise the rigid debate that dominates this issue. Although this subject would appear to be a major source of concern in the UK, little empirical research has been published. There is no reason to believe, however, that the situation will develop very differently from what is well established all over Europe, in diverse national and cultural contexts, and since the nature of migrant sex work in Europe is itinerant and transnational, the best way to conceive of the subject is in any case as 'European'.

What and who is a migrant in Europe?

The first category in need of discussion is that of the 'migrant'. The UK has a longer history of immigration from former colonies into the mother country and a more apparently multicultural society than many other European countries, but the use of the term migrant is more recent here. Confusion arises from different usages of the word migrant in different national contexts.

Although statistics show that in many areas of Europe other *European* migrants are still among the most numerous groups within the migrant whole, the word 'migrant' tends to be used to signify non-European. Similarly, migrants who have now been 'assimilated' and made citizens of a particular European state are sometimes included and sometimes not in popular definitions and census exercises. Official government accountings, which vary across the European Union, do not publish statistics on immigrants per se but on different states related to immigration, such as visa status, residence status, municipal registration or permission to work, in a variety of bureaucratic categories. Many people refer to the dichotomy legal–illegal, but the possibilities are far more complex, taking in workers with definite assignments, transit migrants, suitcase traders, the self-employed, 'forced' migrants, those who are to some extent hiding and those who have escaped being recorded at all. In some countries, migrants move in and out of legal status repeatedly (Singleton and Barbesino 1999: 20). Theories of migration have tended to concentrate on questions of causation – why people move to new countries. Some theorists focus on international structural conditions such as recomposition of capital (for example, in 'export trading zones') or globalisation of markets, without considering the micro-level where individuals decide to migrate. Others look at the national policy level or at household units. Still others consider wage differentials between countries, the focus being on individual decisions. Causes are given as attempts to make better or more secure money than possible at home, loss of land, recruitment by employers abroad, 'family reunification' projects, flight from violence, persecution and war, and the 'feminisation of poverty'. None of these excludes the others; individuals may experience multiple causes at a time and no single condition guarantees that someone will migrate. Nevertheless, considerations of specific migrations are often characterised by discussion of 'push-pull factors' (e.g. see Massey *et al.* 1993).

These factors are conceived as conditions on both sides of the migration, the point of origin and the point of reception. Thus armed conflict and loss of farming land may push people away from home, while labour shortage and personal networks may pull them to another place. The basic concept is unarguable, but envisions human beings as being acted upon, leaving little room for more subtle issues of desire, aspiration, anxiety or other states of the soul. It's questionable whether push-pull terms would be used nowadays for

Europeans, who are less likely to be seen as passive subjects being acted upon and more likely as modern selves searching actively for better situations in which to realise their identities.

In most government accounts of migration, migrants are distinguished from refugees, who are imagined as having no desire to leave, as forced to by natural disaster, armed conflict or violent persecution, and as going wherever they are offered asylum or temporary shelter. Official refugee status is granted by the UN High Commission on Refugees to people fleeing from selected situations, but many similar situations are not officially recognised (wars not recognised as such, for example, because a struggling group is unrecognised by a national government). Individual countries may also make their own distinctions relevant to whether they grant refugee and other statuses to particular groups or not. Thus the identifying characteristic 'passport', and its corresponding state's status (first-world, poor, at war, non-EU), determines how national governments decide to call people migrants, refugees, guest workers, tourists, students or business travellers, and, according to which label is assigned, the traveller has access to more or fewer rights and obligations. In general, those whose problems are not recognised as meriting political asylum and who enter without work contracts come to be characterised as 'economic migrants'. In the UK, the large category available to migrants is 'asylum seekers', which means they need to present themselves as victims or potential victims, not as able, healthy people desiring to work hard and become part of British society.

In the UK as in the rest of Europe, much public discourse reflects the fear that avalanches of opportunists from the global south are set to overwhelm 'welfare' states, but migration research does not bear out this paranoia. If it were true that poor people simply moved to any richer country, then the numbers of migrants would be enormously greater than they now are, given the poverty of much of the world. On the contrary, 'migrations are highly selective processes; only certain people leave, and they travel on highly structured routes to their destinations, rather than gravitate blindly toward any rich country they can enter' (Sassen 1999: 2). This idea applies in places of armed conflict and crop failure as well as in crowded cosmopolitan ghettos. In classic migration theory, of course, the 'certain people' were assumed to be men.

The concept of feminisation of migration

A lot of ink has been spilt in an attempt to prove that there is a 'feminisation of migration'. This idea is, itself, the product of a twentieth-century gender stereotyping that consisted of ignoring women's movements while reinforcing the myth of the tough, lone male migrant. A study of 7,000 English life histories covering 1660 to 1730 found that more than three-quarters of country women left their villages, in greater numbers than did men (Moch 1992). A completely different kind of study, carried out in Africa to determine the geographic range of sex-related DNA, revealed that male chromosomes tend to be more localised, pointing to a rate of female migration eight times higher than the male, owing to traditional practices under which brides move to their husbands' houses (a common practice worldwide) (Stoneking 1998).

Gendered statistics are considered acceptably reliable only since 1960; these describe the number of foreign-born persons to be included in formal censuses of country populations, plus information on the number of formal refugees (remember that no one is counting 'migrants' as an official category). These estimates show that women and girls were already a large proportion of all international migrants in 1960, when they accounted for 47 of every 100 migrants living outside the country where they were born. Since then the proportion has risen to reach nearly 49 per cent in 2000, 85 million females as opposed to 90 million male migrants. An increase of 2 per cent over 40 years is too small to justify as 'feminisation of migration'. Regional differences exist, with slightly higher proportions of women migrants in developed countries, but these differences are still quite small (Zlotnik 2003).

Currently, changes in national economies promote the labour migration of women in particular situations. Structural changes at the global level must be taken into account, particularly industrialised countries' shift to a service economy while manufacturing is moved to developing countries, conditions that lead to informalisation and create a demand for migrant women (Sassen-Koob 1984); one aspect of this is the the increasing dependence by multinational corporations on subcontracting, often to homebased workers (Pyle 2001: 67). And the International Monetary Fund has for decades been imposing policies of 'structural adjustment' on third-world countries who seek or need to refinance loans; these policies mandate severe cuts in government spending, with social programmes the first to be cut. Those who predominate in the social sector and who therefore lose jobs – as teachers, hospital workers, social workers and psychologists, among others – are largely women. These policies are also usually blamed for the disintegration of families under stress from lack of income, with the result that women look for alternatives away from home, and migration becomes a more conventional solution.

Consider the following typical testimonies of migrant women in Europe:

> You work, work, work and then they don't pay you, because there's no money ... I worked in an ashtray factory, and when there was no money to pay me they said 'take ashtrays', 100 ashtrays. So? Can you eat ashtrays? (Ukrainian woman in Spain: Agustín 2004a)

> There wasn't any work and I wanted to be independent. I have a big family, but I didn't get along with them. I wanted to be on my own. I saw the neighbours who are doing okay, who have money because there's someone in Italy. And so you go ... (Nigerian woman in Italy: Danna 2003: 84)

It is an unfortunate commonplace that women are considered the 'least demanding' workforce, so the fact that women predominate overwhelmingly in poorly-paid or unprotected labour is usually treated as a non-event. Mirjana Morokvasíc, a long-time advocate of paying attention to women's migrations, considers that the general lack of surprise at women's undemandingness and concentration in devalorised sectors derives from the idea that their paid employment is not their primary role, an idea held by themselves and also by their employers: 'Their role, or role-to-be, of housewife-mother "justifies" their consideration as subsidiary workers and the level of their wages as complementary wages only' (Morokvasíc 1984: 888).

Migration studies as a field have mostly excluded migrants who sell sex, contributing to the general lack of understanding and further stigmatisation of these people (Agustín 2005a).

The concept of labour migrations

Much of the contemporary conflict in Europe about migrants derives from the change to a post-Fordist economy. Earlier labour migrations to Europe were often formalised and conceived of as temporary: Poles to work in the mines of the Ruhr in later nineteenth-century

Germany, Algerians to pre-Second World War French industry and, the best-known formal programme to stimulate and control a specific migration, the German guestworker system carried out with Turkish labour between 1955 and 1973. These migrants were sought out and came with a contract, and for older generations of Europeans who may themselves have migrated within Europe (for example, the Spanish), this makes all the difference. Formal programmes may also be sponsored by governments of 'sending countries'. Most well known is the Philippines Overseas Employment Administration, which has been sending Filipina women abroad as maids for over 20 years, but Sri Lanka, Bangladesh and Thailand also have such programmes.

In Europe in the present, formal programmes control only a small part of labour migrations. Most of the people being called migrants arrive without documents proving they have a job offer, and in a vast number of cases work in jobs outside the 'formal' economic sector. It may be that their professional qualifications are not recognised across country borders, so that a trained dentist or beautician has to work as a taxi driver or babysitter, or there may be national quotas on professional licences. Or, migrants may simply find that there are plenty of natives to fill posts they are themselves capable of carrying out in their new country; in Europe, immigration policy seeks to conserve these jobs for its own citizens, who continually voice the fear that jobs will be stolen by migrants.

For work to be considered legal, it must belong to the formal sector of the economy, that is be regulated and included in government accounting. Legal migrant workers possess a work permit and the correct visa, by definition in a formal-sector job. However, migrants may also be working in the formal sector *without* a work permit, an illegal activity for both employer and employee. Alternatively, they may be working in a job for which no work permit exists, in the 'informal' sector. An enormously wide range of economic activities exists outside the formal sector, many of them engaged in by legal citizens and considered conventional. Some of these occupations closely resemble formal-sector activities but do not fulfil health and safety regulations or do not operate in locations zoned for them; some are primarily forms of tax evasion; some are crimes that require a victim; others fit definitions of 'alternative' or 'solidarity' economies (mutual-aid, community projects, voluntary work, self-help).[1] Women are disproportionately represented in the informal sector through their dominance in domestic service, sweatshop labour, home piecework, 'caring' labour and the sex industry, a trend many authors have described in terms of the displacement of wealthy women's domestic chores onto poorer women's shoulders. Of all these informalised occupations, commercial sex pays the best. Since all indicators point to there being a boom in this industry, it stands to reason that increasing numbers of migrant women should be found working here (Agustín 2004b).

Being 'trafficked', and other ways of leaving and arriving

Itinerancy has been associated with selling sex for a long time in Europe, for example among those accompanying pilgrims and soldiers. Internal migrations from the countryside or small towns to cities to look for work are still common, and people from Europe used the sale of sex during their migrations to other continents, for example those who travelled to Argentina at the end of the nineteenth century (Guy 1991). The idea that those women were forced to migrate was formulated a hundred years ago just as it is being now.

The phenomenon was called 'white slavery' in the West, in reference to white women supposedly captured and sold into prostitution. Avidly covered by the press, it led to the creation of international organisations and conventions dedicated to its eradication. Numerous authors have written about these events, relating them to anxieties about the nation, 'race', health and women's sexuality (Bristow 1982; Guy 1992; Irwin 1996; Walkowitz 1994) and comparing them to the present (Doezema 2000). Between the last upsurge of 'trafficking' discourse and now, *how* people migrated was not an issue of great interest, but Europe has become so concerned about the number of people who elude its border controls that the question is now addressed everywhere.

For people who want to enter Europe, there two official choices: to enter as a tourist or temporary business traveller with the appropriate visa, or to enter with a job offer and formal working papers in hand. Obtaining a tourist visa can be next to impossible for citizens of many countries, or may require years of waiting because of country quotas. The potential tourist/migrant may be able to get a visa but not have the money to buy tickets and survive while looking for work. Many who want to travel actively search for work-and-travel offers at home, while others search *for* them, to sell them trips and jobs. These vendors in the informal economy are known by a variety of names, from businessmen and travel agents to 'coyotes' on the Mexican border and 'snakeheads' in China. They are often relatives or friends, and they may be tourist acquaintances met during vacations who temporarily enter the field in order to bring friends over to visit or work (Agustín 2003b). Marriage may be part of the deal. They may play a minimal part in the migration project or offer a 'package' which links them closely to the migrant at every step of the way.

Without access to a charge account or formal bank loan, the potential traveller probably contracts a debt at the beginning of the journey. Services offered for money may include the provision of passports, visas, changes of identity, work permits and other documents, as well as advice on how to look and act in interviews with immigration officials (at the border, in airports, on trains and buses, in the street), the loan of money to show upon entrance with a tourist visa, pick-up service at the airport, car transportation to another country or to pre-arranged lodging and contact information for potential employers. These services are not difficult to find in countries where out-travel has become normalised over time, and in certain countries, formal-sector travel agents offer them. In either case, the debt is a typical element of migration, as noted by a Dominican woman running a flat offering sexual services in Pamplona, Spain:

> People come here that have a debt, for example one girl I have right now. They've all come on their own feet, they have a debt they have to pay ... The last girl had to pay a million [pesetas] (€6,010) ... After five months she was finished. (Agustín 2004a)

All these conditions characterise travels to Europe, no matter what job is eventually undertaken, for people without a work permit. And the traveller's necessity continues once inside Europe, where to get a safe job with decent pay and without egregious labour abuses, she or he needs people to provide advice, addresses of safe and inexpensive places to stay, information on whom to trust and whom not and so on. Such contacts, or intermediaries, will provide transport, translations, information on labour and cultural norms, medical references and other, conventional travel advice. Migrant workers in any sector need this kind of help, as do tourists and business travellers. The entry of outside agents into the migration network attempts to redress the imbalance between the number of people seeking entry and the limited visas offered. A lucrative niche is thus created for those interested in making a profit from people's movements (Massey et al. 1993: 450). Such networks have always existed, but only with heightened attention to the sex industry has the entrepreneurial side been attacked as morally corrupt and cruel, leading to abundant proposals for its criminalisation. Travel which results in selling sexual services is positioned, according to this view, as different from all others.

Travelling to work in the sex industry

The sex industry, largely unregulated and outside official government accounting, by definition operates through informal networks, including people who facilitate the finding of jobs. To gain access to news of current employment opportunities, the newcomer must meet at least one insider, who may charge money for information and services or not. The haphazard nature of these contacts is evident in one Ukrainian woman's story:

> Once I was talking with a friend and she asked if I wanted to go to Spain. I knew why, so I said: 'Ah, do you want to?' … and I don't know where she met this guy, he got the papers for us, made the passport, everything, the money and we left … This guy went to look for work, where are the best places to work … I worked in Logroño a month or so, I don't remember, then back to Málaga … He talked first with the boss of this place, asked if there was an opening, said he was looking for work for us. (Agustín 2001)

There is now a small body of empirical studies with migrant women in Europe on the subject of how they migrated. Many who work in the sex industry knew that their labour in Europe would have a sexual aspect if not be directly 'sex work' or 'prostitution'.[2] They may not have understood, however, what working conditions would be like, since commercial sex at home may have little in common with what exists in Europe: standing nude in a window for twelve hours a day, displaying oneself at night next to a road or highway or performing multiple blow jobs, day after day, with no other social contact with clients. Other migrants have been overtly deceived, for example, when part of the migration 'package' included signing a contract without understanding what it meant, the value of foreign money or the language in which the contract was written. Moreover, people over-eager to travel do little research to test what they are told by vendors, allow false documents to be prepared for them that will render them vulnerable abroad and collaborate in other ways in their own deception. Nonetheless, an ethics within the situation is possible, as the following narrative illustrates:

A friend proposed that I come, she knew a girl who could bring me ... You sign a note for seven million pesos (€4.207) and they tell you that you can pay it back working for a month. You know what you're going to be doing. Anyone who says she didn't know, it's a lie, a married lady with children, how can she not know what she's going to be doing here? When you arrive, you crash, because the work is bad and it's a lie that the debt can be paid in a month. You talk with the other girls and see that the debt is more than it cost the girl to bring you. [But] I want to pay her, because she takes a risk, too, to bring you over ... (Oso 2003: 34)

Often enough, those doing the deceiving are family or friends. Sometimes, deceit and control are achieved without physical violence, through the psychological dependency recently-arrived and disoriented migrants feel. In the worst cases, migrants are threatened and held against their will, their personal documents are withheld and they are forced to have and sell sex.

As soon as I was brought to Turin I understood that I had ended up in a blind alley: I found myself with a 'madame' who ordered me onto the sidewalk and wanted 50 million [lire] (€25,800). It was a real nightmare, I cried all the tears I had ... (Kennedy and Nicotri 1999: 36)

It is these worst cases that have prompted not only an appropriate public outcry but also a moral panic that erases all shades of meaning in other testimonies. 'Force' is made into a monolith that sweeps away all migrant women, and many kinds of force are bundled together: some people, for example, feel forced who actually *could* physically escape; others start out doing domestic work but feel obligated to sell sex because of the differential in pay. Moreover, people widely understand that any migratory project carries with it risks and dangers, as do many who sell sex: women in Nairobi were asked if they realised it could be dangerous and were told that they were not selling sex in order to live safely but to earn money and be independent (Pheterson 1996: 18).

The purpose of showing the diversity of forms migration can take is not to deny that some forms are worse than others but rather to avoid homogenising hundreds of thousands of women's experience. Here is the nub of the conflict: if I now refer to those facilitating migrations as agents or entrepreneurs, I appear to condone the kinds of abuses committed by criminals. If, on the other hand, I refer to all facilitators as criminals, I appear to erase the agency of migrants who knew they would be selling sex or who prefer it to other jobs. This point leads me to the debate on 'trafficking'.

The drive to define

The lack of a coherent definition of the term 'trafficking' has inspired an avalanche of meetings, conferences and reports all over Europe (and, indeed, the world). In multiple sessions held in Vienna between 1998 and 2000, the UN Commission for the Prevention of Crime and Penal Justice argued over concepts of trafficking, trade and smuggling of human beings, with the emphasis often on women and children. Two lobbying groups tried to influence the Commission on the definitions of words such as consent, obligation, force, coercion, deceit, abuse and exploitation.[3] In October of 2000, agreement was reached on two protocols appended to the new UN Convention against Transnational Organised Crime which with a fortieth country's signature last year has come into force.

The protocols produced two concepts: 'smuggling of migrants' and 'trafficking'. The gender distinction is clear, the 'trafficking' protocol expressing a presumed greater disposition of women – along with children – to be deceived, above all about sex, and a presumed lesser disposition to migrate. In the 'smuggling' protocol, on the other hand, men are seen as capable of migrating but of being handled like contraband (sex is excluded from this protocol). The opposing sides in the debate have both produced annotated guides to the final protocols (CATW 2003; IHRLG 2002).

Numerous authors have attempted to distinguish between the concept of 'trafficking' and migrations of people who sell sex (Alexander 1996; Skrobanek *et al.* 1997; Mai 2001; Agustín 2003a), but in the press and NGO fora, the focus on criminal abuse of migrants continues, and other problems often ignored, such as their persecution by the police, their lack of labour protections and other conditions related to the sex industry's 'informality'. The conflation of migrations that involve selling sex with 'trafficking' has been the subject of numerous critiques (e.g. Irwin 1996; Doezema 2000; Pickup 1998). How do this conflation and the subsequent confusion come about?

The difficulty is that the fundamental terms being used attempt to pin down enigmatic issues of will, consent and choice: examples include the extent to which people travelling with false papers knew and 'chose' what awaited them, whether they understood the possible consequences of using such papers, whether they felt in love with an entrepreneur or agent, whether they knew what a contract meant, how their parents' participation in a deal affected their judgement or if they understood how being in debt would ultimately affect themselves. If such epistemological questions are often unfathomable when involving people secure in their homes, they become more so when those involved have left their homes behind to face cultural disorientation on a grand scale through migration.

Thus statistics on 'trafficking' are unreliable, because definitions of the terms involved have not been agreed to. Methodologies differ, counting projects cannot be compared and activists may exaggerate or extrapolate numbers from little data. Several recent projects are setting up databases of information on 'trafficking', but given the lack of agreed-on definitions, the usefulness of the data is still questionable (UNESCO 2003; Protection Project 2003). The US government compiles its own data to publish an annual report on other countries' records on preventing 'trafficking', ranking them according to 'tiers' (US State Department 2004).[4] The kind of statistical dispute that arises from this situation can be seen in the following Israeli example:

> It is estimated that there are between 1,000 and 3,000 women in sexual slavery in Israel, according to a survey conducted by the Knesset's Centre for Research and Information. This survey aimed to measure the public attitude towards trafficking in women. However, debate rages as to the exact number of women in the sex industry in Israel … Anachnu Shavot (We Are Worthy) believes the figure to be closer to 30,000. (*Jerusalem Post*: 2004)

According to researchers' definitions then, when counting victims they may be referring to everyone who entered a country accompanied by someone else and who now sells sex; they may be referring to people who have agreed to denounce a 'trafficker' according to the local law; they may be referring to everyone who sells sex and gives money to a man or they may be referring to all 'illegal' sex worker migrants. They may be counting victims in countries of origin only, or only in destinations or both; they may be including transit countries, or not; they may be counting only women, or only women and transsexuals and so on. Finally, and most tellingly, it is doubtful that any researcher can gain access to many and diverse subjects, given the clandestine situations they live in. As John Salt says:

> The enormous interest and concern for trafficking and human smuggling in governmental, inter-governmental and non-governmental organizations, in the media and popular opinion, is running ahead of theoretical understanding and factual evidence. (2000: 32)

Part of this concern derives from the positioning of all commercial sex as 'violence against women'.

Role of the discourse 'violence against women'

Although 'trafficking' occurs into sweatshops, domestic service, agriculture, mines and other industries, the Coalition Against Trafficking in Women (CATW) and the European Women's Lobby (EWL) believe that 'trafficking of women for sexual exploitation' is particularly pernicious, and define women migrants as sexually endangered, less capable of defending themselves and archetypal victims (CATW 1991; EWL 2001 2003).[5] According to this view, women who sell sex have by definition been deceived and recruited against their will.

The project to gain visibility for widespread, routine violence perpetrated against women – their victimhood – has been important to the advancement of women. The problem occurs when a temporary victim status turns into a victim 'identity' that implies becoming the passive object of others' actions. This may, however, be the strongest way for supporters to argue for the rescue of victims, as Ratna Kapur points out:

> In the context of law and human rights, it is invariably the abject victim subject who seeks rights, primarily because she is the one who has had the worst happen to her. The victim subject has allowed women to speak out about abuses that have remained hidden or invisible in human rights discourse. (2002: 5)

Consider the following text on migrant women from the Child and Woman Abuse Studies Unit at a London university:

Whatever levels of knowledge and 'consent' are involved, however, women are *never* made aware of the extent to which they will be indebted, intimidated, exploited and controlled. They believe ... that they can travel to a richer country and earn large amounts of money in a short space of time, which they can then use to move themselves and their families out of poverty and despair. *In reality,* they are told they owe a huge debt which must be repaid through providing sexual services, and they are able to exercise *virtually no control at all* over their hours of work, the number of customers they serve, and the kinds of sex they have to provide. (Kelly and Regan 2000a: 5, *my emphasis*)

Here the authors totalise a vast array of diverse experiences, ignoring the fact that many women do achieve the goal of earning a large amount of money in a relatively short time. This position advocates for a discursive change among feminists that would make 'prostitution' by definition a form of violence against women, with issues of women's possible 'consent' being removed from any consideration. Similarly, issues of migration and commercial sex are fused:

The sheer volume of foreign women who are in the prostitution industry in Germany ... casts further doubt on the fact that these numbers of women could have entered Germany without facilitation ... NGOs report that most of the foreign women have been trafficked into [Holland] since it is almost impossible for poor women to facilitate their own migration, underwrite the costs of travel and travel documents, and set themselves up in 'business' without outside help. (CATW 2003: 3)

Here 'facilitated' migration, including conventional forms of help with documents, tickets and contacts, is fused with 'trafficking'. Similarly, CATW proposes that the concept of 'prostitution' be made equivalent to that of 'trafficking', a move evident in Donna Hughes's testimony to the US Congress:

... unless compelled by poverty, past trauma, or substance addictions, few women will voluntarily engage in prostitution *and are thus* victims of trafficking. (2002: 2, *my emphasis*)

Here the act's definition of 'trafficking', which requires that 'force, fraud or coercion' exist, is deliberately (mis)interpreted so that all people who help migrants become 'traffickers', including family, friends, lovers, agents and entrepreneurs, and all kinds of help become 'trafficking'. This project is fully gendered, so that both the presence of women among 'traffickers' and male migrants who sell sex are both ignored.

Role of migrants' voices

When there is an obviously violent case of someone practically shanghaied and forced to work, everyone agrees that it is a crime. Consider the following testimony:

> When I arrived the first day they took me sightseeing and photographed me by the Houses of Parliament, the big clock and in Trafalgar Square. But after that they locked us up … They looked me over and afterwards I was told I had been sold for £20,000. To pay off this debt, I would have to sleep with more than 500 men … (*Bangkok Post*: 1999)

Many migrants' testimonies do not recount this kind of experience, however, but rather a subtle mix of desire, intention, confusion and collusion. The following four selections illustrate this complexity:

> (1) I arrived in Almería through a friend's mediation. I began to work as a domestic, I was badly paid and mistreated. Sundays I came to the edge of the sea and cried. One Sunday a Moroccan man saw me crying, I explained my situation to him, he took me to his house. I was a virgin, he promised he was going to marry me … he got me a residence card … He found me work in a restaurant and let me stay in his studio, he told me I had to pay rent. I began to sleep with some clients from the restaurant … Now, I would like to go to France, I want to get married … My sister who lives in Bézier says she's going to find me a Frenchman, to get a residence card. (Moroccan woman in Spain: Lahbabi and Rodríguez 2000: 18)

This woman's trip to work as a domestic was facilitated by a friend, but her employers abused her. In her time off she was free to take a walk and thus meet a man who offered to help. The relationship appears to have involved friendship and sex. The man obtained legal papers for but also made money from the woman. She began to sell sex, it is not clear how. She wants to migrate again, she wants to marry, and her sister is looking for a man capable of facilitating this project. All parties mentioned try to take advantage of each other at the same time that they seek affection.

> (2) I came to Spain and began working in a [private] house; it was a very hard job because in my country I worked as a secretary in City Hall. I earned little, but here the work is very hard. Then I began to meet people who worked in this [sex] … No one mistreats you, except if you leave to go outside and something could happen to you, but inside nothing can happen … you end up feeling protected. (Ecuadorian woman in Spain: Bueno 1999: 380)

This woman's migrant career also began as a domestic, work she found difficult and ill-paying. She tried out selling sex, is not mistreated and feels safe inside the workplace. This selection is significant because much of the 'victim' discourse about migrant sex work focuses on sites where migrants both live and work, often presented as a form of slavery. As in this case, however, some migrant workers prefer this situation as preventing them from spending money, protecting them from being asked for documents, not having to do the work of looking for venues and maximising their opportunities to make money.

> (3) A lot of the girls were Northerners who, like me, had hitched down to London with lots of high hopes, big dreams and fuck-all else. One or two had escaped from children's homes and crazy fathers who beat or raped them. These were the ones the media and all the 'experts' call 'sick victims'. They were nothing of the sort – they were kids who had the guts to do something about their bad 'home' situation: they ran away, and found sanctuary in the sex industry. That may sound absurd, but it isn't. Those young runaways, some as young as 14, 15, were independent; they had control over their lives, whereas back where they came from they had none. (Roberts 1986: 57)

Nickie Roberts here describes Soho in the 1960s, when she worked as a stripper and met many women like herself who had migrated from abusive family situations in the North. In this testimony, selling sex is made worthwhile when it helps young 'runaways' to find independence.

> (4) It makes me laugh when they think that I am not an honest woman because I do this job. Of course, as a job it's ugly, and I don't understand why in Italy they don't let us do it in organised places; I don't understand what is bad about selling love for money ... With this job I have made it possible for all my brothers to study and I have supported my mother, so I am proud of being a prostitute. (Nigerian woman in Italy: Kennedy and Nicotri 1999: 32)

This woman does not dispute the 'ugliness' of sex work, but is proud of what it has enabled her to do for her family economically. She also problematises European rationality, which impedes working in an 'organised' way.

There are many such narratives found in ethnographic research carried out among migrants selling sex, and each presents a superficial version of a deep story that must not be taken at face value. Nevertheless, there are enough references here to personal assessments of situations, desires and decision-making to make many researchers refuse to characterise all migrants as victims. This point of view can be described as placing a high value on personal agency, and in particular as allowing the possibility that even people with problems may prefer to sell sex than do other work. This perspective also recognises the wide variety of relationships possible between migrants and their families, friends, lovers, commercial agents and even criminals. Research shows that, even when migrants say they feel deceived, they often complain of the working conditions they are forced to accept, and not about the work being sexual *per se*; they prefer to remain in the industry, but in less exploitative conditions. Paying off debts in the shortest amount of time is nearly every migrant's primary goal, so the focus is on the future, not on past abuses. While the most tragic situations so often cited by the media and NGOs come to light precisely because the police have become involved, migrants who have not sought help are often invisible to reporters and activists seeking victims. This nuancing of issues of deceit and coercion does not imply a belief that no 'real' violence and abuse occurs during migrations, whether migrants end up working in sex or any other job.

The UK context

Although general social concern about migrant women in sex work is recent in the UK, British organisations have belonged to two European networks since the early 1990s: Europap and Tampep (European Projects for AIDS Prevention in Prostitution and Transnational AIDS/ STD Prevention Among Migrant Prostitutes in Europe Project). In 1998, they together published a guide, *Hustling for Health: Developing Services for Sex Workers in Europe*, which explained how to set up a health project with migrant workers. A third European network, the European Network on Male Prostitution (ENMP), was founded in 1997.

One long-term health-promotion project found that the London workforce became more international during the 1990s (Ward *et al.* 2004; Cooper *et al.* 2004). The numbers of migrant sex workers mentioned by networks and the press must be understood to be very schematic, since all are not using the same method for counting, do not all have the same type of contact with the industry, do not speak all the languages necessary to communicate with all migrants or operate only in big cities. Most counting projects attempt to make tallies of nationalities or ethnicities, but these are also not reliable indicators, since migrants often give incorrect information and use falsified documents. Finally, projects may or may not count transsexual, transgender and male workers. UK statistics in 1999 were gathered from 17 projects, six in London. Central London projects reported non-UK workers at about 50 per cent, while outside numbers were minimal (1–10 per cent) (Europap 2000; Tampep 1999). Tampep's more recent mapping exercise showed that for 12 projects in London women migrants accounted for 63 per cent of indoor workers, men for 66 per cent, with figures outside London much lower. No projects reported finding migrants in street work.

Reports are often issued but rarely based on reliable research. The Protection Project's UK Country Report cited a variety of newspaper stories for its statistics (2003). Two other reports on the UK provided only sketchy information (van den Anker 2003; van der Kleij 2002). These and other reports all rely on a single Home Office study which attempted to estimate the number of 'women trafficked in the UK' (Kelly and Regan 2000b) – unfortunately, since this study's methodology was unsound. Although its title is *Stopping Traffic: Exploring the Extent of, and Responses to, Trafficking in Women for Sexual Exploitation in the UK*, the major source of information was a questionnaire survey of 43 police forces in England and Wales in which they were asked about the extent of 'trafficking'. Other sources included interviews with 'senior personnel with the police, immigration, government departments and four NGOs', as well as with journalists. Press reports and estimates were reproduced without critical analysis, no migrant workers were interviewed, migration and 'trafficking' were not clearly separated and 'trafficking' itself was not clearly defined for the interviewees beforehand. The actual data uncovered showed 71 women 'trafficked' in the UK in 1998; however, the authors extrapolated in highly questionable ways to arrive at a possible 'real' figure of 1,420 for that year (Kelly and Regan 2000b). Given these weaknesses, it is unfortunate that so many other sources, anxious for information on the UK, have cited this report. The Nationality, Immigration and Asylum Act of 2002 established the offence of 'trafficking for prostitution', which carries a maximum penalty of 14 years; at the time of this writing several cases have found against 'traffickers' in the UK. Eaves Housing for Women's Poppy Project provides direct support to 'trafficking' victims, including the first safe house for adult women of the type now common in numerous European countries. In Poppy's report on their first year, they listed having supported fully 46 women and housed 26 (Poppy 2004). In 2003, the London School of Hygiene & Tropical Medicine published a report resulting from its European Commission's Daphne Programme-funded project on 'health risks and consequences of trafficking', which included the UK and five other countries (Zimmerman *et al*. 2003).[6]

By 2003 the social alarm over 'trafficking' in the UK was evident, along with the relative lack of concern over migrant women in general; put another way, the conflation between migrants who sell sex and 'trafficked women' was striking (Agustín 2003a). Part of this may be due to an issue mentioned earlier, that UK immigration law is constructed so as to recognise only 'asylum seekers' as worthy migrants and all others as economic opportunists. The very category 'migrant' is new in the UK and does not carry positive connotations. Thus being a damaged victim or a desperate refugee is valued more than being a healthy person in search of work. The curious result of this policy implies a high economic cost for helping accepted migrants, while those in a position to contribute to society are excluded. The press publish routinely on migrant sex workers, mostly in sensationalist terms on 'sex trafficking'.

The dearth of research on *both* groups in the UK is odd. Kantola and Squires, in an analysis of legislation and policy debates relating to 'trafficking' in the UK, suggest that the scarcity of information and proposals may be related to the traditional emphasis on 'public nuisance' in relation to commercial sex (kerb-crawling legislation and anti-social behaviour orders). They also suggest that in the UK there may be more interest in the exploitation of children than in the situation of adult women, and that child-support organisations have been the most active protagonists in achieving visibility for 'trafficking' (Kantola and Squires 2002: 11). A recent book on 'child prostitution and child sexual abuse' claimed that these problems have been severe and neglected in the UK since the late nineteenth century (Barrett and Brown 2002).

Conclusion

The social fixation on the worst forms of travel for work and the worst forms of commercial sex need to be combatted by good, responsible research with migrants. This would mean *not* doing what most UK reporting has so far: *not* relying on police reports, *not* relying on informants who deal solely with 'victims', *not* confusing media reporting or project anecdotes with research, *not* conflating 'trafficking' and facilitated migration, *not* proceeding to talk about 'trafficking' with informants without first establishing a single definition that will be stuck to during the research project. Research on migrants who sell sex need not be undertaken less rigourously than any other. The frame used should not begin by victimising but take an open attitude to what experiences migrants may have had, both positive and negative. A migration framework allows consideration of all aspects of people's lives and travels, locates them in periods of personal growth and risk-taking and does not force them to identify as 'sex workers', 'victims of trafficking' or, for that matter, domestic servants or carers – all jobs they may have fallen into by chance and consider temporary. Other issues than jobs should be included in responsible research, for example the social and cultural assets migrants acquire and the social networks to which they belong. Research that relies on migrants' own testimonies considerably destabilises victimising discourses (Agustín 2005).

Migrants working without legal permission in Europe are living without basic civil rights: this is the crux of the larger social problem. Whether they are employed in industrial-scale agriculture, domestic service or selling sex, their labour is bought by Europeans. The fact that governments do not recognise many labour sectors in formal accounting leads to widespread abuse of those who work in them, and this abuse can come from employers, police and, indeed, any kind of opportunist out to make money, some of them outright criminals. The challenge for Europeans is to examine their own need and desire for these services, and their own unjust practices toward the 'others' they are employing in them.

Notes

1 The range of income-generating occupations excluded from accounting in the formal economy is too wide to be coherent, potentially including any kind of unlicensed service or sale.
2 The following studies interviewed women in Ghana, Niger, the Dominican Republic, Thailand, Holland, Russia, Colombia, the Philippines, Italy, Spain, Turkey, Poland and Albania, with similar results: Tabet (1989), COIN (1992), Altink (1995), Skrobanek *et al.* (1997), Casal (2000), Pickup (1998), Ratliff (1999), Nowak (1999), Kennedy and Nicotri (1999), Brussa (2000), Bonelli (2001), Signorelli and Treppete (2001), Agustín (2002), Gülçür and İkkaracan (2002), Likiniano (2003), Oso (2003), Mai (2001).
3 These words do not translate exactly across languages, so even a final list of accepted words in English does not solve the problem.
4 The methodology for this report is described vaguely and cannot be assessed (US State Department 2004: 14).
5 A few organisations (Global Alliance Against Trafficking in Women, Anti-Slavery International) avoid the conflation of 'trafficking' with 'prostitution', extending their concern about abuse to migrants who work as domestic servants and in sweatshops, *maquiladoras*, mines, agriculture and other industries, whether they are women, men or transgender people.
6 Partners included the Child and Woman Abuse Studies Unit of London Metropolitan University.

References

Alexander, Priscilla (1996) *Trafficking v. Sex Migration*. New York: North American Task Force on Prostitution.

Altink, Sietske (1995) *Stolen Lives: Trading Women into Sex and Slavery*. London: Scarlet Press.

Agustín, Laura (2001) 'Mujeres inmigrantes ocupadas en la industria del sexo,' in Colectivo IOÉ (ed.), *Mujer, inmigración y trabajo*. Madrid: Instituto de Migraciones y Servicios Sociales, pp. 647–716.

Agustín, Laura (2002) 'The (crying) need for different kinds of research', *Research for Sex Work*, 5 June: 30–2.

Agustín, Laura 2003a. 'Sex, Gender and Migrations: Facing Up to Ambiguous Realities', *Soundings*, 23, 84-98.

Agustín, Laura (2003b) 'La familia española, la industria del sexo y las migrantes', in O. Guasch and O. Viñuales (eds), *Sexualidades: Diversidad y control social*. Barcelona: Bellaterra, pp. 259–75.

Agustín, Laura (2004a) *Trabajar en la industria del sexo, y otros tópicos migratorios*. San Sebastián: Gakoa.

Agustín, Laura (2004b) 'A migrant world of services', *Social Politics*, 10 (3): 377–96.

Agustín, Laura (2005) 'Migrants in the mistress's house: other voices in the "trafficking" debate', *Social Politics*, 12 (1).

Agustín, Laura (2006) 'The disappearing of a migration category: migrants who sell sex', *Journal of Ethnic and Migration Studies*, 32 (1): 29–47.

Bangkok Post (1999) 'Flesh market', 23 May.

Barrett, David and Brown, Alyson (2002) *Knowledge of Evil: Child Prostitution and Child Sexual Abuse in 20th-century England*. London: Willan Publishing.

Bristow, Edward (1982) *Prostitution and Prejudice: The Jewish Fight against White Slavery 1870–1939*. Oxford: Clarendon Press.

Bonelli, Elena *et al.* (2001) *Tráfico e inmigración de mujeres en España: Colombianas y ecuatorianas en los servicios domésticos y sexuales*. Madrid: ACSUR-Las Segovias.

Brussa, Licia (2000) 'Migrant sex workers in the Netherlands speak out', *Research for Sex Work*, 3 (19). Amsterdam: Vrije Universiteit.

Bueno, Aida (1999) 'Entrevista con mujeres inmigrantes', in T. Calvo Buezas. (ed.), *Investigación epidemiológica de casos en población desfavorecida*. Madrid: CSSS.

Casal, Marta (2001) *Inmigración femenina y trabajo sexual. Estudios de casos en Madrid, Pamplona y Bilbao*. Report from Universidad de A Coruña for Instituto de la Mujer, Madrid.

CATW (Coalition Against Trafficking Against Women) (1991) *Report of the Meeting of Experts on the International Action in the Struggle Against Sexual Exploitation and Prostitution*. State College Penn.

CATW/Janice Raymond (2003) *Guide to the UN Trafficking Protocol*. Amherst, MA.

COIN (1992) *Viajes al Exterior: Ilusiones y Mentiras (Exportación de sexo organizado)*. Santo Domingo: Centro de Orientación e Información Integral.

Cooper, Kate, Day, Sophie, Green, Anna and Ward, Helen (2004) 'Maids, Migrants and Occupational Health in the London Sex Industry.' Under review.

Danna, Daniela (2003) *Donne di mondo: Costruzione sociale e realtà della prostituzione in Italia e nell'Unione Europea*. Milan: author's pre-edition.

Doezema, Jo (2000) 'Loose women or lost women: the re-emergence of the myth of white slavery in contemporary discourses of trafficking in women', *Gender Studies*, 18 (1): 23–50.

Europap (2000) *European Network for HIV/STD Prevention in Prostitution 1998– 2000 Final Report.* London: Imperial College School of Medicine.

Europap and Tampep (1998) *Hustling for Health: Developing Health Services for Sex Workers.* Brussels: European Commission.

EWL (European Women's Lobby) (2001) *Towards a Common European Framework to Monitor Progress in Combating Violence Against Women.* Brussels: Observatory on Violence Against Women.

EWL (2003) Remarks from Grainne Healy, Chair of EWL's Observatory on Violence against Women, New York, 11 March.

Gülçür, Leyla and İlkkaracan, Pinar (2002) 'The "Natasha" experience: migrant sex workers from the former Soviet Union and Eastern Europe in Turkey', *Women's Studies International Forum*, 25 (4): 411–21.

Guy, Donna (1991) *Sex and Danger in Buenos Aires.* Lincoln, NE: University of Nebraska Press.

Guy, Donna (1992) ' "White slavery", citizenship and nationality in Argentina', in A. Parker *et al.* (eds), *Nationalisms and Sexualities*, New York: Routledge, pp. 201–15.

Hughes, Donna (2002) *Foreign Government Complicity in Human Trafficking: A Review of the State Department's 2002 Trafficking in Persons Report.* Testimony at the House Committee on Foreign Relations, 19 June.

IHRLG/Ann Jordan (International Human Rights Law Group) (2002) *Annotated Guide to the UN Trafficking Protocol.* Washington.

Irwin, Mary Ann (1996) ' "White slavery" as metaphor: anatomy of a moral panic', *Ex Post Facto: The History Journal*, 5. Available at http://www. walnet.org/csis/papers/irwin-wslavery.html.

Jerusalem Post (2004) '3,000 sex slaves in Israel: survey', 11 February.

Kantola, Johanna and Squires, Judith (2002) *Discourses Surrounding Prostitution Policies in the UK.* Paper presented at PSA Annual Conference, Aberdeen, April.

Kapur, Ratna (2002) 'The tragedy of victimization rhetoric: resurrecting the "native" subject in international/post-colonial feminist legal politics', *Harvard Human Rights Journal*, Spring: 1–37.

Kelly, Liz and Regan, Linda (2000a) 'Trafficking in women', *Network Newsletter*, 20. The British Council.

Kelly, Liz and Regan, Linda (2000b) *Stopping Traffic: Exploring the Extent of, and Responses to Trafficking in Women for Sexual Exploitation in the UK,* Police Research Series Paper 125. London: Home Office Policing and Reducing Crime Unit.

Kennedy, Iyamu and Nicotri, Pino (1999) *Lucciole nere. Le prostitute nigeriane si raccontano.* Milan: Kaos.

King, Russell and Wood, Nancy (eds) (2001) *Media and Migration: Constructions of Mobility and Difference.* London: Routledge.

Lahbabi, Fatima and Rodríguez, Pilar (2000) 'Les immigrés marocains en Andalousie: Le cas des femmes marocaines prostituées a Almería.' Unpublished doctoral research, Université Toulouse-le-Murail and Universidad de Almería.

Likiniano (2003) *Tráfico y prostitución: Experiencias de mujeres africanas.* Bilbao: Likiniano Elkartea.

Mai, Nicola (2001) 'Transforming traditions: a critical analysis of the trafficking and exploitation of young Albanian girls in Italy', in R. King (ed.), *Mediterranean Passage: Migration and New Cultural Encounters in Southern Europe.* Liverpool: Liverpool University Press, pp. 258–78.

Massey, Douglas *et al.* (1993) 'Theories of international migration: a review and appraisal', *Population and Development Review*, 19 (3): 431–66.

Mayhew, Henry (1851) *London Labour and London Poor,* [reprint 1968] Vol. IV *Those That Will Not Work, comprising Prostitutes, Thieves, Swindlers and Beggars.* New York: Dover.

Moch, Leslie Page (1992) *Moving Europeans. Migration in Western Europe since 1650.* Bloomington, IN: Indiana University Press.

Morokvasíc, Mirjana (1984) 'Birds of passage are also women', *International Migration Research*, 18 (4): 886–907.

Nowak, Anna (1999) 'Political transformation in Poland: the rise of sex work', *Research for Sex Work*, 2: 9–11.

Oso, Laura (2003) 'Estrategias migratorias de las mujeres ecuatorianas y colombianas en situación irregular', *Mugak*, 23: 25–37.

Pheterson, Gail (1996) *The Prostitution Prism.* Amsterdam: Amsterdam University.

Pickup, Francine (1998) 'Deconstructing trafficking in women: the example of Russia', *Journal of International Studies*, 27 (4): 995–1021.

Poppy Project (2004) *Poppy Project Newsletter*, 2, April. London: Eaves Housing for Women.

Protection Project (2003) *United Kingdom Country Report.* Baltimore: Johns Hopkins University (online at: www.protectionproject.org/main2.htm).

Pyle, Jean L. (2001) 'Sex, maids, and export processing: risks and reasons for gendered global production networks', *International Journal of Politics, Culture and Society*, 15 (1): 55–76.

Ratliff, Eric A. (1999) 'Women as "sex workers," men as "boyfriends": shifting identities in Philippine go-go bars', *Anthropology & Medicine*, 6 (1): 79–101.

Roberts, Nickie (1986) *The Front Line.* London: Grafton Books.

Salt, John (2000) 'Trafficking and human smuggling: a European perspective', *International Migration*, 38 (3): 31–56.

Sassen, Saskia (1999) *Guests and Aliens.* New York: New Press.

Sassen-Koob, Saskia (1984) 'From household to workplace: theories and survey research on migrant women in the labor market', *International Migration Review*, XVIII, 4 (4): 1144–67.

Signorelli, Assunta and Treppete, Mariangela (2001) *Services in the Window: A Manual for Interventions in the World of Migrant Prostitution.* Trieste: Asterios Editore.

Singleton, Ann and Barbesino, Paolo (1999) 'The production and reproduction of knowledge on international migration in Europe: the social embeddedness of social knowledge', in F. Anthias and G. Lazaridis (eds), *Into the Margins: Migration and Exclusion in Southern Europe*. Aldershot: Ashgate, pp. 13–33.

Skrobanek, Siriporn, Boonpakdee, Nataya and Jantateero, Chutima (1997) *The Traffic in Women: Human Realities of the International Sex Trade*. London: Zed Books.

Stoneking, Mark (1998) 'Women on the move', *Nature Genetics*, 20: 219–20.

Tabet, Paola (1989) 'I'm the meat, I'm the knife: sexual service, migration and repression in some african societies', in G. Pheterson (ed.), *A Vindication of the Rights of Whores*, Seattle, WA: Seal Press.

Tampep (1999) *Health, Migration and Sex Work: The Experience of Tampep*. Amsterdam: Mr. A. de Graaf Stichting.

UNESCO Trafficking Statistics Project (2003) Available at: www.unescobkk. org/culture/trafficking/matrix/matrix.asp.

US State Department (2004) *Trafficking in Persons Report*. Washington, DC.

van den Anker, Christien (2003) *Trafficking in the UK – A Country Report*. Paper presented at the NEWR workshop, Amsterdam, April.

van der Kleij, Aika (2002) *Provisions for Victims of Trafficking in Bonded Sexual Labour, i.e. in Prostitution in 6 European Countries*. Amsterdam: Bonded Labour in Netherlands.

Walkowitz, Judith (1994) *City of Dreadful Delight: Narratives of Sexual Danger in Late-Victorian London*. London: Virago.

Ward, Helen, Day, Sophie, Green, Anna, Cooper, Kate and Weber, Jonathan (2004) 'Declining prevalence of STI in the London sex industry, 1985 to 2002', *Sexually Transmitted Infections*, 80: 374–6.

Zimmerman, Cathy *et al.* (2003) *The Health Risks and Consequences of Trafficking in Women and Adolescents. Findings from a European Study*. London: London School of Hygiene and Tropical Medicine.

Zlotnik, Hania (2003) *The Global Dimensions of Female Migration*. Washington, DC: Migration Policy Institute. (Available online at: http://www.migrationinformation.org/Feature/display.cfm?ID=109).

Chapter 6

Murder made easy: the final solution to prostitution?

Hilary Kinnell

I am down on whores and I shan't quit ripping them till I do get buckled … [1]

I killed the women for the sake of God, and for the protection of my religion because they were prostitutes and were corrupting other people.[2]

They're shite, killed by shite. Who gives a shite?[3]

The first of these quotes is from a letter to the press, sent by someone claiming to be Jack the Ripper, the notorious Whitechapel murderer, in 1888; the second is the self-justification offered by Saeed Hanaie, who confessed to killing 16 sex workers in Iran in 2001 and was subsequently hanged. The third quote is attributed to an unidentified police officer, in a press article about unsolved murders of sex workers in 1995.

Murderers who claim to believe they are cleansing society by killing sex workers may or may not be lying, but either way, they are appealing for clemency on the basis that their fellow citizens also want rid of prostitution, but are not as direct in their methods. This chapter looks at violence against sex workers, including an analysis of 84 homicides[4] which occurred between January 1990 and May 2004. It seeks to show that the vulnerability of sex workers, so grotesquely demonstrated in notorious serial killings, continues today. It argues that society's abhorrence of commercial sex, even when voiced by those who regard all sex workers as victims, has resulted in laws and law enforcement strategies that prevent neither violence, nor exploitation, nor even public nuisance. Instead, the legal framework makes all forms of sex work more dangerous, while proposals for making sex work safer are rejected lest they 'encourage prostitution', indicating that many view violence against sex workers as an important deterrent to discourage the sale of sex, and a punishment for those who do.

Some assert that sex work is 'in and of itself, violence against women'. These commentators not only exclude female clients, and male and transgender sex workers,[5] but also fail to distinguish between acts to which the sex worker has consented (however mistakenly), and acts which leave her physically harmed or dead, thus denying any obligation to prevent or reduce the latter kind of violence. This chapter is predicated by the view that commercial sex can be consensual or non-consensual; if the latter, it is a crime of violence. It understands violence to mean non-consensual sexual acts, and acts which cause physical harm or fear of physical harm. It argues that violence within the sex industry is not inevitable and can be prevented or at least reduced. It will explore the circumstances in which it happens and does not happen, how the criminal justice system responds to it, and the relationship between violence and enforcement strategies designed to discourage and punish the sale or purchase of sexual services.

Sex workers experience violence from clients, or men who pretend to be clients, from vigilantes, muggers and robbers, and from partners, pimps and managers. Violence from clients, vigilantes, muggers and robbers is nearly always carried out while the victim is at work, whether engaged in street soliciting or indoor work. At street locations, the public nature of soliciting exposes sex workers to aggression from 'people on the street' (Benson 1998), to street crime, and to hostility from people who resent their presence, as well as to violence from clients.

Indoor workers may operate alone, making them vulnerable to attack; where they operate together, they may be targeted for robbery since the more workers there are in one place, the more cash is likely to be on the premises.

In all scenarios, perpetrators may be encouraged to commit these acts, or at least disinhibited from committing them, by beliefs that sex workers deserve punishment, that they will not report crimes to the police, that police will not accord such crimes much priority, and perhaps that acts which are normally considered crimes are not crimes if committed against a sex worker (O'Neill and Barbaret 2000; Sanders 2001).

Context of violence

Research on client violence against sex workers in Glasgow, Edinburgh and Leeds (Church *et al.* 2001) demonstrated that risk of violence was strongly related to working environment: 81 per cent of 115 street workers had experienced violence from clients, compared to 48 per cent of 125 indoor workers. This picture is similar to that found in Birmingham in 1993 (Kinnell 1993) where all forms of violence were strongly associated with street work.[6] Of 110 women interviewed in Birmingham, 68 per cent had experienced violence while at work: 83 per cent of those engaged in street work at the time of interview compared to 53 per cent of 56 indoor workers, most of whom were reporting on incidents that had taken place when they were doing street work. Benson (1998) also found high levels of violence in Nottingham, while a multi-centre survey of street workers for Channel 4 TV (Dodd 2002) found that 73 per cent had been attacked in the previous year.

The apparent relative safety of indoor sex work will be explored first, to determine whether, and if so how, indoor environments reduce levels of violence. This section draws on information from an analysis of 243 incidents reported to the London Ugly Mugs List (Kinnell 2002), which occurred between May 2000 and January 2002. The term 'Ugly Mug'[7] (or 'Dodgy Punter') refers to reports made by sex workers about clients and others who have assaulted, robbed or abused them. Outreach projects for sex workers turn these reports into warning flyers or bulletins describing the assailant, for distribution to other sex workers.

The London Ugly Mug List (LUML) is a compilation of reports given via sex work projects in the Greater London area. The LUML can only reflect the experiences of those sex workers who have contact with a project which encourages reporting of attacks. Variations in prevalence of violence may therefore be partly an artefact of how the LUML is produced. However, since it is compiled from reports from a variety of agencies, and relates to sex workers in a variety of locations, it offers a better source of information about violence against sex workers in the area it covers than is available elsewhere.

Indoor work

Many towns and cities have brothels which advertise as saunas or massage parlours, although in London the 'sex flat' is more common.

These are private addresses where one or more sex workers operate, attracting custom by word of mouth, advertising in the personal columns of newspapers or contact magazines, or on the Internet. This type of work happens in rural and suburban areas, as well as in towns and cities.

There are also escort agencies, through which sex workers may meet clients in hotels or private premises. Of these methods, only a woman working alone, in premises she owns herself, who does not advertise, operates within the law, and even she may be liable to prosecution for 'keeping a disorderly house'[8] or, under civil law, for running a business without planning consent. All other forms of indoor work are criminalised by the 1956 and 2003 Sexual Offences Acts, which make the premises in which sex work occurs, those responsible for the premises and those involved in the management of sex work the focus of criminalisation.

Whittaker and Hart (1996) explored strategies for avoiding customer violence among indoor sex workers at sex flats in London. They identified several factors which contributed to relative safety: a lighted environment which is the sex worker's 'territory'; the almost universal presence of a 'maid'[9] able to intervene if there is any trouble; screening clients through 'spyholes' (now CCTV is also used for this purpose); and willingness to call for police assistance in emergencies. They also utilised some of the same strategies reported by street workers, including 'intuition' about a client's potential for violence, adopting an assertive stance towards clients, and building up a clientele of 'regulars' (Sanders 2001).

Reports of violence and other incidents at indoor premises in London have increased greatly in the past decade. At one project, the number of such reports rose from under 10 in each year 1990 to 1993, to 58 in 1999 (Fereira da Silva 2000). However, only 17 per cent of mainly indoor workers at one London service (Azevedo *et al.* 2002) had ever experienced an assault while they were at work.

This apparent contradiction is elucidated by examination of the nature of the incidents reported to the London Ugly Mugs List between 2000 and 2002, which showed that 47 per cent of all reports from indoor premises were about events which, though frightening, did not result in violence, and frequently described the effectiveness of having more than one person on the premises, of CCTV and security devices, in averting or reducing the severity of incidents. For example:

The maid timed 20 minutes and then knocked the door to check that the working girl was OK.

He pretended to go but he didn't see the camera and the maid saw him come back in … the maid asked him to leave which he did.

The woman called to her partner saying the man had a gun. The woman's partner than charged towards the door with a large stick and the man ran off.

Sexual violence was far less commonly reported to the LUML by indoor workers than by street workers, in relation to the total number of reports from different venues, as was violence unconnected with robbery. Out of 205 reports from indoor workers only thirteen (6.3 per cent) described sexual assault, and only three of these are described as rape, one at a flat, one in a sauna and one on a visit to the client's home. However, indoor workers were nearly three times more likely to report robberies with violence than street workers, and over twice as likely to report other property crime.

Eighty-one per cent of all indoor robberies involved violence, often severe, and many robberies were perpetrated by assailants known to have targeted other indoor premises. In 39 per cent of robberies a weapon was used or shown: nine involved firearms, others involved knives, machetes and, in one case, an axe; in two CS gas was used. Reports also referred to flat workers, maids, clients, even passers-by, being attacked. Similar incidents have occurred elsewhere in the country, including at saunas in Birmingham and a massage parlour in Stoke-on-Trent which was held up at gunpoint.[10]

It appears that indoor premises have become targets for robbery, perhaps because it is expected that such premises will hold considerable sums of cash or because the offenders do not expect the victims to contact the police. This is an important change since 1994, when Whittaker and Hart (1996) found that women in sex flats felt able to report incidents to the police. The same authors (Whittaker *et al.* 1996) reported that during the year 1994/5, women from former Soviet Union countries began working in sex flats in central London. By 1999, the same service reported that 48 per cent of their female sex working clientele were migrant women (Brussa 1999).

This chapter does not address trafficking and migration issues; however, London projects have reported that new immigration patterns, and law enforcement responses to them, have had considerable impact both on the nature of crimes committed against sex workers, and on sex workers' willingness to report such crimes. Trafficking legislation does not distinguish between those who have been coerced into sex work and those who are essentially working in the sex industry as economic migrants, both being liable to summary deportation. Therefore, those who in the past had no hesitation in contacting the police may now feel unable to do so, as the presence of women with irregular immigration status is something which has to be hidden.

Indoor workers who operate alone can be inferred to be at greater risk of attack than those working with other people, because they cannot rely on anyone else to intervene if a client turns violent. This is borne out by the work style characteristics of murdered sex workers (see discussion below). Only nine reports to the LUML (3.7 per cent of the total) were made by escorts, but this may reflect lack of contact between projects and escorts rather than their relative safety. All these incidents occurred either in the client's home or in hotels. Six incidents (two-thirds) involved violence, the same proportion as in reports from street workers.

It therefore appears that, among indoor workers, risk of violence unconnected with property crime largely depends on whether the worker is alone when meeting clients. Lone workers are least likely to contravene prostitution laws but most vulnerable to attack. Group working reduces the risk of sexual violence, but its criminalisation ensures that attacks which do occur, especially in the course of robberies, frequently go unreported to the police, allowing for their continuance and escalation.

Street work

Since 1959 police in England and Wales have used the Street Offences Act against female street workers; kerb-crawling was criminalized in 1985, and made an arrestable offence in 2001.[11] Police, local authorities and magistrates now also have the power to use Anti-Social Behaviour Orders (ASBOs) against sex workers and clients. ASBOs typically ban the subject of the order from an area, which may include the sex worker's home, as well as the premises of agencies sex workers need to access for health and welfare services. Some ASBOs ban the sex worker for soliciting anywhere in the country. If the ASBO is breached, this can result in a prison sentence of up to five years, even though soliciting is not an imprisonable offence.

These approaches to reducing street sex work increase the dangers for street sex workers. The threat of arrest and of ASBOs increases the incentive to avoid being seen by police or CCTV cameras, so women take less time to assess potential customers and work later at night, in darker and more isolated areas. Enforcement directed at kerb-crawlers means fewer customers, so women have to work longer hours in dangerous environments to make their money. Among sex workers surveyed for the Channel 4 TV documentary, 71 per cent said they took more risks as a result of police crackdowns and 65 per cent said they worked longer hours (Dodd 2002).

Anti-kerbcrawler policies also disrupt contact between sex workers and their regular clients. Sanders (2001) and Benson (1998) report that sex workers regard a clientele of regular customers as an important safety strategy, but 'regulars' are more likely to be caught by anti-kerbcrawler initiatives than occasional visitors, leaving sex workers with proportionately fewer regulars among their clientele. In addition, pimps may beat up women who have failed to make enough money; clients vent their anger at having come to police notice on the sex workers; desperate sex workers are driven to robbing clients, who then take revenge:

> Did business and demanded money back, girl refused, he punched her several times in the face giving her a black eye, said he had been ripped off by another girl.[12]

Sex workers and clients are also likely to disperse from their usual areas of business during periods of heavy policing. In 1999, Hull police claimed a victory over kerb-crawlers when a record number of local men were stopped for kerb-crawling in Sheffield: 'A spokesman for South Yorkshire Police said officers had never before stopped such a significant number of motorists from East Yorkshire in Sheffield's red light district.'[13] Five years later, Hull police were still pursuing anti-kerbcrawler policies, indicating that this 'victory' was short-lived, while the displacement effect of the much-vaunted 1998/9 Leeds Kerb-Crawler Rehabilitation Programme was acknowledged in the evaluation published by West Yorkshire Police: 'As a result of their positive approach to the policing of street prostitutes and their clients, the prostitutes have moved their business into surrounding divisions …'

During this anti-kerbcrawling activity, in April 1999, a Leeds sex worker went to work in London, where she was murdered by David Smith.[14] The Leeds sex worker 'had been given a lift to London by friends but had jumped out of the car near Paddington station. She was arrested for soliciting on the night of 24 April ... but was released about midnight and was last seen asking for directions back to (Paddington). Her next 'punter' was Smith.'[15] Smith was known as a dangerous client to women in Paddington, and was easily recognisable, his nicknames being 'the Honey Monster' and 'Lurch', but an outsider would not have known of his reputation. Several other murdered sex workers were newcomers to the area where they were killed.

These examples show that anti-street work enforcement strategies fail to solve problems for communities, while increasing the dangers for sex workers, sometimes with fatal consequences.

'Cleaning the streets'

Street workers are exposed to harassment and threats from members of the public (McKeganey and Barnard 1996). Verbal abuse, spitting and throwing objects ranging from stones to fireworks and bottles are common occurrences. In many areas sex work projects have reported that highly publicised anti-street work operations coincide with raised levels of violence, not only from clients, but also from members of the public. It is possible that local politicians and police forces perceive the need to placate local communities as a higher priority than taking action when such acts take place under the cover of 'community protest'.

Vigilantism has occurred in Birmingham, Nottingham, Sheffield, Bradford, Derby, Leicester, Edinburgh, Liverpool and London (Hubbard and Sanders 2003; Kinnell 1995).

Lowman (2000) has described the 'rhetoric of disposal' used by the Canadian media and action groups opposed to their areas being used for street prostitution, and has drawn associations between the intensity of such rhetoric and the incidence of murder of sex workers, arguing that the social acceptability of using language which equates sex workers with rubbish legitimises the actions of those who attack and kill them. In the UK, anti-street work drives are routinely accompanied by media pronouncements that assert the socially polluting nature of commercial sex and validate society's abhorrence of it. For example:

War on vice cleans up sex rat-run.[16]

Hull has *declared war on vice girls* operating on a city estate and warned kerb crawlers they face immediate arrest and public shaming if they persist in trawling for prostitutes. Humberside Police is launching a major new initiative to *wipe out street prostitution.*[17] (Emphases added)

Hull is a city which has seen intense anti-sex work policing operations and where at least five sex workers have been killed since 1996.

The perception of sex workers as social pollutants has exacerbated assertions that they menace innocent citizens with sexually transmitted diseases. In 2003, Reading police also descended to using this tactic, claiming a local sex worker 'had AIDS' to try to scare clients away,[18] while in 2001, Wolverhampton police even used the arrest of a multiple rapist to raise fears about HIV:

A police force today warned men about the possibility of contracting HIV from prostitutes after a man with the condition was charged with rape.[19]

In November 1999, Aberdeen police fuelled fears of sex workers by warning clients that they were likely to be robbed or attacked by them. They 'urged men visiting prostitutes to be conscious of their personal safety and (appealed) for any victims who have stayed silent to come forward.'[20] Kenneth Smith, who had a history of violence against sex workers in Aberdeen, raped again not long after this inflammatory statement, in February and June 2000.[21]

These examples of the 'rhetoric of disposal' and deliberate raising of public fears about the dangers posed by sex workers to their clients and through them to the rest of the population show a staggering disregard for sex workers' safety which could easily be seen as legitimising the violence they suffer.

Client violence

Violence from clients most commonly occurs when the client and sex worker have left the soliciting area. Street workers typically get into clients' vehicles and are then driven elsewhere, so that sexual encounters take place somewhere relatively private. In the past, street workers often took clients to their own indoor premises, where the presence of other people helped protect them. Information from agencies working with street sex workers indicates that this is now a less common modus operandi, partly because many social housing providers will evict tenants for using the premises for the purposes of prostitution, and partly because at the present time, a high proportion of street sex workers are homeless – often literally roofless – so have nowhere to take clients to even if they wished to do so.

Instead sex worker and client usually have sex in the vehicle, or outdoors, in alleyways, industrial units, parks, car or lorry parks, derelict buildings or country areas outside town, or go to the client's home. Once in a vehicle, sex workers have little control over where clients take them, and they may be trapped by central locking devices or by clients parking close to a wall. The vulnerability of women in these situations is reflected in the experience of those interviewed for the Channel 4 survey: 64 per cent had been attacked in a car, 42 per cent in an alleyway and 31 per cent in or near an industrial estate in the previous 12 months (Dodd 2002).

Media reports of attacks on sex workers can also illustrate the inherent dangers.

- Two men convicted of kidnapping and raping a sex worker in 2003 had picked her up in Derby, and driven her 15 miles to Nottingham, where she was attacked.[22]

- Eamonn Kelly attacked two Glasgow sex workers in 2000, leaving one for dead, after driving them down a dead-end road by a loch.[23]

- Michael O'Meara, convicted of raping sex workers in Coventry in 2000, 'drove his victims to a secluded area of (an) industrial estate and attacked them'.[24]

- A gang of Rochdale men convicted of raping one sex worker and robbing another had lured their victims into cars by one of the gang posing as a client while the others hid nearby. 'The victims were then driven to a pre-arranged spot where the other men were picked up, trapping the frightened women in the car.'[25]

The environment which affects sex workers' vulnerability to violence is not only the location of work, but the behaviour of other people who may or may not come to the sex worker's assistance if there is any trouble. The advantage of working close to people who will help if there is trouble is illustrated by reports of attacks in the Midlands, North West and Lincolnshire:

A man wanted his money back, the woman refused and got out of the car, he ran after her, held a knife to her throat and demanded his money again. A passerby stopped and the woman got into their car and was driven to a nearby pub.[26]

The 23-year-old woman was allegedly beaten up on wasteland in Scunthorpe, north Lincolnshire. She managed to escape and knocked on the door of a nearby property ... The resident of the house called an ambulance.[27]

Others are not so fortunate. One rape report describes how the woman fought back despite the fact that her assailant had tried to slash her throat with a knife, and kept beeping the horn to try to attract attention, but this did not lead to her gaining any assistance.[28]

Trigger factors
Research among street workers carried out for the Channel 4 documentary (Dodd 2002) found that 52 per cent had experienced attacks for no apparent reason, but where there did seem to be a 'trigger' the main rationalisations for clients becoming violent were:

- sex workers refusing the types of sexual services the clients wanted (44 per cent);
- disputes over money – clients refusing to pay (42 per cent);
- the sex worker saying 'time up' before man could ejaculate after being paid (29 per cent);
- client being unable to get an erection, or ejaculate (32 per cent).

Clients' problems with erection or ejaculation are frequently related to alcohol use, which in itself has potential for violence. Since much street work takes place late at night, as pubs and clubs are closing, street workers will be vulnerable to the effects of excess alcohol on their clientele. Another 'trigger factor', frequently mentioned in sex workers' reports of attacks, although not referred to in the above list, is insistence on condom use.

The 43-year-old women both told the court that Smith had turned violent when they insisted he wore a condom.[29]

Use of condoms is a standard part of the ritual inherent in the commercial transaction,[30] and although sex workers have always reported client resistance to condom use, any man approaching a sex worker for 'business' ought to anticipate the expectation that condoms will be required. Also, when a man who has approached a sex worker as a client reacts violently as soon as he is asked to pay, it begs the question whether this person has ever been a client, since by definition a client is someone who pays for sex? All these suggest unwillingness by some men to accept the commercial nature of the transaction, and with it the limits imposed by sex workers regarding time, money and sexual practice. The violent reactions when the limits of the commercial transaction are enforced suggest that it is the role of client which is being resisted.

The most obvious factor which facilitates violence against street workers is the physical location: interactions with clients take place in dark, isolated places where most attacks happen. Clients, and others who attack sex workers, may also be disinhibited from violence because they share common social attitudes that sex workers are worthless human beings, degraded women who deserve punishment. It is difficult to see how such attitudes could be altered as long as policies and public statements about sex work reinforce a rhetoric of abhorrence and adopt strategies that rely on the shaming and humiliation of clients.

Clients' potential for violence

The question of clients' potential for violence was explored by Brooks-Gordon's study of kerb-crawlers in London (Brooks-Gordon 1999). Under 6 per cent had a criminal record, and only eight out of over a thousand were found to have convictions for sexual or other violence. Slightly higher rates (8 per cent) of previous convictions for violent and sexual offences were found among men apprehended for kerb-crawling in Southampton (Shell *et al.* 2001), and those with previous convictions were also likely to be repeat offenders. This suggests that a relatively small proportion of clients may be responsible for a disproportionately large number of attacks.

Data from the London Ugly Mugs List supports this hypothesis. A substantial minority of offenders (30 per cent) were reported as being known as regular clients, as offenders who had previously attacked other sex workers or other premises, or as being known to the police. Examples of serial attackers elsewhere include:

- Dean Cartwright, given life for raping a Middlesborough sex worker in 2003, had previous convictions for raping two other women and indecently assaulting a teenage girl within the previous ten years.[31]

- George Kamau was convicted of raping two sex workers and indecently assaulting a third, all within a month, in Northampton in 2002.[32]

- Robert Freitas was given nine years in 2004 for raping two Bristol sex workers and indecently assaulting a third, all within a month.[33]

- Martin Rogers, who raped three Stoke-on-Trent sex workers and stabbed another, was jailed for life in October 2001. Rogers attacked three of his victims during one evening and had raped a 22-year-old sex worker in the same area a month earlier. He had told one of his victims that 'he fantasised about what it would be like to kill a prostitute'.[34]

Martin Rogers may have only fantasised about killing sex workers, but there is evidence that a high percentage of murders are committed by men with previous convictions for violence, not only against sex workers, and not only against women.

Murder of sex workers

Potterat *et al.* (2003) estimate that sex workers in the USA are 18 times more likely to be murdered than women of similar demographic characteristics. They concluded that the 'homicide rate is many times higher than that for any occupation in developed countries or any population of women previously studied.'[35] In Canada, police publish statistics on murders of sex workers, categorised by the type of assailant, i.e. client, partner, etc. (Lowman 2000).

In Britain, no such research or data is publicly available. However, Ward and Day (1999) have estimated that the mortality rate among 402 women attending a GU service for sex workers in London between 1985 and 1994 was 12 times the normal rate for women in this age group. Of the four deaths confirmed in this group, two were murders. Brookman and Maguire (2003) refer to 17 sex worker deaths by homicide between 1996 and 1999, and acknowledge that sex worker deaths are likely to go unrecorded, since the 'coding system does not include in its record of "key occupation" those women who have other forms of unemployment and/or whose involvement in prostitution is hidden from official view'. The largest single group of homicide victims, 40 per cent of the total, was among those categorised as unemployed, which may conceal deaths among sex workers.

Sex worker deaths 1990 to 2004

The following is an analysis of information from press and other reports about the deaths or disappearances of 84 sex workers which have resulted in murder investigations, from January 1990 to May 2004.

Only one of these 84 sex workers was male, a 15-year-old killed by two other teenagers in what may have been a homophobic attack. Since these deaths were analysed, another murder of a male sex worker was reported, in July 2004, an indoor worker aged 32. Other male sex workers may have been killed in the past 14 years, but if so, their deaths have not been associated with sex work in the media reports accessed. Connell and Hart (2003) have described violence experienced by young male sex workers in Glasgow, but no other murders have been reported by projects that work with male sex workers.

Two of the sex workers are missing, presumed dead. There are many other sex workers who have disappeared in suspicious circumstances, but these are the only two where it is known that a murder investigation is ongoing.

Age at death is known for 72 sex workers: 61 per cent were aged under 25 years; eight were under 18 years (10.8 per cent). The mean age was 24, with a range of 14 to 46. A very similar, but usually slightly older mean and range, is found in most larger surveys of sex workers in the UK. This might suggest that younger women are more at risk of murder than older women, but may also reflect the preponderance of street workers, who are more likely to be younger on average than off-street workers.

Risk of murder and location of work

Working method is known for 72 sex workers. Fifty-nine were street workers (82 per cent), of whom 47 (65 per cent) were last seen alive while working; three others worked from pubs and lorry parks, their bodies found outdoors, indicating similar location risks to street workers. Only one indoor worker, a clip-joint hostess, was killed at premises where other people were present at the time of the murder,

and she was close to the door when her assailant ran in
street and attacked her.

Eight other indoor workers, and three whose working r
not clear, were found dead either in their own premises
homes of men subsequently convicted of their murders. One of
these was killed by a former partner, two in the course of robberies,
but five were killed by clients, which indicates the dangers of solo
working, whether in one's own premises or visiting clients at theirs.
This suggests that the deaths of at least 53 (63 per cent) sex workers
were directly related to their isolated situations while engaged in sex
work.

Judicial outcomes

At the time of writing,[36] charges are known to have been brought,
or a chief suspect named, in connection with 53 (63 per cent) of
these deaths.[37] It is noticeable that 'clients' were more likely to be
convicted of murder or manslaughter than any other category of
presumed assailant (23/29, 79 per cent). Two-thirds of cases where
an acquaintance or drug dealer was charged resulted in a conviction
for murder or manslaughter, but among partners, only half were so
convicted.

Table 6.1 shows the categories of relationship believed to exist
between the 53 victims and persons charged or named, against the
main judicial outcome. Where more than one person was charged
in relation to one death, the most severe judicial outcome is listed;
for example, where two persons were charged and one convicted of
murder, the other of manslaughter, the outcome is listed as murder. In
only one such case were those charged believed to have approached
the victim as clients. Conversely, four persons were charged in relation
to nine deaths: in all these cases, the person charged is believed to
have approached his victims as a client.

Partners

Many sex workers perceive the person others would describe as their
pimp as their partner, husband or lover. Violence unquestionably
takes place within these relationships, but studies that have carefully
examined relationships between sex workers and 'third parties' (May
et al. 2000) have demonstrated that violence is not universal. Whether
or not violence from sex workers' partners should be regarded as
qualitatively different from other forms of domestic violence, eight

Table 6.1 Sex worker deaths and judicial outcomes in relation to category of persons charged or named as suspects

Category*	Deaths n (%)		Murder	Mans/l	Acquit	Other outcome**
'Clients'	29	(55)	20	3	4	2
Acquaintances and dealers	9	(17)	5	1	2	1
Partners	8	(15)	3	1	2	2
Robbers	2	(4)	0	1	1	0
Other/not known	5	(9)	1	0	1	3
Total	53	(100)	29	6	10	8

 * Persons charged or named as suspects:
- *'Clients'*: it is believed these persons approached their victims as clients, although it is not known whether all had ever paid for sex.
- *Acquaintances and dealers*: includes one case where other sex workers were charged with murder, and cases where drug dealers were also acquaintances.
- *Partners*: includes former and current boyfriends or husbands.
** *Other outcome*: includes convictions for preventing lawful burial, cases where a suspect has been named but not charged, and cases where the outcome of judicial proceedings is not known.

deaths (15 per cent) were attributed to partners, but only half resulted in a conviction for murder or manslaughter. For example:

- Darren Adams, from Hull, was convicted of the murder of his sex worker partner in May 1998. Her dismembered remains were dumped on a waste tip.[38]

- Stephen Price, also of Hull, killed his sex worker partner in 1996. The court was told he assaulted and verbally abused her in the street for not making enough money, that she was scared of him, and was seen with black eyes and bruises. Price was convicted of manslaughter, after a retrial, in 1999.[39]

Extreme levels of abuse and violence in sex workers' private relationships is also illustrated by other cases. For example:

- Steven Wilson, from Birmingham, murdered his two children, boys of seven and eight, in February 2002, in revenge when his wife left him after nine years of physical abuse. He had forced his wife into sex work as a teenager.[40]

- Ashley Wright, also of Birmingham, was convicted of four rapes and two robberies in June 2002. At his trial it was alleged he had raped, beaten or tortured 12 sex workers over a 20-year period.[41]

Acquaintances and drug dealers

Nine (17 per cent) deaths were attributed to acquaintances and drug dealers. In 2003, Rose Broadley, a drug dealer in Glasgow, murdered a sex worker she had repeatedly assaulted and 'treated like a slave'.[42] Arguments between sex workers may be common, but attacks by other working women are rarely reported. However, such aggression can go to extremes, as illustrated by the murder of a Doncaster sex worker in 1993 by two other working women, in an attack which was thought to have been instigated by rival pimps.[43] Another murderer who had relationships with sex workers without being either a client or partner is Kenneth Valentine, convicted of murdering a Bradford sex worker in 1996. He befriended street workers, allowing them to use his flat for business. Valentine also had a previous conviction for manslaughter of a young woman, whom he killed by sexually assaulting her with a pool cue. He convinced the court that this was a sex game which went wrong.[44]

Clients

Although the above categories of partner, acquaintance and drug dealer account for 32 per cent of cases, attesting to the violence facing sex workers in their personal lives, the majority of deaths were caused by those approaching sex workers as clients (55 per cent). Canadian data ascribes a similar proportion of sex worker murders to clients (56 per cent: Lowman 2000). Potterat et al. (2004), however, found that 16 of the 21 (76 per cent) sex workers killed in Colorado Springs (USA) were murdered while actively soliciting, implying that they had been killed by clients. However, these authors do not report on persons charged or judicial outcomes for the whole sample.

It has been argued above that, while a high proportion of sex workers experience violence from clients, only a small proportion of clients are violent. Over the past 14 years only 29 deaths have been attributed to clients, and four of these men were acquitted, giving less than two deaths a year definitely caused by clients. Given the very large numbers of men who pay for sex every year (see Chapter 9 on clients), it is safe to say that only a tiny proportion of clients are potential murderers.

.owever, there is evidence that many clients who do murder have past histories which illustrate their potential for extreme violence. In 26 cases out of 53 (49 per cent), the person charged or named as chief suspect, is known to have previous or subsequent convictions for violence, 23 of them clients.

In 22 of the 35 cases (63 per cent) which resulted in a conviction for murder or manslaughter, the person convicted is known to have more than one conviction for murder, manslaughter or other violent offence, 19 of them clients. Three who were acquitted of murder are known to have attacked other sex workers, one later being convicted of murdering another sex worker, and one convicted of attacks which took place within six weeks of his acquittal for murder. Many offenders also had convictions for attacking non-sex workers, including men and children, for example:

- Deepak Bouri, convicted with Adam Bowler for the murder of a sex worker in East London in July 2003, had a previous conviction for indecently assaulting a 14-year-old, and was a registered sex offender.[45]

- Geoffrey Porter, given life for murdering a 17-year-old involved in prostitution in Bolton, in November 2001, had previous convictions including indecent assault on girls aged from 8 to 11, dating back 20 years.[46]

- Paul Brumfitt, convicted of murdering a sex worker in Wolverhampton in February 1999, and of raping a 17-year-old in March 1999, had pleaded guilty in 1980 to manslaughter for beating a shopkeeper to death in Essex and strangling a bus driver in Denmark. He served 15 years but was paroled in 1994.[47]

These cases indicate that more stringent monitoring of those convicted of violent offences should reduce the threat they pose to sex workers and others. They also demonstrate that the popular assumption that those who attack and murder sex workers do not pose a threat to non-sex workers is incorrect. This is further illustrated by cases where those who have attacked sex workers, but have not been apprehended, went on to attack or kill non-sex workers:

- Alun Kyte, convicted in 2000 of murdering two sex workers in the Midlands in 1993 and 1994, was in prison for raping a Bristol woman when DNA connected him to the earlier murders.[48]

- Victor Farrant, sentenced to 12 years for rape, false imprisonment, grievous bodily harm and unlawful wounding in 1988, was released November 1995. The following month, he viciously attacked a sex worker at her home in Hampshire, and six weeks later, murdered another woman who was not a sex worker.[49]

- Michael Sams, who murdered a sex worker in 1991, went on to kidnap estate agent Stephanie Slater, who was lucky to escape alive.

Despite such cases, and the historic example of Peter Sutcliffe, five of whose 13 victims were not sex workers (Yallop 1981), in April 2002, a senior officer investigating the murder of a sex worker in Norwich, the third in ten years, said 'there is nothing to suggest from our enquiries that there is any threat to any other members of the public'.[50]

While not wishing to stigmatise people with mental health problems, failure of mental health services to monitor or even identify potentially violent patients is evident in seven deaths and other attacks that have occurred at the hands of people known to have a history of psychiatric disorder:

- Anthony Hardy, 53, was convicted in November 2003 of the murder of three London sex workers, two of whom had been found dismembered in bin bags near his home the previous December. The third had been found dead in his flat several months earlier, but the post-mortem concluded she had died from natural causes.[51] Hardy had a history of psychiatric disorder, including detention under the Mental Health Act.

- Mark Corner 26, was convicted in December 2003 of killing two Liverpool sex workers in July of the same year. Like Hardy, he had dismembered his victims, whose body parts were found in bin bags on the street and in the freezer at his home. However, he successfully pleaded guilty to manslaughter on the grounds of psychiatric disorder, having been known to mental health services since he was 17.[52]

- George Leigers, convicted of the murder of a sex worker in Middlesbrough in August 2003, had been convicted of the manslaughter of his wife in 1986. He had served 16 years in a secure hospital, but killed again six months after release.[53]

- Peter Slack, 39, convicted of manslaughter in 2002, after strangling a sex worker in Nottingham, had been detained in a secure unit for more than ten years after previous stabbings.

- Noel Dooley, a paranoid schizophrenic who was given two life sentences in November 2001[54] for knifing a Bradford sex worker 43 times, had previously served 19 years for murdering a woman in Coventry in 1979, and was released on licence in 1998.

- James Aird Walker, convicted in 2001[55] for eleven offences against sex workers in Plymouth, including two rapes, four indecent assaults and four false imprisonments, had appeared in court on 56 previous occasions going back to 1962. In 1978 he had been made subject to a hospital order in Scotland.

The failure of agencies tasked with monitoring offenders in the community is also illustrated by the case of Kenneth Valentine (see above). Despite his previous conviction for the sexual killing of a young woman, after release from prison he was rehoused in Bradford's area of street soliciting, and it was to these premises he lured other sex workers, one of whom he murdered, and another was found imprisoned in his flat when he was arrested.

Failure of murder investigations

Over a third of the 84 deaths (31) are not known to have been resolved. Some of these may have been, but it has not been possible to obtain the relevant information from police sources. Of the 42 most recent deaths (May 1998 to March 2004), no one is known to have been charged in 12 cases; in a further three cases, the person charged was acquitted, or convicted of another offence (i.e. preventing lawful burial and conspiracy to rob). Of the 42 least recent deaths (January 1990 to February 1998), no one is known to have been charged in 19 cases, and in seven, the person charged was acquitted, three on 'not proven' verdicts. Therefore only 35 of the 84 deaths (42 per cent) are known to have resulted in a conviction.

Among the acquittals is the case of a sex worker who had cancer but died soon after a brutal sexual attack. The defendant was also accused of numerous robberies from indoor sex workers; there was DNA and photographic evidence against him, but he was acquitted of murder, even after admitting to repeated lying in court. He has continued to menace sex workers in the same area since his acquittal. Gary Allen was acquitted of the murder of a Hull sex worker in January 2000: six weeks later he was arrested for attacking sex workers in Plymouth. David Smith was acquitted of murdering one sex worker in 1993, but subsequently convicted of murdering another in 1999. Only five of the eight murders of sex workers in Glasgow since 1991 have resulted in a trial, and three of these resulted in 'not proven' verdicts.

Clearly, it is in no one's interests to convict an innocent person, leaving the real killer free; however, acquittals which appear to result from prejudice on the part of juries against sex worker victims or witnesses, or from idiosyncrasies in the judicial process, or from failures of the police to gather sufficient evidence, are unacceptable.

Obtaining evidence in the criminalised, stigmatised world of commercial sex is difficult: police need the cooperation of clients, sex workers and their associates at these times, but several recent cases suggest that reducing the public nuisance of street prostitution continues to be the main police priority, even when a murder investigation is taking place. In 2000, police in Middlesbrough appealed for public cooperation in the investigation of the murder of a local sex worker, at the same time as running an anti-kerbcrawling operation. Kerb-crawlers were brought to court in the week before Christmas, with police announcing:

> We have repeatedly warned that men who come to Middlesbrough looking for prostitutes will be prosecuted. I accept that their families are also victims and it is a terrible thing to happen in the run-up to Christmas, but kerb crawlers must accept the consequences of their actions.[56]

At the same time, police from the same force complained about lack of public cooperation in the murder enquiry:

> A Cleveland Police spokeswoman said: 'Officers are dismayed yet again at the lack of response to pleas for help. This latest appeal … has not resulted in a single call to the incident room.[57]

Repressive policing also reduces contact between outreach projects and sex workers: sex workers alter their usual soliciting times and locations to avoid detection, and may have less time to talk, even if outreach workers can find them. Such services play an important role in mediating between sex workers and police at times when cooperation is needed for the investigation of serious crimes, so control strategies that reduce such contact are likely to interfere with collection of intelligence. In Middlesbrough, at the time of the 2000 murder investigation, the local news website reported a nurse at the drop-in centre as saying:

> ... there are not so many girls using the centre. It would be foolish to think they have stopped. We do not know where they are. I think it is because of the crackdown.[58]

Middlesbrough police have continued to promote their anti-kerbcrawler strategy, but the murder is still unsolved. Similar cases have occurred in Stoke-on-Trent (2001), Liverpool (2000) and Bradford (2001), where murders which coincided with anti-sex work enforcement drives are also still unsolved. Such cases, where hostile policing has either coincided with murder or interfered with investigations, indicate the extent to which control policies, pursued to reduce the neighbourhood nuisance of street sex work, increase sex workers' vulnerability, decrease their ability to limit their own risks, decrease contact with helping agencies and decrease the likelihood of cooperation between sex workers, clients and police over the investigation of serious crimes.

Responses to violence

Police cannot respond appropriately unless sex workers report attacks and other crimes to them. However, sex workers are frequently unwilling to go to the police (McKeganey and Barnard 1996). Only 38 per cent of violent incidents reported to the LUML by indoor workers were also reported to the police, and this was more than twice the rate of reporting by street workers (15 per cent: Kinnell 2002). Among women interviewed for Channel 4, 69 per cent said they reported no or hardly any attacks to the police (Dodd 2002).

They may not expect sympathetic treatment: police may respond by saying she 'shouldn't be out there in the first place'. The main reason for not reporting among the Channel 4 group was that they did not think the police would be sympathetic (60 per cent). If there are warrants out against them, or they are subject to ASBOs, they may fear being locked up if they go to the police; those in the country illegally may fear deportation. Those who have not been arrested for prostitution-related offences may fear to identify themselves to the police. Those working from private addresses may not wish to draw attention to themselves or to their premises. Those under pressure from pimps or supporting a drug habit may be deterred from reporting by the amount of time it will take. If they do approach the police, they may be detained for long periods and questioned about matters that are nothing to do with the incident they wish to report.

The following account from an outreach worker shows how difficult it can be for police to give priority to crimes against sex workers, or to encourage sex workers to report attacks, when they are also tasked with enforcement:

> A woman was in a marked police vehicle having just given details of a violent incident that had taken place earlier in the evening. Our local 'man on a mission' [police officer] approached and the officer who had taken details left his vehicle to speak with him. On his return he appeared flushed and uncomfortable and stated that the other officer had told him in no uncertain terms that as the woman had declared she was a prostitute it was his duty to give her a police caution.[59]

Conclusions

Violence against sex workers is intimately related to hostile legislation, law enforcement and public attitudes.

Among indoor workers, lone workers are least likely to contravene prostitution laws but are most vulnerable to attack. Group working reduces the risk of sexual violence, but its criminalisation ensures that attacks which do occur, especially in the course of robberies, frequently go unreported to the police, allowing for their continuance and escalation.

Street prostitution is typically policed solely to reduce or eliminate the presence of sex workers and their clients from public space. Control policies which displace sex workers from familiar areas, reduce negotiation time, reduce contact with known, regular clients and increase levels of client anger towards them, increase sex workers' vulnerability, decrease their ability to limit their own risks, decrease contact with helping agencies and decrease the likelihood of cooperation between sex workers, clients and police over the investigation of serious crimes.

Police need the cooperation of clients, sex workers and their associates if those who attack sex workers are to be brought to justice, but several recent cases suggest that reducing the public nuisance of street prostitution continues to be the main police priority, even when a murder investigation is taking place. Therefore, while the physical environment of sex work, especially street work, facilitates attacks, the judicial environment militates against their investigation, leaving offenders free to repeat and to escalate the violence.

Those who attack sex workers may also share common social attitudes that sex workers are worthless human beings, degraded women who deserve punishment. It is difficult to see how such attitudes could be altered as long as policies and public statements about sex work reinforce a rhetoric of abhorrence and adopt strategies that rely on the shaming and humiliation of clients.

Society's abhorrence of commercial sex, even when voiced by those who regard all sex workers as victims, has resulted in laws and law enforcement strategies that prevent neither violence, nor exploitation, nor even public nuisance. Instead, the legal framework makes all forms of sex work more dangerous, and proposals for making sex work safer are rejected lest they 'encourage prostitution', indicating that many view violence against sex workers as an important deterrent to discourage the sale of sex, and a punishment for those who do.

Notes

1 *The Enduring Mystery of Jack the Ripper*, online at: http://www.mel.police.uk/history/ripper.htm.
2 'Serial killer of 16 to die today, Iran says', *Toronto Globe & Mail*, 17 April 2002.
3 Michael Bilton, 'Footsteps of the Ripper,' in *The Sunday Times magazine*, 17 September 1995.
4 Cases where the death or disappearance of a sex worker has led to a murder investigation.
5 The focus here is on violence against female sex workers, but it should be remembered that male and transgender sex workers also encounter violence in the course of their work, including murder, as evidenced by the massacre of eight male masseurs in a Cape Town sauna (*'Two guilty of Cape gay massacre'*, 13 March 2004. http://news.bbc.co.uk/1/hi/world/africa/3505514.stm) and the murder of transgender sex workers in Toronto, both in 2003.
6 My 1993 research included all violence encountered while working, not only violence from clients.
7 The term 'Ugly Mug' was first used by sex workers' groups in Australia in the 1980s, and adopted in the UK from 1989 onwards.

8 Disorderly Houses Act 1751.
9 A maid does not offer sexual services, but acts as a receptionist, helping to screen out unwanted clients and giving company and assistance to the sex worker when required.
10 Project Ugly Mug Reports, 2002/3.
11 Section 71 of the Criminal Justice and Police Act 2001.
12 Report from sex worker, March 2002.
13 'Kerbcrawlers forced out of Hull': see Hull & East Yorkshire website, 20 January 1999.
14 A convicted rapist, who had been acquitted of murdering another sex worker in 1993.
15 'Prostitute murderer gets life', BBC News website, 8 December 1999.
16 *Birmingham Evening Mail*, 2 March 1989.
17 'New drive to keep vice girls off streets', *Yorkshire Evening Post*, 10 August 2001.
18 'Police AIDS "witch-hunt" criticized', BBC News Online, Berkshire, 2 July 2003.
19 'HIV warning to men using prostitutes', PA News, 27 April 2001.
20 'Sex clients' robbery risk', BBC News website, 25 November 1999.
21 'Rapist jailed for prostitute attacks', BBC News website, 6 February 2001.
22 'Two convicted of kidnap and rape', 26 May 2004, online at: http://news.bbc.co.uk/1/hi/england/leicestershire/3751495.stm.
23 'Nine years for prostitute attacks', 9 December 2003, online at: http://news.bbc.co.uk/1/hi/scotland/3304023.stm.
24 'Life for man who raped prostitutes', *Coventry Evening Telegraph,* 19 June 2001.
25 'Gang is jailed after attacks on prostitutes', Rochdale Observer 19 April 2000.
26 Incident reports to projects, Midlands and North West, July 2003.
27 'Arrest over prostitute attack', 30 July 2003, online at: http://news.bbc.co.uk/1/hi/england/humber/3109601.stm.
28 London Ugly Mugs List, 2000–02.
29 'Rapist jailed for prostitute attacks', BBC News website, 6 February 2001.
30 Sex work projects do report anxiety that universal condom use has been undermined in recent years, for various reasons, including their continued use by police as evidence of soliciting or of breach of an ASBO.
31 'Life term for prostitute rapist', 28 February 2003, online at: http://news.bbc.co.uk/1/hi/england/2810009.stm.
32 'Prostitute rapist jailed for life', 16 December 2003, online at: http://news.bbc.co.uk/1/hi/england/northamptonshire/3325221.stm.
33 'M32 rapist jailed for nine years', 28 April 04, online at: http://news.bbc.co.uk/1/hi/england/somerset/3667977.stm.

34 'Life sentence for rape of prostitutes', BBC News website, 25 October 2001.
35 It is possible Potterat *et al.* underestimate total numbers of sex workers, making the homicide rate seem very high. They appear to assume that all sex workers will have been identified by police or health departments.
36 July 2004.
37 'Known to have' means known to the author, from media reports or through contact with sex work projects.
38 'Appeals fail over killing of vice girl', *Yorkshire Post* 31st July 2001.
39 'Prostitute was 'scared' of man': see Hull & East Yorkshire website, January 1999.
40 'Boys killed in revenge by 'evil' father', *Guardian*, 26 March 2003.
41 'Face of evil', Sunday Mercury, 9 June 2002.
42 'Drug dealer guilty of vice murder', 29 March 2004, online at: http://news.bbc.co.uk/1/hi/scotland/3580537.stm.
43 'Prostitute's murder "may be part of underworld feud" ', Yorkshire Post, 30 October 1993.
44 'Minimum of 22 years for prostitute's killer', *Yorkshire Post*, 27 March 1998.
45 'Life for pair over burning body', online at: http://news.bbc.co.uk/1/hi/england/london/3562025.stm.
46 'Past sex offender gets life for killing prostitute', *Guardian*, 5 December 2002.
47 'Freed killer murders again', BBC News website, 21 July 2000.
48 'Midlands Ripper unmasked', *The Observer* 19 March 2000.
49 'Rapist gets life for murder', BBC News website, 29 January 1998.
50 'Tests show city vice girl was strangled', *Norwich Advertiser*, 5 April 2002.
51 'Life for killer who mutilated women', *Guardian*, 26 November 2003, online at: http://www.guardian.co.uk/uk_news/story/0,3604,1093124,00.html.
52 ' "Bin bag" killer detained in hospital', 10 December 2003, online at: http://news.bbc.co.uk/1/hi/england/merseyside/3306841.stm.
53 'Double killer is jailed for life', 20 February 2004, online at: http://news.bbc.co.uk/1/hi/england/tees/3507933.stm.
54 'Double life term for knife maniac', *Bradford Telegraph and Argus*, 6 November 2001.
55 'A man with a hatred of women', *Plymouth Evening Herald*, 1 December 2001.
56 'Kerb crawler GP tells of regret', Teesnet news, December 2000.
57 'Family's plea met by silence', Teesnet news, 23.12.2000.
58 Teesnet News, 16 November 2000.
59 Report to UKNSWP, November 2000.

References

Azevedo, J., Ward, H. and Day, S. (2002) *'Health Risks for Sex Workers: Results of a European Study.'* Paper presented to Sex Work and Health in a Changing Europe, EUROPAP Conference, January, Milton Keynes.

Benson, C. (1998) *Violence against Female Prostitutes: Experiences of Violence, Safety Strategies and the Role of Agencies.* Dept of Social Sciences, Loughborough University.

Brooks-Gordon, B. (1999) *'The Criminal Careers of Kerb-Crawlers.'* Paper presented to the National Police Vice Conference, June.

Brussa, L. (ed.) (1999) *Health, Migration and Sex Work: Transnational AIDS/STD prevention among migrant prostitutes in Europe.* TAMPEP (Transnational AIDS/STD prevention among Migrant Prostitutes in Europe Project), International Foundation.

Church, S., Henderson, M. and Barnard, M. (2001) 'Violence by clients towards female prostitutes in different work settings: questionnaire survey', *BMJ*, 322, 3 March.

Connell, J. and Hart, G. (2003) *An Overview of Male Sex Work in Edinburgh and Glasgow: The Male Sex Worker Perspective*, MRC Social & Public Health Sciences Unit, Occasional Paper No. 8, June.

Dodd, V. (2002) 'Law increases danger, prostitutes say', *The Guardian*, 16 June.

Fereira da Silva, C. (2000) *Prostitution in the Nineties: Changing Working Practices, Changing Violence.* MA Criminology dissertation, Middlesex University.

Hubbard, P. and Sanders, T. (2003) 'Making space for sex work: female street prostitution and the production of urban space', *International Journal of Urban and Regional Research*, 27, 1 March.

Jeffereys, S. (1997) *The Idea of Prostitution.* North Melbourne: Spinifex Press.

Kinnell, H. (1993) *'Prostitutes' Exposure to Rape: Implications for HIV Prevention and for Legal Reform'.* Paper presented to the VII Social Aspects of AIDS Conference, South Bank University, London, June.

Kinnell, H. (1995) 'Prostitutes' exposure to rape and other violence as an occupational hazard', in D. Friedrich, and W. Heckman (eds), *AIDS in Europe – The Behavioural Aspect; Vol. 2: Risk Behaviour and Its Determinants*, Ergebnisse sozialwissenschaftlicher Aids-Forschung, Bd. 16.

Kinnell, H. (2002) 'Violence against sex workers in London: the London Ugly Mugs List, October 2000 to February 2002'. Unpublished paper.

Lowman, J. (2000) 'Violence and the outlaw status of (street) prostitution in Canada', *Violence Against Women*, 6 (9).

May, T., Harocopos, A. and Hough, M. (2000) *For Love or Money: Pimps and the Management of Sex Work*, Police Research Series Paper 134. Home Office: Policing and Reducing Crime Unit.

McKeganey, N. and Barnard, M. (1996) *Sex Work on the Streets.* Buckingham: Open University Press.

O'Neill, M. and Barberet, R. (1999) 'Victimisation and the social organisation of prostitution in England and Spain', in R. Weitzer (ed.) *Sex for Sale: Prostitution, Pornography and the Sex Industry*. New York and London: Routledge.

Potterat, J. J., Brewer, D. D. *et al.* (2004) 'Mortality in a long-term open cohort of prostitute women', *American Journal of Epidemiology*, 159 (8).

Sanders, T. (2001) 'Female street sex workers, sexual violence and protection strategies', *Journal of Sexual Aggression*, 7 (1).

Shell, Y., Campbell, P. and Caren, I. (2001) *It's Not a Game: A Report on Hampshire Constabulary's Anti-Kerb Crawling Initiative*. Hampshire Constabulary.

Ward, H., Day, S. and Weber, S. (1999) 'Risky business: health and safety in the sex industry over a 9-year period', *Sexually Transmitted Infections*, 75 (5).

West Yorkshire Police (2000) *The Kerb-Crawlers Rehabilitation Programme: An Evaluation from the Police Perspective*. West Yorkshire Police.

Whittaker, D. and Hart, G. (1996) 'Research note: managing risks: the social organization of indoor sex work', *Sociology of Health and Illness*, 18.

Whittaker, D., Hart, G., Mercey, D., Penny, N. and Johnson, A. (1996) *Satellite Clinics and Delivery of Sexual Health Services to the 'Hard to Reach': An Evaluation. Final Report to the North Thames Regional Health Authority*, March. Academic Department of STD, University College London Medical School and Central London Action on Street Health.

Yallop, D. A. (1981) *Deliver Us from Evil*. London: Macdonald Futura Publishers.

Chapter 7

Sex work and problem drug use in the UK: the links, problems and possible solutions

Tiggey May and Gillian Hunter

There is much evidence documenting the connections between drug use and street sex work and a growing concern, from many quarters, about the impact this has on sex workers and on the communities where sex markets are based. The government's review of prostitution (Home Office 2004) is largely motivated by the need to address 'its close links with problematic drug use'. In this chapter we draw on the findings of our own work in this area and review key UK research evidence about the extent and nature of drug use among *street* sex workers. We examine the degree to which drug use may influence routes into street sex work and consider the health and other issues affecting sex workers who are problem drug users. Lastly we look at the evidence for *good practice* for providing drug treatment and harm reduction services to sex workers.

We focus here on adult female *street* sex workers, thus drug use among women working as escorts or from massage parlours and other indoor venues is not dealt with in any detail. That is not to say that problematic drug use does not exist in these settings; however, current research shows much lower levels of problem drug use among women working from indoor markets and, where it does exist, it tends to be more hidden (Cusick 1998a; May *et al.* 1999; Church *et al.* 2001; Sanders 2004). Issues relating to these groups are discussed by Sanders in Chapter 4.

The organisation of sex work

Sex is sold in a variety of ways, with a clear demarcation between street and off-street sex work. The mobility between the two 'sectors' tends to be restricted (Benson and Matthews 1995) (Box 7.1). Ethnographic studies have found that street sex workers value the flexibility of street markets, though it is equally likely that they lack the access to other safer indoor market systems. Those working off-street tend to regard themselves as better organised, more mature and reliable than those working from the street, and often want to distance themselves from the negative stereotypes attached to street sex work (Cusick 1998a; May, Harocopos and Hough 2000).

There are also differences in the way in which sex work is managed. For example, in off-street markets some sex workers are – to all intents and purposes – employees; others pay a rental or a percentage to those who provide premises or other means of meeting clients; others are self-employed and autonomous.

The extent to which 'pimps' manage sex workers is unclear; indeed the nature of the relationship between pimp and sex worker can range from the coercive and exploitative to the supportive and cooperative. There is no evidence to suggest that it is the norm for street workers to be managed by pimps; if anything, the reverse is true for adult sex workers (May, Harocopos and Hough 2000).

Box 7.1 Organisation of sex markets

Street
- *meeting face-to-face on street*
- *kerb-crawling, usually in a 'red light district'*

Off-street
- *visiting brothels or working flats*
- *responding to small adverts in local newspapers or magazines*
- *responding to Internet advertisments*
- *calling escort agencies or visiting hostess clubs*
- *visiting massage and sauna parlours*

Source: Adapted from May, Edmunds and Hough (1999).

Problem drug use among sex workers

We know that a significant proportion of those working in the sex industry are heavy users of both licit and illicit drugs (Plant 1997), although the size of this proportion varies across different sectors of sex work. For example, at one end of the spectrum sex work may be used as a primary means to fund problem drug use. Also, the environments in which some sex workers make contact with their clients – in and around bars, clubs and other licensed premises – may encourage substance use (Plant 1997; Cusick 1998a). Drugs can be used to cope with the physical and emotional demands of sex work, for example to deal with negative feelings about sex work or fear of violence from clients, or to manage the long working hours or to deal with boredom and isolation (Plant 1990; Barnard 1993; Gossop *et al.* 1995; Cusick 1998a). More recently attention has focused on the increasing use of crack-cocaine among sex workers. Its use has been reported among women operating in both indoor and street sex markets and variously described as being a treat, being used recreationally, as well as being an addiction (Green, Day and Ward 2000; Lindsell 2003).

Problem drug use[1] is more common among street-based sex workers than those working off-street (McCullagh *et al.* 1998; Church *et al.* 2001; Taylor 2003; Hester and Westmarland 2004). In part this is due to the fact that 'chaotic' or problem drug use would not be tolerated in indoor venues and women working in that sector are often keen to distance themselves and their work from any association with drug use (Cusick 1998a; Taylor 2003). Keeping drug use discreet is one strategy to deflect police interest in indoor venues (Cusick 1998; May, Edmunds and Hough 1999; Cusick, Martin and May 2004). It is also likely that women who are using drugs problematically would be unable or unwilling to work the shifts required of indoor sex work (Benson and Matthews 1995). There are various accounts in the research literature of women moving from indoor to street-based work as a result of heavy drug use (Cusick 1998; Green, Day and Ward 2000; Lindsell 2003) and, although less common, reports of women who have moved from the street to indoor sex work because they have been able to stop using drugs (Sanders 2004; Campbell and Van Nooijen 2005).

Church and colleagues (2001) compared the recent drug use of 115 street and 125 indoor sex workers in Leeds, Edinburgh and Glasgow and reported a significantly higher prevalence of injecting drug use (49 per cent v. 3 per cent), heroin (78 per cent v. 5 per cent) and crack cocaine use (32 per cent v. 4 per cent) among street sex workers. Only the use of amphetamines (30 per cent v. 11 per cent) and tranquillisers (79 per cent v. 37 per cent) was higher among indoor workers.

In addition, 63 per cent of street sex workers stated that their main reason for engaging in sex work was to pay for drugs whereas indoor workers cited household expenses and children as the impetus (74 per cent of indoor workers compared to 28 per cent of street sex workers in the Church *et al.* study). We found that street sex workers were spending on average between 75 per cent and 100 per cent of their income from sex work on drugs (May, Edmunds and Hough 1999; May, Harocopos and Turnbull 2001).

Table 7.1 summarises the findings from a number of studies conducted in cities and towns in England and Scotland of drug use among street sex workers. These show that the large majority of women were using and often injecting Class A drugs.

Drug use as a reason for entry into sex work

Routes into sex work vary. Some commentators focus on sex work as a rational, if a somewhat restricted choice, often as a response to poverty and economic necessity. Others have noted the role of coercion from pimps or of peer association or pressure (O'Neill 1997; Barnardos 1998). The causal relationship between problem drug use and involvement in sex work is hard to demonstrate in any precise way. However, drug use and street sex work largely share the same set of interconnecting risk factors, including disrupted family lives, socio-economic deprivation, child sexual abuse, experience of local authority care, homelessness, involvement in crime, disrupted schooling and low self-confidence and self-esteem (Faugier and Cranfield 1994; O'Neil 1997; Shaw and Butler 1998; Crosby and Barrett 1999; Phoenix 1999; Ayre and Barrett 2000; Campbell 2002; Cusick 2002; Melrose *et al.* 1999; Pearce, Williams and Galvin 2003; Cusick, Martin and May 2004; Hester and Westmarland 2004).

Problematic drug use is often reported as a mitigating factor for entry to street sex work. A number of studies have reported that raising money to buy drugs is the most common reason given by women for their involvement in street sex work (May, Edmunds and Hough 1999; Church *et al.* 2001; Campbell 2002; Hester and Westmarland 2004). Unlike women working from indoor locations, few street sex workers report starting sex work to pay for household bills or to supplement other incomes. In studies focusing on the sexual

Table 7.1 Drug use among women street sex workers

Author	Sample size and study site	Drug use in past six months
Hester and Westmarland (2004)	228 sex workers, Hull, Manchester, Kirklees, London	87% were using heroin and 64% were using crack cocaine
Pitcher and Aris (2003)	76* sex workers, The Midlands	70 were using heroin and 71 were using crack cocaine
MacDonald et al. (2003)	20* sex workers, Medway Kent	15 were injecting drugs
Campbell (2002)	70* sex workers in Liverpool	66 were using heroin and 57 were using crack cocaine
Church et al. (2001)	115 sex workers, Leeds, Edinburgh and Glasgow	93% were using illegal drugs 78% were using heroin and 32% crack cocaine
Dorset Working Women's Project (2001)	30* street sex workers, Bournemouth	All were using heroin (19 injected the drug), and one-third crack cocaine
May, Harocopos and Turnbull (2001)	100 sex workers, London	53% were using heroin and 73% crack cocaine
May, Edmunds and Hough (1999)	56* sex workers, three large towns in England	37 were using heroin and 53 were using crack cocaine
McCullagh et al. (1998)	317 sex workers, North West	58% were injecting drugs
McKeganey and Barnard (1996)	167 sex workers, Glasgow	75% were injecting drugs

*For samples of less than 100 sex workers, numbers rather than percentages are provided.

exploitation of young people, drug use has been identified as an important factor. For example, Melrose and colleagues (1999) found that 'to get drugs' was a frequent reason given by young people for their involvement in street sex work and drug use was more likely to have preceded sex work than vice versa. Pearce et al.'s (2003) study of the sexual exploitation of young women found that all (N = 55) had problems with alcohol use and just over half were using heroin on a weekly basis. Further, a significant proportion (21 of 55) of the young women spoke about selling sex on the street.

Cusick and colleagues (2004) noted that sex work precedes drug use as often as the reverse. Some commentators have pointed to the easy availability of drugs in the settings where sex work takes place (an issue we discuss below), thus increasing the likelihood of eventual drug use for those involved in street sex work (May, Edmunds and Hough 1999; Cusick 2002).

In a study of 125 sex workers in the South of England (Cusick, Martin and May 2004), the average age at first Class A drug use was 16 years and age at first involvement in sex work was 19 years. Between 1997 and 2001, in three separate studies conducted in London and four towns in England, we interviewed 158, mainly street-based sex workers. Ninety per cent were problem drug users and, of those, 63 per cent reported their dependent drug use had pre-dated their involvement in sex work. In some cases respondents chose to sex work rather than commit acquisitive crimes as a means to fund drug use, seeing it as more lucrative and less likely to attract a custodial sentence. Many other crimes do not provide the same earning potential on a daily basis that sex work does as the following quotes from our interviewees illustrate:

I needed the money for drugs, it [sex work] was an easy chore compared to shoplifting.

I didn't want to go to prison anymore, it [sex work] was an easier way to fund my habit.

I started work [sex work] to fund my habit. Shoplifting and fraud were just not doing it.

Street sex workers are often not only working to fund their own drug use but also that of their sexual partner (Cusick 1998a; May, Harocopos and Hough 1999; Stewart 2000; Campbell 2002; Hester and Westmarland 2004), and women can feel some pressure to enter or remain in sex work because of a partner's drug use. In our study examining the nature of pimping (May, Harocopos and Hough 2000), we found that both 'classic' pimps and partners relied heavily on sex workers to pay for drugs. For example, those sex workers who had a sexual partner who was also a drug user (9/17) paid an average of

£500 per week to fund their partner's habit. Fourteen of the 19 pimped sex workers we interviewed also disclosed paying for their pimp's drug use.

Links between sex and drug markets

A key issue for those developing harm reduction strategies for street sex workers is to understand the connections between sex and drug markets. We have carried out a research study specifically examining these links in three sites in England. These sites were selected because of the co-existence of a sex and drug market (May, Edmunds and Hough 1999). While the structure of the drug markets differed from site to site, and included 'open', 'semi-open' and 'closed markets' (see Box 7.2), we found that sex workers had some degree of impact on every type of drug market.

Box 7.2   Organisation of drug markets

Open drug markets
These tend to operate in geographically well-defined areas at defined times and there are no barriers to access; someone completely unknown to sellers would be able to buy drugs in an open market.

Closed drug markets
These can be prearranged meetings on the street or at off-street premises. Access is limited to known and trusted participants. An unknown buyer needs someone to introduce them or to vouch for them before they can make a purchase.

Semi-open drug markets
These are often, but not exclusively, pub- or club-based markets where unknown buyers will be able to purchase drugs, 'if they look the part'.

'Dealing houses/crack houses'
This describes a range of properties from which drugs are sold. They are often tenanted and sometimes empty or semi-derelict. They are often occupied for a short period until enforcement intervenes. In some cases the crack dealer may have forced the rightful tenant to use the house. These can also be used as centres for obtaining stolen goods or firearms. Users may be able to stay for extended periods using drugs and obtaining other services such as commercial sex. Sex workers can introduce new buyers to the crack house.

Source: May *et al.* (2000); Home Office (2003a).

Street sex workers are significant customers for drug dealers

The most obvious way in which a sex market can support a drug market is by providing a sufficient core of drug buyers to ensure that the drug market reaches a threshold of viability (cf. Edmunds *et al.* 1997). In our study the view among sex workers and professionals was that there were clear links of this sort, as two interviewees explained:

> Wherever you find a prostitute you will find a drug seller looking for quick money. Wherever you find a drug seller standing selling his drugs you'll find a prostitute looking for the drugs. (Sex worker)

> It is about time that all professionals realised the impact sex workers can have on a drug market, especially once crack infiltrates and takes a hold. (Agency worker)

However, the situation is not clear-cut. All of the markets we examined operated on more than one level, combining more than one mode of operation. In one site, street sex workers comprised a significant proportion of drug buyers in the semi-open market but were less central to the closed market. In another site, they were an important purchasing group for the closed market and played a significant part in the operation of the open market.

The level of income generated by sex work can be extremely high. Drug users engaging in sex work can earn considerably more than those committing acquisitive crime. For example, Edmunds *et al.* (1999) reported that street sex workers within a sample of arrest and probation referrals were spending in excess of £600 on drugs per week compared to an average of £300 for those who were being arrested for acquisitive crimes. In a study conducted in Kent, street sex workers had more than doubled their weekly drug spend since starting sex work (McDonald, Brown and Wake 2003). Thus they are likely to be targeted by drug dealers because of their buying power (McKeganey and Barnard 1996; May, Edmunds and Hough 1999).

Sex workers assist drug dealers

Where street sex and drug markets are co-located it is not unusual to find sex workers assisting drug dealers. In our study sites over half (53 per cent) of our interviewees stated that they had bought drugs for clients. Many sex workers also used drugs with clients. In one

176

site, they played a more active part including holding and selling drugs for sellers, selling drugs to their clients and others and hiding drugs in body cavities to avoid police searches.

Male drug dealers act as 'pimps'

Two-thirds of the sex workers reported working independently and there was no evidence that the stereotypical pimp/exploiter was a common feature of sex work. However, it was found that the role of dealer, partner and pimp had become interwoven and that many women had close relationships with dealers and were dependent on them for their drug supply (May, Edmunds and Hough 1999). In some cases drug dependence has been substituted for violence as a means of securing compliance from sex workers with women heavily reliant on a largely male-dominated drug scene (O'Connell Davidson 1998; May, Harocopos and Hough 2000).

The impact of crack cocaine on sex markets

Over recent years the availability and use of crack cocaine has steadily increased and this is reflected in research findings of drug use among street sex workers. For example, among street sex workers we interviewed in London in 2000, crack cocaine was as frequently cited as heroin as a *drug of choice* with more money being spent on that drug (an average of between £80 and £100 per day on crack cocaine compared to an average of £50 per day for heroin) (May, Harocopos and Turnbull 2001). Pitcher and Aris (2003) found similar proportions of street sex workers in the Midlands reporting regular use of heroin and crack cocaine in the past month (92 per cent and 93 per cent respectively) and Campbell (2002) has noted the increasing popularity of crack cocaine among street sex workers in Merseyside.

Crack cocaine was key in pulling together sex and drug markets and was identified as the most significant factor in the development of the markets in all our study sites (May, Edmunds and Hough 1999). It was easily obtainable, as the following quote illustrates:

> If you wanted crack you used to have to make a phone call at one time. You don't even have to move off the street corner now, they drive past you and throw it out of the window ... it is just totally manic. (Sex worker)

Ward and colleagues (2000) found that crack use and the organisation of crack distribution were closely linked with the sex industry and that the drug was being used in all sectors of sex work, including by clients (Green, Day and Ward 2000). American research (Feucht 1993) has also highlighted sex workers' role within 'marketplace economics' of crack distribution in terms of carrying drugs, exchanging information, and selling and bartering goods and services including sex for drugs exchanges.

The so called 'crack house' is a more recent feature of some drug markets. These are properties where drugs (including, but not only, crack cocaine) can be bought and used on site and where commercial sex is often available. Sex workers can play a role in bringing new buyers to these locations (Home Office 2003).

To summarise then, there is a strong association between an involvement in *street* sex work and problem drug use. It is in that 'sector' that most women are likely to be using sex work as a means to fund drug use. Furthermore, there is a 'co-dependency' in the way in which street sex and drug markets operate which extends well beyond their geographic proximity.

The level of harm that can flow from integrated sex and drug markets includes a range of health and other problems for sex workers. Although different, the harms caused by integrated markets also impact on local communities. Of late, government policy has focused strongly on the need for health and enforcement agencies to develop coordinated strategies to 'tackle' sex and drug markets as part of 'neighbourhood renewal' and crime reduction schemes (Home Office and Department of Trade, Local Government and the Regions 2002). In the remainder of this chapter we look at some of the key needs of street sex workers, review the available evidence for providing services to meet the complex needs of this group, and look at how service providers 'manage' their role with crime reduction and enforcement agencies.

Health and other issues for sex workers who are problem drug users

Blood-borne viruses and other drug-related harms

There are a number of ways in which involvement in sex work has been shown to exacerbate problematic drug use and increase heath risk and vice versa. A key issue, as noted above, is the level of income generated by sex work, which is likely to increase the quantity and frequency of drug use. There are obvious health implications of problematic drug use, including, if injecting drugs, blood-borne viruses (BBV) such as HIV, Hepatitis B (HBV) and Hepatitis C (HCV), abscesses and overdose. There are few recent published studies of BBV among women sex workers in the UK; however, in a review of research in the mid-1990s the prevalence of HIV among this group was deemed to be relatively low, with the *potential* exception of those who were injecting drugs (see McKeganey and Barnard 1996, for a review of UK studies). This mirrors the prevalence rates of HIV reported among injecting drug users (IDUs) generally, which have remained low throughout the 1990s with research and surveillance studies reporting rates of under 1 per cent outside London and around 3.6 per cent in London (Health Protection Agency *et al.* 2003). However, rates of HBV and HCV are considerably higher. Studies in England and Wales conducted from the late 1990s suggest HBV prevalence among IDUs at 22 per cent and HCV at 38 per cent (Health Protection Agency *et al.* 2003). One study of HBV among sex workers in the North West of England found that 38 per cent of their sample of street sex workers had been exposed to HBV (McCullagh *et al.* 1998).

It is hard to assess the extent to which sex workers who are using drugs may expose themselves to risk of BBV via sharing of injecting equipment or unprotected sex. Behavioural surveys tend to underestimate such risk practices with interviewees providing socially desirable responses (Cusick and Rhodes 1998; Stimson *et al.* 1998). Thus, while indiscriminate sharing of needles and syringes is uncommon, the sharing of injecting equipment with sexual partners or those defined as close friends is much more frequent (Hunter *et al.* 2000) and, as noted, many street sex workers report partners who are also using drugs. Risk factors associated with HCV transmission among IDUs extend beyond the sharing of needles and syringes and include all injecting paraphernalia such as filters and spoons used in drug preparation, the duration and frequency of injecting and the overlap between injecting and use of crack cocaine (Rhodes, Davis and Judd 2004).

The regular use of condoms with clients is a well-established practice among sex workers. Ward *et al.* (1993) found 98 per cent of over 200 sex workers claimed to have used condoms with all clients. McKeganey and Barnard (1996) also found that condom use with clients was reportedly very high in developed countries. However, there is a resilient demand from clients for unprotected sex and exceptions have been reported in situations where drug use is involved

(Gossop *et al*. 1995; McKeganey and Barnard 1996). Sex workers have associated drug or alcohol effects with loss of control, leading to reduction of condom use (Cusick 1998b). Ward and colleagues (2000) have found that women will sometimes make exceptions to their condom rule for a man who is supplying them with crack cocaine or whom they describe as a crack-smoking partner. We found that only a minority of sex workers (5 of 65) said they would always practise safe sex. Unsurprisingly sexual partners were often exempt from condom use; however, nearly a quarter of women stated that if a client paid enough they would consider unsafe sex (May, Harocopos and Hough 1999).

A key agency working with sex workers in London noted the increase in the number of women with multiple health problems associated with the use of crack cocaine, including unwanted pregnancies requiring late terminations, sexually transmitted infections (STIs), depression and widespread social problems (Ward, Green and Day 2000). We found women suffered a range of health problems that they attributed to their drug use, including not being able to sleep for long periods of time, significant weight loss and suffering from constipation, which many attributed directly to their use of crack cocaine. For others, however, health concerns were more serious including depression, anxiety attacks, irregular periods, miscarriages, constant chest pains and abscesses (May, Harocopos and Turnbull 2001).

Risk of violence

There are also the potential risks to women's safety of working while under the influence of drugs and working excessively to fund drug use. Women involved in street sex work often work daily, for long periods of time, sometimes while suffering from withdrawal or the effects of overdose, in order to raise sufficient funds (Campbell *et al*. 1996; McKeganey and Barnard 1996).

Kinnell, in Chapter 6 of this book, has highlighted the extent and nature of violence suffered by street sex workers. In our study examining the links between sex and drug markets (1999) just over three-quarters of our sample (N = 67) said that clients had subjected them to physical, sexual or other forms of violence. Fifty had been assaulted while working and 32 had been raped or subjected to other forms of sexual violence. Drug use can make women more vulnerable to violence from clients in that their usual self-defence strategies, such as working in pairs and negotiating arrangements before entering a car, are less likely to be adhered to, or their ability to make assessments about 'punters' may be impaired if under the influence of drugs (Campbell, Coleman and Torkington 1996; McKeganey and Barnard 1996; Europap 1998; Pearce 1999). In addition, women can experience sexual and physical violence from sexual partners and be pressurised by partners to sex work in order to fund their drug use (Hester and Westmarland 2004).

Homelessness

A recurring theme in our interviews with street sex workers has been the difficulty women experience in finding secure housing. Over half of our interviewees reported they were either living in either temporary accommodation or were homeless. Homelessness or insecure housing has been highlighted in other studies of street sex work as a common issue and a factor which is likely to inhibit help-seeking for drug problems or engagement in drug treatment programmes (Campbell 2002; Pitcher and Aris 2003; Hester and Westmarland 2004).

Providing services for sex workers who are problem drug users

Street sex workers then have a range of service needs over and above specific problems with their use of illicit drugs and there is indeed 'official' acknowledgment that drug problems cannot be tackled in isolation from other issues such as housing (Home Office and DTLR 2002; Home Office 2004).

The Home Office Crime Reduction Programme (CRP) 'Reducing Crime and Disorder Associated with Prostitution' has identified a number of principles for effective service provision for women street sex workers (Hester and Westmarland 2004). The central tenet of this is the need for a holistic, coordinated multi-agency approach to provision whereby drug services are linked to health, housing and legal agencies to offer women support for a whole range of issues that need to be tackled alongside their drug problems (Hester and Westmarland 2004). Their research found that seeking help was often triggered by a crisis event, for example when women had experienced extreme violence, and they stress that services must be able to meet women's immediate needs and help them to stabilise their lives. They also highlighted the importance of outreach services, ongoing and one-to-one support and the ability to offer fast-track access to drug treatment and other services (ibid.). Much of this advice echoes what key services for sex workers have been providing, or certainly have been aiming to provide, for their clients for some time.

Historically the development of services for sex workers has been influenced by public health concerns about the transmission of STIs, and most recently HIV, from sex workers to others (May, Edmunds and Hough 1999; Phoenix 1999; Hester and Westmarland 2004). As discussed above, such fears were unfounded; however, funding for services for sex workers increased from the late 1980s as part of the public health response to HIV/AIDS. As with service development for drug users more generally at that time, there was an emphasis on harm reduction and making projects attractive and accessible to potential clients via low-threshold 'drop-in' facilities, the expansion of treatment facilities and of outreach to encourage a more proactive approach to contacting clients, particularly those deemed 'hard to reach', as well as the distribution of free condoms and sterile injecting equipment.

Over more recent years, service development for problem drug users, and indeed funding, has been influenced less by harm reduction and public health and more by a crime reduction agenda. This has involved the introduction of various interventions within the criminal justice system, such as arrest referral schemes and drug treatment and testing orders aimed at diverting drug-using offenders into treatment and 'out of crime'. For sex workers who are problem drug users, the rhetoric has been about helping women to 'exit' sex work via drug treatment and other support.

While criminal justice interventions targeting sex workers are limited, dedicated arrest referral services and court diversion schemes, whereby women can forego fines for soliciting if they agree to meet with a drugs worker, have been and are being piloted (May, Harocopos and Turnbull 2001; Pitcher and Aris 2003).

Street sex workers have always been defined as a 'hard to reach' and challenging group by drug service providers and they can face a number of barriers to getting access to drug treatment and harm reduction facilities. At the most basic level, their working patterns – including working throughout the night – can make it difficult for sex workers to keep daytime appointments at drug services, or attend daytime drop-in services and needle exchanges. Drug service workers do not always understand the issues faced by sex workers and women have reported fears of a negative reaction from staff if they admit to sex work (Hunter et al. 2004). Having responsibility for funding a partner's drug use can add further complications when seeking assistance for one's own drug use, and as is the case generally for women drug users, there are fears about children being taken into care if drug use becomes known (McKeganey and Barnard 1996; May, Harocopos and Hough 2000; Hester and Westmarland 2004).

To improve access for sex workers to drug treatment services, a number of key methods have been recommended. These include providing drug treatment at services dedicated to sex workers so they can receive help for drug problems from a service they are already familiar with, the extension of drug service opening times to accommodate sex workers and the provision of drug treatment to partners of sex workers. Some projects operate low-threshold methadone programmes whereby women can be assessed, receive a prescription for methadone and be supported on a reduction or maintenance programme at the sex worker project.

Outreach teams remain essential for contacting women, for passing on vital safety information, and condoms and clean needles. They can also help women to access full health checks including Genito-Urinary Medical (GUM) services and can be the first port of call in referring women to drug treatment agencies (McKeganey and Barnard 1996; Europap 1998; May, Edmunds and Hough 1999; Hester and Westmarland 2004). One development of outreach provision has involved taking services to sex work areas via a mobile unit which can carry stocks of condoms and sterile injecting equipment but also has space for women to talk to service workers off the street and can provide a whole range of services including primary heath care, STI testing and hepatitis B vaccination.

Projects have also sought to encourage women to report violence from clients, if not to the police then at least to project workers. The operation of 'dodgy punter' or 'ugly mugs' schemes whereby projects disseminate to women descriptions of men (or their cars) who have been violent towards sex workers is a facility provided by many agencies. Evidence suggests that where these schemes operate there has been a greater willingness to report violent incidents, which in some areas has contributed to successful convictions (Penfold *et al.* 2004). As well as promoting zero tolerance towards violence to sex workers, responding effectively to such reports can provide the opportunity for services to intervene and offer help in relation to drug problems and other issues.

There is also the emphasis on the securing of emergency and longer-term accommodation for sex workers (Pitcher and Aris 2003; Hunter *et al.* 2004; Home Office 2004). As noted above, this is seen as an essential first stage in providing women with some stability while linking them into drug treatment and other services (Stewart 2000; Home Office 2004). The Prostitution Review states that 'appropriate housing is a crucial element of a successful exit strategy'. It can also allow women to leave violent relationships. Examples of how this has been practically applied include partnership agreements between sex worker projects and housing authorities to assist in the rehousing of women or the setting up of hostel accommodation dedicated to sex workers and linked to local drug treatment services. In Glasgow a 'Rough Sleeping Initiative' has made use of a system of 'scatter flats' to provide stable accommodation for street sex workers while drug treatment and other issues are discussed (Stewart 2000). There is also the government-funded 'Supporting People Health' pilot programme which was set up in April 2003 to provide coordinated housing and support services to vulnerable people, including sex workers.

Thus the coordinated multi-agency approach to service provision is the 'gold standard' for providing services to sex workers, with good practice advice stressing that all treatment interventions must be provided in the context of a 'holistic strategy' that includes longer-term help with housing, health and other social issues.

As noted above, funding sources for such service developments are largely linked to community safety and crime reduction monies, and managing the tension between harm reduction and crime reduction agendas can pose difficulties for health providers. Services for sex workers often have to be delivered in an environment where enforcement operations are aiming to move sex workers out of an area. This can make it difficult for services to remain in contact with women and can inhibit women from approaching outreach services because this will identify them as sex workers or drug users to the police. Recent Home Office guidance (Hunter *et al.* 2004) has emphasised the importance of combining any enforcement activity with packages of drug treatment and support for sex workers. Service providers, then, need to be central to any local plans to target street sex markets and while health projects may be uneasy at such 'collaboration', this is essential to ensure that outreach and other harm reduction initiatives are not disrupted by police activity and that health service development is factored into local planning. There is also a growing consensus among criminal justice agencies that helping women to deal with their drug problems and other health and social issues is the only way to effect any longer-term change.

There is much empirical evidence to suggest that arresting sex workers, particularly those who are problem drug users, is an ineffective deterrent that can result in their temporary displacement to another location or a possible prison sentence for fine default. We found considerable movement by sex workers between sex markets; a number of sex workers attributed this to avoiding arrest.

For services to be able to work with sex workers on a longer-term basis women need to feel safeguarded from arrest. In tackling street sex markets the Prostitution Review has put forward a number of suggestions to this end. These involve managed areas and/or licensing off-street locations. The government appears less than enthusiastic about either idea – due to a fear that sex work will become viewed as a 'normalised' activity. However, it is these types of solutions – if set up and managed correctly – that may have the potential to reduce the harms sex markets pose for both sex workers and host communities. Managed areas could serve to increase the contact sex workers have with services, thus increasing the likelihood of a possible reduction in drug use and consequently sex work. In initiating any new idea it would seem prudent to learn from experiences abroad and to develop and adapt ideas to fit the UK context. It will be important for those involved in planning such initiatives to take account of local conditions to put in place local solutions. It appears unlikely that one policy will fit all, thus piloting and evaluation will be important.

What must be remembered is that whatever policy either central or local government pursue, drug-using street sex workers need long-term, often intensive assistance in addressing their many complex needs.

Finally, as a further note of caution it is important to acknowledge that 'exiting' is by no means a linear process (Hester and Westmarland 2004) nor necessarily always a goal that sex workers themselves would prioritise. Yet there may be some pressure from funders for service providers to show early results to this effect. Holistic service provision makes good sense but policy-makers and funders need to understand that such interventions demand significant and long-term investment if they are to be effective. See also Chapter 10 of this book for a discussion of the development of services for sex workers.

Acknowledgments

We would like to thank Mike Hough at the Institute for Criminal Policy Research, School of Law, King's College, London for comments on an earlier draft.

Note

1 Following the ACMD (1982, 1988), we define problem use as use that causes social, psychological, legal or physical problems.

References

Advisory Council on the Misuse of Drugs (ACMD) (1982) *Treatment and Rehabilitation*. London: HMSO.

Advisory Council on the Misuse of Drugs (ACMD) (1988) *AIDS and Drug Misuse*, Part One. London: Department of Health.

Ayre, P. and Barrett, D. (2000) 'Young people and prostitution: an end to the beginning?', *Children and Society* 14 (1): 48–59.

Barnard, M. (1993) 'Violence and vulnerability: conditions of work for streetworking prostitutes', *Sociology of Health and Illness*, 15 (5): 683–705.

Barnardos (1998) *Whose Daughter Next? Children Abused through Prostitution*. Ilford: Barnardos.

Benson, C. and Matthews, R. (1995) 'Street prostitution: ten facts in search of a policy', *International Journal of Sociology of Law*, 23: 395–415.

Campbell, R. (2002) *Working on the Street: An Evaluation of the Linx Project 1998–2001*. Liverpool: Liverpool Hope University.

Campbell, R. and Van Nooijen, L. (2005) *Seafarers, Scanias, Saunas and Sexual Health: The Portside Project Promoting Sexual Health in the Port of Liverpool*. North Liverpool PCT and Liverpool Hope.

Campbell, R., Coleman, S. and Torkington, P. (1996) *Street Prostitution in Inner City Liverpool*. Liverpool City Council.

Church, S., Henderson, M., Barnard, M. and Hart, G. (2001) 'Violence by clients towards female prostitutes in different work settings: questionnaire survey', *British Medical Journal*, 332: 524–5.

Crosby, S. and Barrett, D. (1999) 'Poverty, drugs and youth prostitution: a case study', in A. Marlow and G. Pearson (eds), *Young People, Drugs and Community Safety*. Lyme Regis: Russell House.

Cusick, L. (1998a) 'Female prostitution in Glasgow: drug use and the occupational sector', *Addiction Research*, 6: 115–30.

Cusick, L. (1998b) 'Non-use of condoms by prostitute women', *AIDS Care*, 10: 133–46.

Cusick, L. (2002) 'Youth prostitution: a literature review', *Child Abuse Review* 11: 230–51.

Cusick, L. and Rhodes, T. (1998) *Sexual Safety Among HIV Positive Drug Users and Their Sexual Partners: A Qualitative Study*. Final Report to the Department of Health. London: CRDHB.

Cusick, L., Martin, A. and May, T. (2004) *Vulnerability and Involvement in Drug Use and Sex Work*. London: Home Office.

Dorset Working Women's Project (2001) *Survey of Street Sex Workers in Bournemouth*. Dorset Working Women's Project.

Edmunds, M., Turnbull, P. J., Hough, M. and May, T. (1999) *Doing Justice to Treatment: Referring Offenders to Drug Services*. London: Home Office DPAS.

Edmunds, M., May, T., Hough, M., Hearnden, I. and van Rozeboom, R. (1997) *Get It While You Can: An Evaluation*. A Report to Sussex Association for the Rehabilitation of Offenders.

European Network for HIV/STD Prevention in Prostitution (Europap) (1998) *Hustling for Health: Developing Services for Sex Workers in Europe*. Europap UK, Imperial College, London.

Faugier, J. and Cranfield, S. (1994) *Making the Connection: Health Care Needs of Drug Using Prostitutes*. Manchester University: Department of Nursing.

Feucht, T. E. (1993) 'Prostitutes on crack cocaine: addiction, utility, and marketplace economics', *An Interdisciplinary Journal of Deviant Behaviour* 14 (2): 99–108.

Gossop, M., Powis, B., Griffiths, P. and Strang, J. (1995) 'Female prostitutes in South London: use of heroin, cocaine and alcohol and their relationship to health risk behaviours', *AIDS Care*, 7: 253–60.

Green, A., Day, S. and Ward, H. (2000) 'Crack cocaine and prostitution in London in the 1990s', *Sociology of Health and Illness*, 22: 27–39.

Health Protection Agency, SCIEH, National Public Health Service for Wales, CDSC Northern Ireland, CRDHB and the UASSG (2003) *Shooting Up: Infections among Injecting Drug Users in the United Kingdom 2002*. London: Health Protection Agency.

Hester, M. and Westmarland, N. (2004). *Tackling Prostitution: What Works?* London: Home Office.

Home Office (2003) *Disrupting Crack Markets: A Practice Guide*. London: Home Office.

Home Office (2004) *Paying the Price: A Consultation Paper on Prostitution*. London: Home Office.

Home Office and DTLR (2002) *Tackling Drug Use in Rented Housing. A Good Practice Guide*. London: Home Office.

Hope, V. D., Judd, A., Hickman, M., Lamagni, T., Hunter, G., Stimson, G. V. *et al*. (2001) 'Prevalence of hepatitis C among injection drug users in England and Wales: is harm reduction working?', *AJoPH*, 91: 38–42.

Hunter, G., May, T. and the Drug Strategy Directorate (2004) *Solutions and Strategies: Drug Problems and Street Sex Markets. Guidance for Partnerships and Providers*. London: Home Office.

Hunter, G., Stimson, G. V., Judd, A., Jones, S. and Hickman, M. (2000) 'Measuring injecting risk behaviour in the second decade of harm reduction: a survey of injecting drug users in England', *Addiction* 95: 1351–61.

Judd, A., Stimson, G. V., Hickman, M,. Hunter, G. M., Jones, S., Parry, J. V. *et al*. (2000) Prevalence of HIV infection in a multi-site sample of injecting drug users not in contact with treatment services in England', *AIDS*, 14: 2413–5.

Lindsell, H. (2003) *Crack the New Pimp? A Study of Street Sex Workers in Lambeth*. London: West London Mission.

McCullagh, J., Syed, Q. and Bellis, M. (1998) 'Female prostitution and associated drug use in the North West of England', in *Changing Perspectives on Female Prostitution: Conference Proceedings, 7th February 1998*. Greenbank Conference Centre, Liverpool University.

MacDonald, M., Brown, C. and Wake, I. (2003) *Street-Based Prostitution in Medway: Findings of an Action Research Programme*. Medway: Medway Council Health Promotion Service.

McKeganey, N. and Barnard, M. (1996) *Sex Work on the Streets: Prostitutes and Their Clients*. Buckingham: Open University Press.

May, T., Edmunds, M. and Hough, M. (1999) *Street Business: The Links between Sex and Drug Markets*. London: Home Office.

May, T., Harocopos, A. and Hough, M. (2000) *For Love or Money: Pimps and the Management of Sex Work*. London: Home Office.

May, T., Harocopos, A., Turnbull, P. J. and Hough, M. (2000) *Serving Up: The Impact of Low-level Police Enforcement on Drug Markets*. London: Home Office.

May, T., Harocopos, A. and Turnbull, P. (2001) *Selling Sex in the City: An Evaluation of a Targeted Arrest Referral Scheme for Sex Workers in Kings Cross*, Social Science Research Paper No. 14. London: Criminal Policy Research Unit, South Bank University.

Melrose, M. and Barrett, D. (eds) (2004) *Anchors in Floating Lives: Interventions with Young People Abused through Prostitution*. Lyme Regis: Russell House.

Melrose, M., Barrett, D. and Brodie, I. (1999) *One Way Street: Retrospectives on Childhood Prostitution*. London: Children's Society.

O'Connell Davidson, J. (1998) *Prostitution, Power and Freedom*. Cambridge: Polity Press.

O'Neill, M. (1997) 'Prostitute women now', in G. Scambler and A. Scambler (eds), *Rethinking Prostitution*. London: Routledge.

Pearce, J. J. (1999) 'Selling sex, doing drugs and keeping safe', in A. Marlow and G. Pearson (eds), *Young People, Drugs and Community Safety*. London: Russell House.

Pearce, J. J., Williams, M. and Galvin, C. (2003) *It's Someone Taking a Part of You*. York: Joseph Rowntree Foundation and Children's Bureau.

Penfold, C., Hunter, G., Campbell, R. and Barham, L. (2004). 'Tackling client violence in female street prostitution: inter-agency working between outreach agencies and the police', *Policing and Society*, 14 (4): 365–79.

Phoenix, J. (1999) *Making Sense of Prostitution*. London: Macmillan.

Pitcher, J. and Aris, R. (2003) *Women and Street Sex Work. Issues arising from an Evaluation of an Arrest Referral Scheme*. London: NACRO.

Plant, M. (ed.) (1990) *AIDS, Drugs and Prostitution*. London: Routledge.

Plant, M.A. (1997) 'Alcohol, drugs and the social milieu', in G. Scambler and A. Scambler (eds), *Rethinking Prostitution*. London: Routledge.

Rhodes, T., Davis, M. and Judd, A. (2004) 'Hepatitis C and its risk management among drug injectors in London: renewing harm reduction in the context of uncertainty', *Addiction*, 99: 621–33.

Sanders, T. (2004) *Sex Work. A Risky Business*. Cullompton: Willan.

Shaw, I. and Butler, I. (1998) 'Understanding young people and prostitution: a foundation for practice?', *British Journal of Social Work*, 28 (2): 177–96.

Stewart, A. (2000) *Where Is She Tonight: Women, Street Prostitution and Homelessness in Glasgow*. Glasgow: Rough Sleeping Initiative.

Stimson, G.V., Jones, S., Chalmers, C. and Sullivan, D. (1998) 'A short questionnaire (IRQ) to assess injecting risk behaviour', *Addiction*, 93 (3): 337–47.

Taylor, D. (2003) *Sex for Sale: New Challenges and New Dangers for Women Working On and Off the Streets*. London: Mainliners.

Ward, H., Green, A. and Day, S. (2000) *Sex Work and Crack Cocaine – Summary Report*. London: Department of Epidemiology and Public Health, Imperial College.

Ward, H., Day, S., Mezzone. J., Dunlop, L., Donegan, C., Farrar, S., Whitaker, L., Harris, J. R. W. and Miller, D. L. (1993) 'Prostitution and risk of HIV: female prostitutes in London', *British Medical Journal*, 307: 356–58.

Chapter 8

Finding the 'I' in sexual exploitation: young people's voices within policy and practice

J. J. Pearce

This chapter gives an overview of recent developments in policy and practice relating to young people who are at risk of, or experiencing, sexual exploitation. It defines sexual exploitation as the abuse of young men and women who are under 18 years of age by adults who encourage, coerce, persuade or enable them to swap or sell sex in return for favours. It explores some of the contradictions and tensions experienced by young people who struggle to protect themselves, and be protected from, sexual exploitation. Referring to specific case studies, the chapter argues for a coordinated and comprehensive 'young person' centred framework which recognises the demands on the young people, on their carers and on the practitioners working to support them. It also argues that while the important focus on child protection has dominated thinking in this work, it has served to somewhat overshadow the need to develop preventative work, treatment, containment and restraint of those who abuse young people. The chapter proposes a focus on child-centred practice supported by multi-agency work that can both protect the child and gather evidence against abusers.

What is sexual exploitation and how prevalent is it?

A recent review noted that 76 per cent of all local authority Area Child Protection Committees (ACPCs) in England confirmed that there were children involved in prostitution in their area; 28, from a targeted 50 ACPCs providing figures, showed a total of 602 children involved. The findings suggested that an average of 19 girls and three boys were involved in prostitution in an area at any given time (Swann and Balding 2002). The semantics used here are of interest as it is now widely accepted that the term 'prostitution' is out of date and constitutes labelling, both in application to young people's situations (Pearce *et al.* 2002) and to the self-definitions presented by many adult sex workers.

The Department of Health issued guidance for practitioners working to safeguard children who experienced sexual exploitation, overtly recognising that the young people concerned were victims of abuse (DoH 2000). Multi-agency work had led to practitioners and policy-makers recognising that penalising the young people, who were, in fact, victims of abuse, was not tackling the causes of exploitation or working with its effects (Brain *et al.* 1998; Van Meeuwen and Swann 1998). The guidance asserted the need for young people to be worked with under the child protection frameworks, agencies being required to work together under local (welfare based) protocols enacted through the ACPCs to both protect children from abuse through sexual exploitation and prosecute abusers (DoH 2000). The guidelines stated that:

> Children involved in prostitution should be treated primarily as the victims of abuse, and their needs require careful assessment. They are likely to be in need of welfare services and, in many cases, protection under the Children Act 1989. (DoH 2000: 3)

However, the term 'prostitution' was used in the title of the guidance and practitioners, including police, were advised that young people who were seen to persistently and voluntarily return to sell sex on the street could be convicted for crimes associated with prostitution. That these contradictions remain and are endorsed through a recent consultation paper on prostitution from the Home Office (2004a) suggests that there remains a desire to penalise and punish young people for behaviour that results from abuse from adults. This anomaly must be addressed for the welfare of young people to be upheld.

Recent research and project work has recognised that the early stages of vulnerability to abuse are important times for intervention as are times when the young person is actively being used for sexual exploitation. A survey, conducted by Barnardo's in 1998, of 48 agencies reported contact with more than 300 children under 16 years of age who did not self-define as prostitutes, but who were clipping (taking money from a punter and then running without exchanging sex) and/or were 'swapping' sex for money, drugs, accommodation or other goods 'in kind' (Van Meeuwen and Swann 1998). An audit of a total of 21 local services from one London borough and one northern city provided knowledge of 269 young women aged 18 and under, 165 of whom were known to be selling sex. The remaining 104 were known to be swapping sex in exchange for drugs, accommodation or other returns 'in kind' (Pearce *et al.* 2002).

Such audits illustrate the difficulties in collecting reliable data when definitions, policy and practice among different geographical areas and professions vary, illustrating the need for enhanced multi-agency awareness training about the meanings associated with current definitions. Some agencies do not see or recognise sexual exploitation as an issue, focusing instead on problems associated with substance misuse or offending behaviour, overlooking the significance of abusive, older people within the young person's life. Others focus on providing a comprehensive sexual health service, being less mindful of the child protection issues that may be involved in the sexualised risk-taking behaviour of sexually exploited young people. Where different agencies have contact with the same young woman involved in sexual exploitation, wide discrepancies in the definitions used may exist.

Although there are tensions in the task of identifying reliable quantitative data on the numbers of sexually exploited young people because of different understanding of semantics and different levels of awareness and visibility of the range of associated problems, practice interventions, research and evaluations have given qualitative evidence of the complex and varied range of reasons for vulnerability to abuse through sexual exploitation. Truanting from school and running from home or care have been seen to increase a young person's vulnerability to abusive adults. Although poverty is a central contributor to family breakdown and vulnerability (Pitts 1997), young people who run away or go missing can come from a range of different social classes and racial backgrounds, a 'running career' developing over time (Patel 1994; Broadfoot 1998; Ivison 1998). The one refuge for children under 16 years of age in England is based in London and has eight beds, providing accommodation for up to two weeks. During the period April 2001 – February 2002 there were 387 referrals to the refuge with 122 admissions involving 97 young people, 84 of whom were young people referred for the first time. Fifty-seven of the non-admissions were because no beds were available at the time of referral. Of those admitted, 56 young people said that they ran from home or care because of arguments and conflict, 22 saying that they had been told to leave home and therefore felt unable to return (London Refuge 2002). In the absence of alternative support, young people may turn to abusive adults and will try to survive through use of their own resources. A review of runaways showed that 25 per cent of those who ran survived through stealing, small-scale drug dealing and selling sex (Home Office 2001).

Many sexually exploited young people have also been shown to have little, if any, contact with education or training services, a history of truancy and disruptive behaviour often resulting in the young person slipping behind in attendance and achievement (Zigman 1999). Isolated from mainstream support, the young people are increasingly vulnerable to violence and abuse. Melrose *et al.* (1999) undertook a retrospective study into the circumstances of 50 adults selling sex. Thirty-six of the sample started swapping or selling sex before the age of 16, 24 of whom started when they were 14 or younger. Of these, 36 reported experiences of conflict and abuse in their families of origin, 21 noting their first sexual experience to be in the context of abuse. This background of abuse and isolation makes young people easy prey for adults with sophisticated methods of coercion and manipulation for their own gain (Shaw and Butler 1998; Ivison 1998; Dodsworth 2000; Melrose *et al.* 1999). Some of the methods used to exploit young people are illustrated well in the video *Whose Daughter Next* (Van Meeuwen and Swann 1998), which gives a helpful insight into the means by which young people can be manipulated and exploited through coercion by an older adult who poses as a 'friend'. In this particular work the adult male grooms the young woman for selling sex as she falls in love with, and becomes dependent, upon him. He does this through three stages (a) fantasy, (b) grooming then (c) abuse. During the fantasy stage he entices her to believe that he loves her and that he will care for her, increasingly leading her away from her familial/care and peer networks. He then grooms her into sexual activity, often increasing her dependence upon drugs while so doing. Finally he introduces her to prostitution. As a result, the young woman is dependent both upon the abusive male and upon drugs. At a psychological level, any previous experiences of violence and abuse within interpersonal relationships have been repeated, and her self-esteem, temporarily raised through the fantasy stage, is lowered further than before. Although their work was specifically focused on issues for young women, young men have also been shown to be vulnerable to coercion from abusive adults

(Palmer 2001). Barnardo's note that of the young men and women seen by their projects since 1995, those aged between 12 and 14 did not make their own decision to sell sex, but were coerced by an adult aged 18 to 25 (www.Barnardos.org.uk). Whether grooming through the Internet or through face-to-face contact, the methods of coercion result in the young person being alienated from family/carers and friends. However, caution does need to be applied if we are assuming a one-dimensional approach to understanding the processes of sexual exploitation. Many young people may be cautious about seeing themselves or defining themselves as the victim of a perpetrators' desire, a caution that can be shared by parents, carers and practitioners. Phoenix has argued that the young person may rationalise certain actions or behaviours as a means of dealing with poverty and social disadvantage, a rationalisation that underpins a strategy for survival (Phoenix 2004). In other words, if a young person has made a decision to act in a particular way in order to survive they are at least trying to exert some control and power over their own circumstances. To label them as a victim without considering their own sense of agency, their self determination, power, authority and self-confidence may serve to further undermine rather than empower them. Phoenix points out that the crude application of an all embracing 'victim' approach to work with young people who are sexually exploited can inadvertently endorse the contradiction that has been noted above within the DoH guidance (DoH 2000) which allows for prosecution of young people who do not obediently fall within the victim label but who persistently and voluntarily return to selling sex (Phoenix 2002, 2004). Indeed, despite recent campaigning, the Home Office consultation on prostitution (Home Office 2004a) continues this contradiction, separating the good victim from the bad offender and overriding evidence that shows that both are responding, albeit in different ways, to circumstances of violence and abuse. Although explained under the guise that criminalisation will be used as a 'last resort' to 'do something' after all else has failed, all this will and can do is add to the burden of the young person through being proportioned blame and given the additional stigma of offender through entry into the criminal justice system.

With these issues in mind, good practice recognises the need to help the young person maintain an awareness of their own power and self-defined determination while simultaneously helping them to work with the problems they face related to health, self-esteem, financial security and future employment prospects. Similarly, awareness of the young person's attempt to maintain a sense of their own agency means accepting that welfare services may well be repeatedly rejected. However, this rejection can be part of a process where the young person is trying to 'do something', to gain some control when there are few other opportunities available to them to exert their own wishes. This means working with rejection and disobedience as a part of the ongoing work rather than using rejection as an opportunity to close a case or endorse criminal proceedings. However difficult and challenging this may be to service providers, working with the young person rejecting the service rather than accepting rejection and closing a case may be the complex response needed to address the complex problems presented in this work (Pearce *et al.* 2002).

Problem drug use, including heroin, crack cocaine, cannabis and serious alcohol misuse, are also widespread among young runaways and those vulnerable to exploitation (Green *et al.* 1999). There is a complicated relationship between sexual exploitation, substance misuse, violence and prostitution (Phoenix 1999; Scrambler and Scrambler 1997; Barnard et al. 2002). Jarvis et al. (1998) have argued that adolescence is a critical time for interventions around drug misuse, proposing that these interventions need to concentrate on issues of self-esteem and self-worth among young people. There is evidence that the age of first use is declining (Parker *et al.* 1995, 1998), suggesting that interventions should target young people in early adolescence. The 1998 Youth Lifestyles Survey highlighted drug use among vulnerable young people, and reported that half of all truants as well as those excluded from school reported using illicit drugs compared to 13 per cent of all school children. Seven per cent of those excluded from school were found to be using Class A drugs regularly, with drug use being higher for young women than young men. Four out of five rough sleepers had tried an illicit drug and 80 per cent of serial runaways were using illicit drugs (Goulden and Sondhi 2001).

The complicated relationship between sexual exploitation, substance misuse and experiences of violence has been explored by Barnard *et al.* (2002), young people being particularly vulnerable to both problem drug use and related experiences of violence. However, no simple causal link between prostitution and drug use can be drawn (Cusick 1998, 2002). Instead, problems facing young people are rarely identifiable in isolation from each other, a realisation that has supported the drive articulated within *Every Child Matters* towards integrated, multi-agency rapid response teams that provide one lead professional to support the young person through the various issues they are dealing with (DfES 2003). This is echoed in the recent Home

Office publication focusing on the interrelationship between problem drug use and sex work which notes that services for sexually exploited young people need to be integrated and delivered within a multi-agency framework (Home Office 2004). To be effective, these welcomed initiatives will need to be supported by funding that facilitates ongoing joint work, shared inter-agency training and joint evaluation of related service provision.

The 'new' focus within sexual exploitation – the child sex slave trade and the Internet

Although it has been recognised that all young people, irrespective of racial or cultural origin, are vulnerable to sexual exploitation, there has been increasing awareness of the specific issues facing those who are purposefully trafficked into the country for the purposes of prostitution. Sections 57–59 of the Sexual Offences Act 2003 introduce enhanced regulation of trafficking into, within and out of the UK for purposes of sexual exploitation. As with policy and practice within the UK, it has been recognised that trafficked young people are victims of abuse, entering the country involuntarily as a result of force or coercion (Mullenger 2000; www.ecpat.org.uk; www.mrgraaf.nl) This trafficking of youth is not only the work of paedophiles, but is integrated within some of the abusive aspects of the larger-scale global adult sex industry. As within the UK, many women and young people are increasingly vulnerable to exploitation as a result of poverty and deception. Although young people have been trafficked from countries across the world, the economic and political changes within Europe over the last decade have brought specific forms of feminised poverty and have seen the increasing movement of impoverished children within and between European countries (Nistor and Soitu 2000; www.ecpat.org.uk; www.walnet. org/NSWP; Lewis, Gewirtz and Clarke 2000). It was shown that as women have been affected by poverty during the late 1990s, more children have been living in poorer conditions with less scope for support (Munday 1998). However, ECPAT argue that as trafficking has developed over recent years, it is no longer adequate to say that victims are moved only from poor to wealthier countries.

> In many cases the 'direction' or 'flow' may appear illogical. However, one must remember that it benefits the traffickers to keep their victims in a foreign environment where not only

are they vulnerable for having entered a country illegally, but disadvantaged because of their ignorance of the law, culture and language of that country. (ECPAT 2003a: 1)

With these issues in mind, there have been a number of calls for a coordinated strategy within European countries to raise the profile of issues facing young people trafficked for sexual exploitation. For example, Europap (European Network for AIDS/STD Prevention in Prostitution), Tampep (Transnational AIDS/STD Prevention among Migrant Prostitutes in Europe) and the Global Alliance against Trafficking in Women have each argued for greater awareness of the dangers facing young people and their families. Talking of the impact of the changing economies within Europe on the sexual exploitation of young people, Lenihan and Dean (2000: 40) note that there is 'need to ensure that multi-agency work has an international dimension'. The ECPAT newsletter of September 2003 notes that the issue of human trafficking has risen up the political agenda, that a trafficking toolkit, funded by the Home Office, has been developed as a guidance tool for various authorities, such as the police, Immigration, Social Services departments and NGO's (ECPAT 2003b). Despite this, the practical issues facing practitioners who may come across a trafficked young person in their local area have not yet been fully explored and there is an increasing need for local inter-agency collaboration focused on enabling service providers to identify and work with trafficked young people. Essentially, the central theme to the toolkit is that the child protection issues involved in each case should be the central and paramount concern. As such, the dual task of protecting children and prosecuting abusers should be upheld, meaning that practitioners, carers and young people themselves need to be able to identify an abuser and gather evidence against them.

Similarly, abuse through the Internet has been shown to follow similar patterns of 'grooming' as can happen through face-to-face contact. However, the nature of the abuse used to generate images and the knowledge that they can be sold and broadcast across the world provide additional layers of abuse for the child concerned. Palmer and Stacey (2004) focused attention on those abused through the Internet and mobile phones, noting that there is no one agency that has the money or authority to track children abused in this way. They argue that some of the conventional methods of responding to sexual exploitation may increase the damage for the young person concerned. For example, well meaning courts may use the same technology, such as video cameras, that were used to abuse the child in the first place, creating additional trauma for the child concerned. Their report drew from a survey of more than 80 young people who had been victims of this abuse and who were worked with by the children's charity Barnardo's. The single largest group of children were those whose abuse was photographed and placed on the Internet. Many of these young people were in their early teens, but the work identified a trend toward more disturbing images of much younger children (Palmer and Stacey 2004, on www.Barnardos.org. uk).

While the existing child protection framework provides the context for work with sexually exploited young people, there are ever increasing and changing ways that abuse can take place. Although the DoH Guidance 2000 has been helpful in establishing the central premise that the children concerned are victims of abuse, there is a need for further initiatives to look at ways of identifying and challenging abusers and of keeping practitioners, carers and young people up to date with the changing forms of abuse.

What has been done to identify and work with the sexual exploitation of young people?

Despite evidence from practice to show that sexually exploited young people are victims of abuse, many were, prior to 2000, penalised for committing offences related to prostitution. Two thousand, three hundred and eighty cautions and 1,730 convictions were secured against those under 18 years of age for offences related to prostitution in England and Wales between 1989 and 1995 (Aitchinson and O'Brien 1997). Joint work between police, social services and children's charities such as Barnardo's, the NSPCC and the Children's Society has argued that this visible street-based exploitation is just a small part of a bigger picture. There remained under the 'tip of the iceberg' an unknown number of young people selling or swapping sex for accommodation, drugs and other 'returns in kind', being increasingly vulnerable to manipulation by abusive adults (Barrett 1997). Although rarely prosecuting young people for offences relating to prostitution, the police do have an important role to play in identifying vulnerable young people, particularly during anti-social hours when they are most at risk of abuse. A review of young people under 18 years of age taken into police protection under Section 46 of the Children Act 1989 in the London, Soho area, show that 91 young women were brought into police protection from the local streets on 255 different occasions in 1999, 48 on the grounds of being suspected of vulnerability to prostitution. A further 55 young women were brought into police protection suspected to be vulnerable to abuse through prostitution on 101 different occasions during 2000 (Pearce *et al.* 2002).

A number of subsequent government initiatives support strategies for early intervention to prevent abuse. The themes within *Every Child Matters* (DfES 2003) on supporting parents and carers and providing early intervention and effective protection for young people are in line with initiatives for 'joined up' thinking in early intervention. The proposals that local authorities appoint a Children's Director to bring services together as Children's Trusts and that 'Safeguarding Children's Boards' succeed ACPCs intend to raise the profile of young people and their needs within the local authority overall. *Every Child Matters* also calls for 'on the spot' service delivery with rapid-response, integrated, multi-agency teams based in and around schools and for Children's Centres that work to identify young people at the early stages of vulnerability. As noted by Lloyd *et al.* (2001), early intervention based within schools can play an important role in reducing truancy and exclusion. Their work shows that the key to success is in providing the school with support to manage time and staffing pressures created by the additional burden of co-coordinating multi-agency responses to children in trouble. This means all agencies involved being able to commit resources to support the school in their efforts to manage social as well as educational issues.

The Updated Drugs Strategy (Home Office 2003) also advocates a stronger focus on prevention and on the school as a key location for identifying children vulnerable to problem drug use and related problems. As well as increasing the profile of preventative education, it proposes that treatment services are specifically designed for young people. Although there are many problems to be addressed in reaching these stated goals, the focus of recent legislation has been on supporting integrated, multi-agency work to prevent abuse and exploitation. If appropriately resourced to be effective, this strong and justifiable focus on prevention is welcomed. It supports one of the two stated aims of the DoH guidance – protecting children from abuse. However, it leaves open the question of how we gather the valid and credible evidence needed to prosecute abusers, a gap in policy and practice that needs to be addressed.

The Sex Offences Act 2003 has created a number of new possible means of taking a case against an abuser once he or she is identified. Designed to be relevant for those abused through grooming through the Internet as well as through face-to-face contact, sections 9–15, 47–50 and 52 and 53 in Part One of the Act note that 'causing or inciting a child under 16 to engage in sexual activity', 'arranging or facilitating commission of a child sex offence' and 'meeting a child following sexual grooming' are sexual offences, being complete whether or not a sexual act takes place. These can each be used to intervene at an earlier stage of grooming and enticement than has been possible. Part One (sections 16–19) also clarify the definition of 'position of trust', offering new powers that can be used by practitioners and young people in bringing a case against an abuser known to them who has abused their trust. However, taking proactive steps to identify an abuser is notoriously hard for a number of reasons. The abuser's intentions in the early stage of exploitation are often unknown or undetected by those involved, including, in some cases, by the abuser themselves. Previous statutory records of abuse may, if they exist, be incomplete or unknown as abusers move from one location to another. The 'victim' may be emotionally attached, or 'in love' with the abuser and others within the family and friends network may be unaware of the potential danger. In some cases, family or friends may be aware of, but colluding with, the abuse. Professional staff may be focused on developing strategies to protect the young person as their main priority, without knowing when or how to gather evidence that could later be used to identify the abuser or that will be accepted by the crown prosecution service for use in a court case against an abuser (Dodsworth 2000; Iveson 1998; Calder 2001).

The Sex Offences Act 2003 implies that the enhanced scope to criminalise those who sexually exploit young people will help to alleviate the problem. While it may provide further opportunities to temporarily remove the small minority who have been identified and prosecuted, it cannot address the central questions of how all of those involved can distinguish between friends and abusers in a young person's life early enough to prevent abuse from occurring, what is needed to initiate criminal proceedings against an abuser and how parents, carers and practitioners can work together to gather evidence against an abuser while supporting the child throughout. While recent developments in policy and legislation are welcomed, there remains work to be done to provide an equal focus on identifying abusers and gathering evidence that can be used to argue for their conviction and treatment.

Despite the rapid changes in some of the ways that sexual exploitation takes place, and in the increasing range of legislation and policy initiatives that are or will soon be available, some local authorities are still in the early stages of developing their own local protocols for ensuring effective multi-agency work to protect young people. A review of the implementation of Safeguarding Children Involved in Prostitution (DoH 2000) showed that 89 per cent of all Area Child Protection Committees in England had protocols for safeguarding children involved in prostitution in place by 2002, either finalised or in draft form, whereas only 51 per cent had established a sub-committee or steering group to work with young people exploited through prostitution (Swann and Balding 2002). Only 6 per cent of 50 targeted ACPCs were able to say that they were meeting the dual aim of protecting children and helping police to gather evidence against abusers (Swann and Balding 2002). Those agencies which have developed sophisticated services in line with the DoH Guidance work with difficult cases presenting a range of dilemmas. We will look now at a few individual case studies in which some of these dilemmas are discussed.

Dilemmas in the work with young people who experience sexual exploitation

Drawing on findings from research carried out with a total of 55 young women at risk of or involved with sexual exploitation, aged 13 to 18 (inclusive), from a UK London borough and a northern city, specific issues for practice are raised. The research was funded by the Joseph Rowntree Foundation and was developed in partnership with the NSPCC. The NSPCC provided follow-up support services for the young women and supervision for the researchers on child protection issues arising during the work. As an action research project, the aim was to provide recommendations that could be used in the development of policy and practice at a local and national level. Although the work took place with young women, the researchers and associated NSPCC projects were in touch with practitioners developing services for young men. The recommendations supported the ongoing development of work focusing on specific needs of sexually exploited young men (Palmer 2001).

The researchers maintained contact with the 55 young women on an ongoing basis over an 18-month period, developing self-reported case studies through youth work techniques including art and drama projects, photography projects and one-to-one discussions and group work. The purpose of the research was explained to the young women and a confidentiality policy, which noted that NSPCC practitioners would be informed of cases of 'extreme and immediate danger', was agreed by the local Area Child Protection Committees. Nineteen of the young women were contacted through outreach work on the street, 28 were referred from social work, schools and related education departments, homeless persons units and youth offending teams. The remaining eight young women either self-referred or were introduced via a friend. Three of the young women were 13 years old, 19 were 14 and 15 years old and 36 were 16 to 18 inclusive. Thirty-eight of the 55 young women were white of UK origin. Although similar issues raised from the work were found across racial and cultural boundaries, there was an overt difference according to self-defined racial origin in that the majority who self-defined as selling sex were white, meaning that fewer of the black and minority ethnic young women were met through outreach, street-based work. Contact with black and minority ethnic young women was made mainly as a result of referral from agencies or by self-referral. To maintain confidentiality, the young women were given false names once their cases studies were documented.

Analysis of the case studies placed the young women into one of three categories: those at risk of sexual exploitation, those who spoke of swapping sex for accommodation, cigarettes, drugs or other favours, and finally those who self-defined as selling sex. Different issues and dilemmas arose in work with young women in each of the three categories, some of which are discussed below.

Preventative work in schools

Although 35 of the total 55 young women were of school age, only 13 were still officially on a school roll. The 22 who were of school age yet not on school roll had been excluded because of difficult behaviour or had left through persistent truanting. The recommendations from the research supported previous and ongoing work which argues that schools need more support in identifying the potential problems and in accessing services that may be able to help at the early stages of abuse. In developing this argument it is important to note that no one young woman presented any one problem. For instance, of the 19 young women in the at risk category (the majority of whom were aged between 13 and 15), all had problems with serious alcohol misuse, five used heroin at least once a week, 18 had histories of running away from home or care, 11 had relationships with boyfriends who were violent towards them, four had been abducted, nine had been raped and four had been pregnant. Ten of the young women were regularly self-harming, seven of whom had made suicide attempts. It is evident that these young women were carrying a number of interrelated problems, often exacerbated though diminishing contact with statutory services such as schools and health providers.

An example of helpful intervention lead by a school able to pick up on concern at an early stage was illustrated by work with Anne, aged 14, who was abducted by two older men she had met over a period of time when out in the evenings drinking and 'hanging around' with mates. She saw one of the two men as her boyfriend, but following an evening at his flat was held against her will for a week. Prior to the abduction she had no previous history of running away from home, but subsequently started to act aggressively at school and was sexually provocative towards boys in her class and male teachers. Her sexualised behaviour resembled another case of a young woman who was demonstrating extreme sexualised risk-taking behaviour. She claimed that she had 'shagged 26 blokes in seven months, I'm not worried about AIDs' and noted that she would 'return to this if I'm not allowed to go home to live with my Mum' (Julie in Pearce *et al*. 2002). This overt sexualised behaviour became the main focus for concern and intervention rather than her deeper needs of understanding why her mother could not care for her. These two cases illustrate the way that many young women will draw attention to themselves through sexualised risk-taking behaviour. Returning to Anne, the school encouraged her to attend their club for young people who had been bullied. Taking up this offer she was able to maintain contact with the school and slowly start to explain some of the things that had happened to her. If she did truant or go missing, she felt able to approach the club on her return rather than try to fit straight back into the school routine. Through patient work between the school, education social work and local police, she was eventually able to identify her abductors and take a case out against them. Such examples of good practice show that with appropriate support to the school, continued outreach can be maintained and young people at risk can be diverted from further harm. However, such cases are rare, and do depend upon the local providers having sensitivity and understanding of the issues involved and access to time and resources to work with them. Connexion workers, teachers, youth workers and specialist young people's charities play a key role in providing this localised support for vulnerable young people. For the aims of preventative work as outlined in the government strategies noted above to be effective, training and support must be directed to these practitioners.

Child-centred practice – listening to the young person's story

As noted in the discussion about empowering young people's own sense of agency while recognising that they are victims of abuse, one of the dilemmas for practice is in working with the conflict that can arise when a young person has decided that they want to continue with a lifestyle that practitioners and carers may consider to be against the young person's best interests. The following examples touch on some of these dilemmas. The first arises from work with Jo, a 17-year-old who was placed in category two: young women who spoke of swapping sex for favours, cigarettes, drugs or accommodation for a night.

Jo spoke of intermittently running away from home during the previous two years in attempts to make new starts and to move away from the hardships she had experienced. Explaining her feelings about being at home with her elder sister, her carer who had abused her physically and sexually, Jo says she

> used to stay in my bedroom for two months, I couldn't get out. I even tried to commit suicide as well … I tried to take some tablets. I just didn't see point in living no more and because of what my sister was doing to me it kind of like, topped it all, and made it worse …

After reaching a point when she did eventually decide to run, she was raped on the street. This led her to services for support. However, once placed in a children's home she continued to run, swapping sex for accommodation when on the run. Running away was for her a way of coping. It was a positive method to cope with her confusion.

> Just going out and just putting it behind me and raving … I stayed out one night, coming in the next day and also they thought that 'Jo is not handling it, since she got raped and she is not handling the situation very well', but people find different ways to handle things … some people might like going for walks to clear their heads and some people might like to not even talk about it, put it behind them and just move on.

For Jo, running provided an outlet for 'clearing her head', an outlet that she needed and relied upon as a method of coping with the confusions in her mind about how to handle her situation. The second example shows Angela, a young woman aged 14 deciding that the best way of escaping from her circumstances at home was to run away. Running gave her a sense of control over her unbearable home conditions and a sense of her own power over those at home who were hurting her. She ran, staying overnight with a man in his early 30s who she slept with because he let her stay with him. For this brief time, she considered the man to be her boyfriend. She explained that while she was there she was asked to sleep with other men, being encouraged to bring other 'girls' into the flat. She met about 12 men aged 20 and over, with about six young women aged between 14 and 15 intermittently attending the flat. This continued until one young woman came to the flat and spoke of feeling very unsafe. This young woman shocked Angela by saying that Angela's boyfriend was a sex dealer. It was at this point that she decided to move on, returning to the street and eventually to home.

In both cases the young women took what they saw as positive steps in running from home, taking enormous risks in so doing. At the early stages, neither were receptive to being 'rescued' from circumstances they were trying to control in their own way. Although clearly vulnerable to abuse from exploitative adults, neither would have defined themselves as victims. Jo saw running as a means of sorting things out in her head and Angela considered swapping sex with her 'boyfriend' to be an effective way of getting a bed for the night rather than having to return home to abuse. Practitioners found that rather than undermine Jo's attempts to 'sort herself' through running, it was best to acknowledge that she may feel the need to run again. This did not undermine their offer of support and resources which they accompanied with advice about the dangers associated with running. Similarly, although Angela was unable initially to approach support from professionals prior to moving in with her 'boyfriend', her contact with the peer who alerted her to the abuse taking place in the flat meant that she followed leads suggested by the peer to use the support that had previously been offered by professionals. Eventually with this support her home circumstances were addressed and she also felt able to report the 'boyfriend' to the police.

Implicit within the cases above is the fact that although the child protection framework is the appropriate context for work with young people who are sexually exploited, the work often involves teenagers who are developing their own sense of self-determination and who are experimenting with or rehearsing adulthood. They may well challenge interventions that are offered by carers, parents or practitioners and may find it difficult to identify a 'boyfriend' as an abuser. The resulting tensions create specific dynamics around the process of engagement with the young person and around attempts to control their behaviour. It also creates problems in the gathering of evidence against an abuser who may have coerced the young person into believing they have their best interests at heart.

To illustrate this point further, one final example is used. Nina, aged 16, described as an 'A' star GCSE pupil by her school, where she maintained intermittent attendance, lived at home with her aunt, had a history of running from home to avoid physical violence, had been diagnosed as clinically depressed and had a history of self-harming. She discussed the reasons that she did not leave her boyfriend, a heroin addict aged somewhere between 25 and 35. She did not leave, despite the fact that he introduced her to 'street life', abducted her for a week, raped her, kicked her and tried to strangle her. Although she wanted to return to study, she explained that she could not because she 'loves him'. In an unsent letter to him she says:

> I never loved anyone the way I loved you, but no one ever hurted me the way you have, to make me hate you in the way I do now, could never hate anyone the way I hate you, will never love anyone the way I loved you.

She explained the complicated tangle between love and hate as an obsession: 'he takes up all my head space'. Although she wanted to maintain her school work, the researcher's notes recorded her argument that she was going back to him because:

- if she left him before the police did anything her family may suffer;
- she has had a miscarriage with his baby and she wanted to tell him so he knew how much she has suffered;
- she thought that if she stayed with him for long enough she could change him – make him treat her differently;
- he was dependent upon her, needing her for money for his drugs – he has asked her for £50 and she gave it to him because she has no one else to give it to;
- when he forced her to have unprotected sex it was only because it was his birthday.

The boyfriend, clearly able to exploit the fraught and unresolved contradictions that Nina felt in her familial relationships, continued her understanding of interpersonal relationships as abusive. He expected her to accept that violence is acceptable. She, on the other hand, felt that if she were to stay with him for long enough she could change him. This sentiment is often one used by victims of domestic and interpersonal violence. Project staff found that adopting approaches commonly used in work with victims of domestic violence was as helpful as those that may be used within child protection frameworks. For example, they accepted that Nina may not feel ready to leave her boyfriend immediately, that 'rescuing' her from the situation may not provide a long-term, client-centred resolution and that she may continue to feel in love with her boyfriend and return to be with him. They tried to link Nina into a group with other young women who had experienced interpersonal violence and continued to offer alternative accommodation that could be ready for use if and when she felt able, an offer that few local areas would be resourced to make. They recognised that short of forcibly removing Nina from the area by trying to make a case for secure accommodation (a case that Phoenix (2002) argues is inappropriately made under the guise of protection, Nina would probably find ways of returning to her 'boyfriend'. Instead, they maintained an open-door approach, offered support with education and employment and encouraged her to see alternative ways of living her life. Over an eleven-month period, Nina had disassociated herself from her boyfriend and was attending a local college, although she explained that he 'still takes up her head space' and, at this stage, was not prepared to press charges against him for abduction, rape or coercion. It is in situations such as these that a broader perspective of child protection is needed, accommodating a partnership with the young person which accepts their status as a developing adult while maintaining the provision of support that can be used over time.

Conclusion

Drawing on policy, practice and research it is evident that we have come a long way in understanding the changing nature and contexts within which the sexual exploitation of young people takes place. We have also learnt much about the complexities involved in providing support to the young people concerned and in gathering evidence to prosecute abusers. Early intervention through multi-agency work initiated by schools which are properly resourced to provide support outside of the classroom is an effective way of preventing the escalation of abuse. An open door policy that works in partnership with the young person by respecting their autonomy and interests and that involves them in decision-making provides some scope for working with those who may otherwise continue to run and reject service provision. A combination of approaches to the work that draw on lessons learnt from detached youth work and from the field of domestic and interpersonal violence can complement the child protection framework and potentially lead to further empowerment of the young person and a greater onus on conviction of offenders. While helpful moves have been made in legislation and policy within this field, it is evident that we still face an uphill battle in changing the law so that sexually exploited young people are not criminalised for actions that result from abuse. The scope to criminalise young people who have been sexually exploited for offences related to prostitution must be removed. So too must the rhetoric of inter-agency work be resourced so that supervision and career development opportunities are directed towards supporting workers with experience and expertise in the area. All too often staff 'burn-out' results in a rapid turnover of skilled and experienced staff who could play a significant role in developing training and service development for sexually exploited young people. It is this very staff expertise that we need to be able to foster to ensure a coherent and accessible service is available to those young people who are most in need.

References

Aitchinson, P. and O'Brien, R. (1997) 'Redressing the balance: the legal context of child prostitution', in D. Barrett (1997) (ed.), *Child Prostitution in Britain: Dilemmas and Practical Responses*. London: Children's Society, 32–59.

Barnard, M., Hart, G. and Church, S. (2002) 'Client violence against prostitute women, working from street and off street locations: a three city comparison', available at: http://www.rhul.ac.uk/sociopolitical-science/rvp/findings/rfbarnard.DPF.

Barrett, D. (ed.) (1997) *Child Prostitution in Britain: Dilemmas and Practical Responses*. London: Children's Society.

Brain, T., Duffin, T., Anderson, S. and Parchment, P. (1998) *Child Prostitution: A Report on the ACPO Guidelines and Pilot Studies in Wolverhampton and Nottinghamshire*. Gloucestershire Constabulary.

Broadfoot, A. (1998) 'A father's perspective', in I. Ivison (ed.), *Stopping the Pimp* CROP (Coalition For the Removal of Pimping) Conference Report, Leeds Metropolitan University, Research Paper No. 16: 29–31.

Calder, M. (2001) 'Child prostitution: developing effective protocols' *Child Care in Practice*, 7 (2): 98–118.

Cusick, L. (1998) 'Female prostitution in Glasgow: drug use and occupational sector', *Addiction Research*, 6 (2): 115–30.

Cusick, L. (2002) 'Youth prostitution: a literature review', *Child Abuse Review*, 11: 230–51.

Dodsworth, J. (2000) *Child Sexual Exploitation/Child Prostitution' Social Work Monographs* No. 178. Norwich: UEA.

Department for Education and Skills (DfES) (2003) *Every Child Matters*. Available at: www.dfes.gov.uk/everychildmatters/downloads.cfm.

Department of Health (DoH) (2000) *Safeguarding Children Involved in Prostitution: Supplementary Guidance to Working Together to Safeguard Children*. Department of Health, Home Office, Department for Education and Employment, National Assembly for Wales.

ECPAT (2003a) Background information/home page. ECPAT UK, available at: www.ecpat.org.uk/hmepage/background information Page 1.

ECPAT 2003b) *September Newsletter*. ECPAT UK, available at: www.ecpat.org. uk.

Goulden, C. and Sondhi, A. (2001) *At the Margins: Drug use by vulnerable young people in the 1998–99 Youth Lifestyle Survey*, Home Office Research Studies 228.

Green, A., Day, S. and Ward, H. (1999) Crack Cocaine and Prostitution in London in the 1990s, *Centre for Research on Drugs and Health Behaviour*, Executive Summary No. 65.

Home Office (2001) *Consultation on Young Runaways*, Social Exclusion Unit, CAB017658/0401/D16.

Home Office (2003) *Updated Drugs Strategy*. London: Home Office.

Home Office (2004a) *Paying the Price: A Consultation Paper on Prostitution*. London: Home Office Communication Directorate.

Home Office (2004b) *Solutions and Strategies: Drug Problems and Street Sex Markets*, available at: www.drugs.gov.uk/Reportsand Publications/ Communities/1089989115.

Ivison, I. (ed.) (1998) *Stopping the Pimp*, CROP (Coalition for the Removal of Pimping) Conference Report, Leeds Metropolitan University, Research Paper No. 16.

Jarvis, T., Copeland, J. and Watson, L. (1998) 'Exploring the nature of the relationship between child sexual abuse and substance use among women', *Addiction*, 93 (6): 965–875.

Jeffreys, S. (1999) 'Child versus adult prostitution: a false distinction' in European Commission (ed.), *Child Sex Tourism, First European Meeting of the Main Partners in the Fight against Child Sex Tourism*, 25/5 November 1998. Brussels: European Commission, 65–71.

Lenihan, T. and Dean, P. (2000) 'Child Protection in England', in D. Barrett with E. Barrett and N. Mullenger (eds.), *Youth Prostitution in the New Europe*. Lyme Regis: Russell House, 26–41.

Lewis, G., Gerwirtz, S. and Clarke, J. (eds) (2000) *Rethinking Social Policy*. London: Sage, in association with the Open University.

Lloyd, G., Stead, J. and Kendrick, A. (2001) *Hanging On In There: A Study of Interagency Work to Prevent School Exclusion in Three Local Authorities*. London: National Children's Bureau and the Joseph Rowntree Foundation.

London Refugee (2002) *The London Refuge: A Safe House for Children and Young People: Annual Report 2001–2002*. NSPCC.

Melrose, M., Barrett, D. and Brodie, I. (1999) *One-Way Street: Retrospectives on Childhood Prostitution*, London: Children's Society.

Mullenger, N. (2000) 'Immigrants and illegal youth sex workers in Italy', in D. Barrett with E. Barrett and N. Mullenger, *Youth Prostitution in the New Europe*. Lyme Regis: Russell House, 57–76.

Munday, B. (1998) 'The old and the new: changes in social care in Central and Eastern Europe', in B. Munday and G. Lane (eds), *The Old and the New: Changes in Social Care in Central and Eastern Europe*. Kent: European Institute of Social Services.

Nistor, D. and Soitu, C. T. C. (2000) 'Youth prostitution in Romania', in D. Barrett with E. Barrett and N. Mullenger, *Youth Prostitution in the New Europe*. Lyme Regis: Russell House, 94–108.

Palmer, T. (2001) *No Son of Mine!* London: Barnardo's.

Palmer, T. and Stacey, L. (2004) *Just One Click*. London: Barnardo's.

Parker, H., Aldridge, J. and Measham, F. (1998) *Illegal Leisure: The Normalisation of Adolescent Recreational Drug Use*. London: Routledge.

Parker, H., Measham, F. and Aldridge, J. (1995) *Drug Features: Changing Patterns of Drug Use among English Youth*. Institute for the Study of Drug Dependence.

Patel, G. (1994) *The Porth Project: A Study of Homelessness and Running Away Among Vulnerable Black People in Newport, Gwent*. London: Children's Society.

Pearce, J. J. with Williams, M. and Galvin, C. (2002) *It's Someone Taking a Part of You*. London: Joseph Rowntree Foundation and Children's Bureau, available at: www.ncb.org.uk.

Phoenix, J. (1999) *Making Sense of Prostitution*. London: Routledge.

Phoenix, J. (2002) 'In the name of protection: youth prostitution policy reforms in England and Wales', *Critical Social Policy*, 22 (2): 353–75.

Phoneix, J. (2004) 'Rethinking youth prostitution: national provision at the margins of child protection and youth justice', *Youth Justice*, (3) 3: 152–67.

Pitts, J. (1997) 'Causes of youth prostitution, new forms of practice and political responses' in D. Barrett (ed.), *Child Prostitution in Britain: Dilemmas and Practical Responses*. London: Children's Society, 139–58.

Scambler, G. and Scambler, A. (1997) *Rethinking Prostitution: Purchasing Sex in the 1990s*. London: Routledge.

Shaw, I. and Butler, I. (1998) 'Understanding young people and prostitution. A foundation for practice?', *British Journal of Social Work*, 28: 177–96.

Swann, S. and Balding, V. (2002) *Safeguarding Children Involved in Prostitution: Guidance Review*. Available at: http://www.DoH.gov.uk/acpc/safeguarding childrenreview.pdf.

Taylor-Brown, J. (2002) *More Than One Chance! Young People Involved in Prostitution Speak Out*. London: ECPAT UK.

Van Meeuwen, A. and Swann, S. (1998) *Whose Daughter Next: Children Abused through Prostitution*. London: Barnardo's.

Zigman, M. (1999) 'Under the law: teen prostitution in Kensington', *Critique of Anthropology*, 19 (2): 193–201.

Chapter 9

Clients of female sex workers: men or monsters?

Hilary Kinnell

Since the early 1980s, the burden of moral censure heaped upon the sex industry has been incrementally extended and, to a degree, transferred from women who sell to men who pay (Brooks-Gordon and Gelsthorpe 2003a). Kerb-crawling was first criminalised in 1985, and became an arrestable offence in 2001.[1] The Home Office consultation document *Paying the Price* sets out options for future prostitution law and policy in the UK, including increased penalties for kerb-crawling and the Swedish approach of criminalising the purchase of sexual services. Targeting clients is loudly advocated by those who see sex work as intrinsically abusive to the seller, and by those who regard commercial sex as immoral and offensive.

The current climate of public opinion is quite receptive to proposals which aim to extend the criminalisation of clients, but despite the odium heaped upon clients by those who feel menaced by kerb-crawlers and by those who see them as predators against the vulnerable, and despite the confidence of those who assert that targeting the purchasers will bring the sex industry to an end, there is minimal public awareness of basic information about clients. Any anti-client enforcement strategy must at least concern itself with the size of the population whose behaviour it seeks to change; social policy-makers should perhaps also inform themselves about clients' demographic characteristics such as age, ethnicity, occupation, marital status, reasons for seeking commercial sex and frequency of doing so. Those whose concern is to prevent violence against sex workers need to know more about the circumstances in which such violence occurs and about those who commit it.

I have argued that sex work policy should promote sex workers' safety, health and human rights and have written about sex workers' vulnerability to violence, especially from clients (see in this volume Chapter 6, 'Murder made easy'), as have many other commentators on the sex industry. However, I am concerned that such research and concern about client violence against sex workers is not interpreted simplistically. This chapter suggests that clients, far from being a tiny minority of men, with abnormal desires and predilections for violence, are a substantial subsection of the male population, broadly representative of it on most demographic variables, with fairly mundane reasons for engaging in commercial sex, and rarely violent. It will also offer some insight into the reasons why enforcement aimed at clients is unlikely to achieve the hoped-for withering away of the sex industry, and may instead increase abuse and violence against sex workers. Its publication may be too late to influence the government's present deliberations, but as history demonstrates that the sex industry is largely unresponsive to policy innovations, it may still add to the somewhat meagre body of knowledge about sex workers' clients and inform future policy decisions.

A variety of information sources are utilised, including press reports and working documents from agencies that provide services to sex workers. It also reports on research carried out by the author among clients of sex workers in Birmingham in 1988/1989 to investigate risk factors for HIV. Some findings were reported in various papers focusing on HIV issues,[2] but much of the information about clients was never published. Despite a time lapse of over 15 years since this data was collected, it is felt to be still relevant, partly because the research itself indicated that a substantial proportion of the men interviewed 15 years ago will still be paying for sex now, and partly because more recent studies of clients have found similar demographic patterns to those found in Birmingham in 1988/9, suggesting that the sub-group of the male population that pays for sex has some predictable characteristics which do not change greatly over time.

The Birmingham client surveys 1988/9

Two methods were used to elicit information from clients. First (Survey 1), an interview schedule was administered to 126 clients by sex workers and outreach workers, or self-completed, between April 1988 and February 1989. It was anticipated that this method might not obtain a representative sample, so a second method was also used (Survey 2), in which eight sex workers operating by various methods kept consecutive records of all their clients up to a maximum of 50. Three hundred records were collected by this method between August and December 1988, covering basic demographics and brief information relevant to the role of being a client. These two methods produced very similar results on most demographic variables, and on details of sexual practice, giving some confidence that the information obtained gave a reasonably accurate picture of sex workers' clients in Birmingham. These results will be referred to below in the context of more recent studies and claims made about clients of sex workers.

How many clients are there?

McLeod (1982) calculated the number of clients in Birmingham by estimating the number of sex workers and their average number of client contacts over a given period of time. Agustín (2001) has commented on the use of this method in France, Spain and Italy. For example, if a sex worker averages 20 clients a week and works for only 40 weeks of the year, she will have had 800 client contacts during that year. This is similar to estimates made by Brewer *et al.* (2000), who calculated an annual average of 868 male partners per sex worker per year in the USA.

A widely accepted current estimate of the numbers of sex workers in the UK is 80,000 (Home Office, 2004). If their average yearly clientele was 800 each, there would be a total of *64 million commercial sex transactions in a year.*

All the values used in the above calculations can be questioned. If the average numbers of clients per sex worker per week, or the number of weeks worked per year per sex worker, or the total number of sex workers were lower, the total number of commercial sex transactions in a year would also be lower.

Numbers of sex workers and their 'working year'

In 1999, the author estimated a total number of sex workers in the UK of just under 80,000, or approximately 1.3 per 1,000 of the population. This was based on information from 17 sex work projects (six in London) and extrapolated for the whole country. Confidence in this speculative figure was increased when colleagues in the Netherlands and Belgium calculated similar proportions in relation to their own populations. The figure of 80,000 has since been repeated by other authorities including the police, indicating that it is consistent with their own sources of information.

Estimating the average 'working year' of sex workers is more speculative, as it has not been possible to find other commentators who have reported on the subject. The author's own research on sex workers in Wolverhampton (Kinnell 1993) included a question about the number of weeks worked in the previous year: the average was 45 weeks.

Ratio of clients to sex workers

The above calculation suggests a national average of 20 clients per week per sex worker. May *et al.* (1999) found that average numbers of clients per week varied over three sites: 15 in 'Midtown', 22 in 'Oldport' and 30 in 'City Way'. May *et al.* (2000) also reported an average per week of 27 clients for sex workers with a pimp and 14 for those without. O'Neill and Campbell (2001) found an average of 17 clients per sex worker per week in Walsall. However, research among indoor sex workers in London (Whittaker and Hart 1996) gave an average number of clients per sex worker per week of 76: were this applicable to all sex workers in the UK, the predicted number of commercial sex transactions would be nearly quadrupled.

It therefore seems reasonable to base calculations on a total of 80,000 sex workers, and relatively conservative to posit a national average of 20 clients per week and an average working year of 40 weeks per sex worker.

Frequency of client visits

The figure of 64 million commercial sex transactions per year, based as it is on reasonable estimates of numbers of sex workers and of their yearly clientele, forces us to consider the likely number of clients participating in these transactions. The lower the mean annual frequency of clients' visits, the larger the whole client group has to be to account for the number of episodes of commercial sex. According to the 2001 Census, there were only 20,393,129 males aged 15 to 79 in the whole population, so either every male in this age group must pay for sex at least three times a year, or a smaller number must do so more frequently. To determine the size of the client population, it is necessary to discover the average frequency of client visits.

Johnson *et al.* (2001) found that 4.3 per cent of males aged 16 to 44 reported paying for sex in the past five years. Applying this percentage to all males aged 15 to 79 would give a client population of 876,904, based on 2001 census figures, a client to sex worker ratio of eleven to one (based on 80,000 sex workers), so that clients would have to pay for sex 73 times a year *on average*, i.e. more than once a week, to account for the level of business estimated for sex workers. However, if the episodes of commercial sex reported were equally distributed over a five-year period, the annual client population would be only 175,380, and every client would have to pay for sex every single day of the year to account for all episodes of commercial sex.

The authors point out that because paying for sex is a highly stigmatised activity, 'estimates derived should probably be regarded as minima'. In other words, it is reasonable to assume that a higher proportion of men pay for sex than admit to it, even in confidential questionnaires.

Men whose role as client is criminalised are even less likely to give honest answers about the frequency with which they engage in commercial sex. Elliott *et al.* (2002) reported that 82 per cent (36/44) of men arrested for kerb-crawling in Middlesbrough claimed it was their first time. Brooks-Gordon and Gelsthorpe (2003b) found only 1 per cent of men stopped for kerb-crawling in London (n = 518) volunteered the information that it was an habitual practice.

However, the scale of the sex industry could not possibly be sustained if most clients paid for sex only once in their lives. In contrast, Shell *et al.* (2001) reported that, among kerb-crawlers attending a rehabilitation programme in Southampton, participants' comments suggested that 'this behaviour is habitual and often of a longstanding nature'.

Reports on the frequency of client visits in academic literature are scarce and variable. Faugier and Cranfield (1995) reported that only 26 per cent of clients in Greater Manchester had paid for sex within a week of interview, and in Merseyside 36 per cent had done so (Campbell *et al.* 1996). In Glasgow (Barnard *et al.* 1993), the mean reported length of time since the last visit to a sex worker was 60 days, an annual rate of 6 visits per client, giving a ratio of 133 clients per sex worker, and indicating a client population of 10,640,000, over 50 per cent of the entire male population aged 15 to 79. In contrast, Morgan Thomas *et al.* (1990) indicated that clients in Edinburgh averaged 28 visits per year, a ratio of 28 clients per sex worker, suggesting a client population of 2,240,000, or 11 per cent of the adult male population. In Birmingham (Kinnell 1989) clients were asked both how often they 'looked for business' (i.e. commercial sex) and how long it was since they last 'did business'. The mean on the first question was 'every two weeks', producing 26 episodes of commercial sex per year per client, a ratio of 30.5 clients per sex worker. However, on the second question, 'how long since your last visit?', the mean was five weeks, an average of ten visits per year, a ratio of 80 clients per sex worker. Applying these values to the estimated 64 million commercial sex transactions per year would give a client population of between 2,460,000 and 6,400,000 (12 per cent or 31 per cent of males aged 15 to 79).

Even the lowest of these estimates of client numbers – 11 per cent of males aged 15 to 79 – begs the question, should the government decide to criminalise the purchase of sexual services, what levels of law enforcement would be effective in changing the behaviour of such a large group?

Client characteristics

This section draws on client profiles contained in various studies, ranging from Matthews' work in Finsbury Park in the mid-1980s (Matthews 1986), to the 2002 report on kerb-crawlers in Middlesbrough (Elliott *et al*. 2002). It is noticeable that all the most recent studies are of kerb-crawlers. These samples may be affected by police selectivity regarding who is apprehended for kerb-crawling, and client responses about marital status, frequency of paying for sex and their motivations for doing so, may reflect the exigencies of the criminalised situation in which these clients found themselves. They also exclude the great majority of clients who visit off-street sex workers.

The other studies all included clients who accessed sex workers in a variety of ways. Faugier and Cranfield (1995) accessed 61 per cent of clients via police and sex workers in 'red light districts' of Greater Manchester, so unsurprisingly, 67 per cent of their sample visited street workers, but 22 per cent visited saunas. The Merseyside sample (Campell *et al*. 1996) comprised mainly men who visited saunas, as did the Edinburgh group (Morgan Thomas *et al*. 1990). The Birmingham surveys (Kinnell 1989) were obtained via sex workers and outreach in sex work venues, including street soliciting areas.

Survey 1 did not investigate what style of sex work clients accessed, but the method favoured indoor venues. In Survey 2, 61 per cent of client contacts were via indoor workers.

While demographic variables are quite similar between kerb-crawler and non-kerbcrawler samples, it is likely that clients' accounts of their motivations and behaviour are more accurately reflected in samples obtained through non-criminalised situations.

Age

Table 9.1 shows clients' ages in nine studies. Information on age groups in the male population from the 2001 Census is also given.

The Southampton and Birmingham samples show a very similar age distribution to each other, and to the general male population aged 20 to 49, although men over 50 are somewhat under-represented. The Merseyside and West Yorkshire samples are not strictly comparable as the age ranges used do not match the Census groups, but suggest over-representation of younger men and under-representation of men over 50, while in Middlesbrough the 30 to 49 age group is over-represented, and over-fifties under-represented.

The age profile of men found kerb-crawling does not seem to differ greatly from men who contact sex workers in other venues, nor does it differ greatly from age patterns in the general population. Although they do indicate that men over 50 are less likely to be apprehended for kerb-crawling, this may be an effect of policing selectivity.

Shell *et al.* (2001) noted that the age profile of their sample was older than other offenders under the supervision of Hampshire Probation, with only 22 per cent of kerb-crawlers being aged 18 to 26, compared to 53 per cent of other offenders. Only 12 per cent of the Birmingham sample were in this age group, and only 13 per cent of the West Yorkshire sample (18–25).

Age profiles of clients therefore suggest that they are similar to men in general, but dissimilar from male offenders.

Length of involvement

Campbell *et al.* (1996) found that 70 per cent of Merseyside clients had first paid for sex between the ages of 18 and 29. In Birmingham (Survey 1), 63 per cent first paid for sex before they were 30, 95 per cent before they were 50. The mean length of time since initiation was 10.4 years (range 0–55 years). Wellings *et al.* (1994) found that

Table 9.1 Client age

	Type of sample	Age range	Mean age	20–29	30–49	50–59
Census 2001	UK male population	20–59		23%	53%	23%
Middlesbrough 2001, n = 44	Kerb-crawlers	19–56	37	16%	64%	16%
Southampton 2000/1, n = 45	Kerb-crawlers	18–69		21%	50%	15%
West Yorks 1998/9, n = 71	Kerb-crawlers	19–61		28% (19–30)	58% (31–50)	10% (51–60)
London 1997/8, n = 518	Kerb-crawlers	17–77	39			
Merseyside 1996, n = 28	Advert and phone interview	18–71		46% (18–29)	43%	
Manchester 1995, n = 120	Various*	19–61	39			
Glasgow 1993, n = 143	GUM clinic, advert and direct interview	21–63	36			
Edinburgh 1988/9, n = 203	Direct interview	18–60	33			
Birmingham 1988/9, Survey 1, n = 126	Direct interview or self-completed	19–80	41	21%	50%	18%

* Self-completed questionnaires handed out by police and sex workers in 'red-light districts', plus adverts and phone interviews.

Sources:

Middlesbrough: Elliott *et al.* (2002); Southampton: Shell *et al.* (2001); West Yorks: WYPA (1998/9); London: Brooks-Gordon and Gelsthorpe (2003); Merseyside: Campbell *et al.* (1996); Manchester: Faugier and Cranfield (1995); Glasgow: Barnard *et al.* (1993); Edinburgh: Morgan Thomas *et al.* (1990); Birmingham: Kinnell (1989).

reporting of ever paying for sex rose through the age bands, with 10.3 per cent of men aged 45 to 59 having done so.

It appears that clients remain in the market for commercial sex for several years. Using a conservative estimate of ten visits a year, a client aged 40 will, on average, have already made over 100 visits to a sex worker in his lifetime. This calls into question the efficacy of attempts to reduce the market for commercial sex activity by moral exhortation, education or police activity.

The estimated numbers of clients, the frequency of their contact with prostitutes and the number of years they remain as clients all indicate the strength and persistence of the demand for commercial sex.

Area of residence

Wellings et al. (1994) found that men who worked away from home were significantly more likely to report paying for sex, which appears to support a rationalisation of clients' behaviour as fulfilling sexual urges that would otherwise be catered for in non-commercial relationships. There is also a substantial literature covering 'sex tourism' which suggests that the 'away from home' factor is important. A survey in Finland (1995) found that, while 10 per cent of men had paid for sex abroad, only 3 per cent had done so in Finland. Some clients in the British studies already cited engaged in commercial sex away from home. In Birmingham (Kinnell 1989) 12 per cent had done so elsewhere in Britain or Ireland; 6 per cent with sex workers abroad, all in western Europe. In Manchester (Faugier and Cranfield 1995), 25 per cent had paid for sex elsewhere in Britain, and 18 per cent had done so abroad. Higher rates of paying for sex abroad (43 per cent) were reported by clients in London (Day et al. 1993), predominantly in Europe but also in other countries.

Clients are often regarded as 'outsiders', bringing shame and disruption to otherwise respectable communities. The social psychology of communities wishing to distance themselves from disgraceful behaviour is not difficult to understand, but much of the evidence suggests that, although few clients reside in the areas of street soliciting, most are using the nearest sex market to their homes.

In 1991, a Luton newspaper reported: 'Figures recently released show half the kerb-crawlers in Luton live in the town. This quashes previous theories that most punters came from elsewhere'.[3]

On both Birmingham surveys a majority of clients were resident in Birmingham (60 per cent, 56 per cent). In Merseyside, 64 per cent lived in Liverpool, and only one man was not resident in the North West region. In Manchester, 88 per cent lived in the Greater Manchester area, and the remainder in neighbouring counties. In West Yorkshire, 72 per cent were resident in West Yorkshire, and were found kerb-crawling in the same area where they lived. Matthews (1986) found that 77 per cent of kerb-crawlers in Finsbury Park lived either in Finsbury Park or nearby. In Middlesbrough, however, 84 per cent of kerb-crawlers lived outside the city, but the authors attribute this to the fact that Middlesbrough is one of only two places in the region with a street sex market.

It therefore appears that most clients are accessing sex workers in an area close to their homes, and that, certainly in sites not renowned for their tourism, commercial sex is not primarily a service industry to visitors from outside the region or a form of tourist entertainment.

Clients' occupations

Table 9.2 provides details of clients' occupations.

Variations in the way occupational data is reported in different studies makes comparisons very difficult. Employers, managers and professionals formed a much larger proportion of the Middlesbrough kerb-crawler group than managers and professionals did in the Manchester, London or Birmingham surveys. The 1990 NATSAL survey found that men in social classes I and II were most likely to report paying for sex, but the substantial proportions in the blue-collar/manual categories in the above three studies suggests that perhaps NATSAL reflects more the social class of men willing to admit to paying for sex than anything else.

One occupational characteristic common to 32 per cent of the Birmingham sample was a job that entailed mobility, either locally or regionally, e.g. drivers, sales reps, meter readers, milkmen, postmen, building trade workers, etc. These occupations may have facilitated clients' contact with sex workers, as their whereabouts during the working day would be variable and often unmonitored.

One common finding where occupation is reported is that the great majority of clients were employed: in addition to the samples included in Table 9.2, 71 per cent of clients in Merseyside and 82 per cent of kerb-crawlers in Southampton were employed. Shell *et al.* (2002) note the contrast with 'other offender groups' in

Table 9.2 Clients' occupations

Birmingham 1988/9 Survey 1	[%]	Middlesbrough 2002	[%]	Manchester 1995	[%]	London 1985	[%]
Managerial/professional	14	Managerial/professional/employers	41	Managerial/professional	28	Managerial/professional	15
Small business	13			Self-employed	12	Tradesmen	29
White collar	14	Non-manual	10	White collar/service/retail	15	Service and salesmen	19
Blue collar	45	Manual	49	Manual/transport	31	Manual	18
Armed forces	0						
Retired	7						
Student	0						
Unemployed	6	Unemployed	9	Unemployed	13	Unemployed	19

contact with Hampshire Probation, only 48 per cent of whom were employed.

Clients' marital status

Reports of clients' marital status also vary. In Birmingham, on direct interview, 66 per cent reported non-sex worker partners but only 29 per cent described themselves as married, compared to 44 per cent in the consecutive records kept by sex workers. The West Yorkshire study reported 44 per cent married and 15 per cent cohabiting; in Southampton 51 per cent were married, and another 14.5 per cent had a partner; in Merseyside, 54 per cent were married or cohabiting, and another 14 per cent in a steady but non-cohabiting relationship, and in Middlesbrough, 54 per cent were married, although 73 per cent had a regular partner. These findings all indicate that a majority of clients do, theoretically, have sexual partners who are not sex workers.

The research available on the socio-demographics of men who pay for sex indicates that they are a cross section of the population and rather ordinary. McCleod (1982) noted that apart from a minority of exceptions sex workers referred to their clients as 'Mr Average'. Campbell *et al.* (1996) found that many of the street sex workers they spoke to referred to the majority of their clients as 'normal';

Most of them are just ordinary fellas.

You get a few weirdo's but most are normal.

Reasons for seeking commercial sex

When celebrities such as Wayne Rooney, Angus Deighton or Hugh Grant are exposed as clients, there is often public amazement as well as opprobrium – they are not 'dirty', 'desperate', 'undesirable', 'geeky' men – it seems beyond public imagination that a rich, even attractive man would ever 'need' to pay for sex. What is being challenged are 'stereotypes' about men who pay for sex and a limited understanding about their varied motivations for doing so. When these men become visible it is difficult to sustain the stereotypes, as McKeganey points out:

The secret world of the client is sustained by the belief that the men who buy sex are never our father, brother, husband or boyfriend, but someone else, who we do not know and may not even wish to know. (McKeganey 1996)

In Birmingham (Survey 1, Kinnell 1989), clients were asked why they paid for sex. There were both open-ended questions and a list of options. While responses suggested that some interviewees were unused to verbalising or analysing their motivations, most gave more than one reason, and only two did not give any reasons. Answers tended to vary depending on whether the client had a regular private partner or not. Age also had some effect, but the most frequently recorded explanations applied across the age range (see Table 9.3).

Do these responses from 15 years ago have any relevance today? Comparisons are given with more recent accounts from brothel clients in Australia, which suggest that client attitudes and motivations have not changed.

'I do not want emotional involvement'

The most common reason for seeking commercial sex was the wish to avoid emotional involvement. It was as important to men with non-sex worker partners as it was to those without, and applied across the age range. The wish to separate sexual activity from emotions was expressed by some partnered clients as a strategy to protect their relationships. Some clients felt commercial sex did not count as 'being unfaithful' to the person they loved; others positively wished to avoid the emotional ties of any single relationship.

Got involved once with a woman and never again. Go to a working girl because of no involvement. My wife will never find out. (Client, 42, Birmingham 1988/9)

In a way, I think this helps my marriage. Sometimes my wife doesn't want to have sex. It could start an argument. But I come here, and that's it – we don't have an argument. (Client, 39, Australia 2002)

Cannot get any (wife in hospital). Do not want to be unfaithful to the wife as I love her. (Client, late 30s, Birmingham 1988/9)

Table 9.3 Reasons for seeking commercial sex, Birmingham Survey 1, 1988/9, n = 126*

	Partner	No partner	20s	30s	40s	50s	60s	All
No emotional involvement	42.0	46.0	37	50	41	48	33	44
No other sex partner**	7.0	85.0	37	23	45	56	78	42
Not enough sex at home	54.0	2.0	37	35	34	17	22	30
Other sexual services	39.0	9.0	29	20	41	17	22	26
Sex workers are experts	28.0	22.0	18	10	31	35	33	25
Shyness	7.0	39.0	11	17	20	26	55	21
No chat up	24.0	18.5	33	17	17	17	22	21
Like them!	18.0	22.0	7	6	24	26	55	19
Excitement	22.0	5.5	26	18	14	9	0	15
Sex boring with partner	22.0	0	18	12	14	9	0	12
In control	16.0	5.5	18	37	0	4	0	10
Alternative to masturbation	–	9.0	7	3	10	4	0	5
Loneliness/old age	–	5.5	0	0	0	0	55	4

*Values are percentages of each sub-group giving the reasons stated for seeking commercial sex. Partner/no partner refers to non-commercial partners.

**The 7% of men with a partner who gave this reason stated there was no sex within this relationship.

I've been married once and I don't want to do that again. I don't want to get involved in another relationship. (Client, 52, Australia 2002)

The attraction of sex detached from social interaction was also expressed by clients who used phrases like 'no chat up', 'guaranteed sex' and 'no strings' to describe the advantages. A third of men in their twenties used these terms, but they were less common among older men.

To relieve myself without the hassle and expense of chatting up a bird and not getting anything at the end of the night. (Client, 25, Birmingham 1988/9)

'No other sex partner' or 'Not enough sex with wife/girlfriend'

Absence of other sexual partners was the next most common reason, expressed mainly by unpartnered men, 85 per cent of whom gave this reason, but 7 per cent of partnered men said there was no sex within their relationships. It was mentioned least frequently by men in their thirties, most often by men in their sixties, 78 per cent of whom gave this reason. More than half of men with private partners cited insufficient sex in that relationship. It was twice as important to men aged 20 to 49 than to men in their fifties.

Enjoy the company. Too old to enter into a relationship, and no one at home to enjoy sex with. (Client, 68, Birmingham 1988/9)

My wife is deceased and I still have some sexual urges ... When my wife was alive, that was it for me. There were no other activities. (Client, 70, Australia, 2002)

No sex within marriage. (Client, 59, Birmingham 1988/9)

In the past six months I've been separated from my missus and I've only had sex three times ... If you don't have sex for a while you sort of blow up. (Client, 30, Australia, 2002)

Need to have sex sometimes. Wife thinks you stop it when you reach 40. (Client, 47, Birmingham 1988/9)

'Other services'; 'Excitement'; 'Sex boring with wife/girlfriend'

A quarter of all clients wanted sexual experiences, usually oral sex, which they could not get from other partners. It was much more common among clients with a private partner, (39 per cent), than unpartnered clients, only 9 per cent of whom felt there were specific sexual services unavailable from private partners, perhaps because no sexual service was readily available to these. Only partnered men cited boring sex in other relationships as a reason for paying. A quarter of all clients regarded sex workers as 'experts', with men over 40 finding it a more important factor than younger men.

> I like a blow job. Girlfriend says I'm a pervert and sex once or twice a week is okay. (Client, 28, Birmingham 1988/9)

> My wife won't do oral sex. She just reckons: 'Yuck!' I can see her point there. (Client, 44, Australia 2002)

> Because no strings attached and can ask for things without feeling embarrassed. Girlfriend is a bit shy to experiment sexually. (Client, 28, Birmingham, 1988/9)

> I've got a steady girlfriend at the moment … she's a bit nervous about it and won't do a lot of things … I would probably be suspicious if she was too eager or knew too much. (Client, 23, Australia, 2002)

> Gets a bit boring with the same woman in the same position year in and year out. (Client, 37, Birmingham, 1988/9)

Men with partners were also much more likely than those without to use phrases like 'excitement', 'a turn-on', 'feel the urge', 'bit of fun', but the older the client, the less likely they were to use these expressions. In the same vein 10 per cent of partnered men mentioned 'freedom of choice' or 'variety': no unpartnered man used these terms. The 'monotony of monogamy' expressed above affected younger men more strongly, declining in relative importance in the older age ranges.

Alternative to masturbation

While younger, partnered men might seek 'variety' and 'excitement', 9 per cent of unpartnered men expressed the need to escape from solitary sexual activity. None of those with a private partner gave this reason.

> If I'm sexually frustrated I can masturbate, it's no problem. But it's not all that much fun, is it? (Client, 26, Australia, 2002)

> Sick of doing it myself. (Client, 32, Birmingham, 1988/9)

'I like them!'

Nineteen per cent of all clients explained their choice of commercial sex simply in terms of liking sex workers and enjoying their company, not feeling shy, and being able to express their sexual needs without embarrassment. These reasons were progressively more important with age, mentioned by 7 per cent of men in their twenties, 24 per cent of men in their forties, and 63 per cent of men aged over 60, (p < 0.003).

> Enjoyment, satisfaction, fun, excitement, like them, and enjoy their company. (Client, 45, Birmingham, 1988/9)

> Enjoy their company, know them well, they are more like friends than pros. (Client, 59, Birmingham, 1988/9)

Sex workers experience some clients as emotionally demanding, and some client responses betray a depth of commitment to the client role which belies their common denials of emotional involvement. It is possible that the resilience of the demand for commercial sex is strengthened by clients' emotional involvement, even if this aspect is unacknowledged by them:

> He wanted more than he wanted to pay for. I personally think he just wanted my company – female company. (Sex worker, Birmingham 1992, describing a 29-year-old widower)[4]

> I try to see the same woman each time, mainly because I like her ... I reckon I must have been seeing her for about two and a half years. If she moved parlours, I'd follow her. (Client, 52, Australia, 2002)

> I don't need to use working girls and never have needed to, but it has become a habit over the last 12 years. (Client, 30, Birmingham, 1988/9)

It might sound crazy, but this is really the only place where I feel I can be a man, the way men are supposed to be, without feeling guilty or that I'm a social misfit. (Client, 36, Australia, 2002)

Shyness, loneliness and old age

Shyness was cited more frequently by men without a private partner, 39 per cent of whom gave this reason, compared to 7 per cent of men with partners (p < 0.0001). With increasing age, shyness was mentioned progressively frequently, by 11 per cent of men in their twenties, 20 per cent of men in their forties and 54 per cent of men over sixty. Five men in their sixties, 55.5 per cent of this age group, mentioned loneliness or 'too old to go courting', but none of the three men in the sample aged over 70 listed these reasons.

Control

In recent feminist literature, the assertion is made that clients are expressing a dominant masculine identity through gendered control of women (O'Connell-Davidson 1999). However, on the Birmingham Survey, only 10 per cent of clients said they paid for sex because they liked to be 'in control of the situation'. If this factor were associated with abusive behaviour towards sex workers – and this study gives no evidence for such an association – it might be important to note that it was more important to men with private partners (16 per cent) than those without (5.5 per cent), and to men in their twenties (18 per cent) and thirties (37 per cent), but of negligible importance to men over 40.

Conversely, eight men (6 per cent) stated that they wanted to be dominated or chastised by the sex worker (only three of them in social classes 1 or 2), although none offered the insight given by one of the Australian clients:

I'm not so much into being beaten or whipped or tied up, as wanting the woman to be the person who calls the shots ... to be honest, it can be a bit of a drag always having to be the one who seduces. Here ... she is dictating the terms. I am the one who is submissive and I have to do what the woman wants. (Client, 43, Australia, 2002)

Whatever observers imagine client motivations to be, the responses above indicate that clients themselves think their behaviour is largely about otherwise unmet sexual needs, which they are unable or unwilling to fulfil in emotionally significant relationships. Since sexual behaviour is notoriously difficult to change, the results suggest that the demand for commercial sex will persist, despite police enforcement and social disapproval.

Abusive behaviour by clients

So far it has been suggested that clients are, in one sex worker's phrase, 'just ordinary fellas'[5] whose capacity to detach sexual desire from emotion may be annoying or upsetting, but is hardly deviant or criminal. However, although it is important to stress that only a minority of interactions between sex workers and clients involve violence (McKeganey and Barnard 1996; Brooks-Gordon 1999), when one looks at sex workers' experience of violence in the course of their work (rather than violence in private relationships), client behaviour has to be reassessed.

It is argued in Chapter 6, 'Murder made easy', that the unprotected environment in which many commercial sex encounters take place is key to levels of violence, both from clients and from others. It is also possible that such attacks arise out of the client's shame and self-disgust with his own sexual behaviour, with transference of anger towards the sex worker who has allowed him to give in to urges he cannot accept in himself, and that some clients may be disinhibited from violence because they share common social attitudes that sex workers are worthless human beings, degraded women who deserve punishment. It is suggested that policies and public statements about sex work which reinforce a rhetoric of abhorrence and adopt strategies that rely on the shaming and humiliation of clients can only perpetuate some clients' aggression and sex workers' vulnerability.

Clients and the law

Under UK law at present, only clients who kerb-crawl[6] and those who purchase sex from under 18-year-olds are defined as offenders.[7] Calls to suppress street sex work by increased penalties against kerb-crawlers do not take into account the likelihood of clients being either caught or deterred by anti-kerbcrawler operations, nor the detrimental effects such operations have on sex workers and others.

Although kerb-crawling was not made an arrestable offence until 2001, it has been an offence in England and Wales since 1985. Since then, police have used various anti-kerbcrawler tactics, including verbal warnings, sending warning letters to clients' homes, summons to court and kerb-crawler rehabilitation programmes. In 1988, as the first Birmingham client survey was beginning, the local paper reported 'Success of blitz on vice'[8] in relation to the strategy of sending warning letters to clients' homes, with police claiming that none of the 80 men targeted had returned to the street soliciting area. However, by February 1989, when the Birmingham survey was completed, only 10 per cent of clients reported ever having been warned for kerb-crawling, and 15 years on, Birmingham police are still targeting kerb-crawlers and regularly announcing imminent success in their efforts to end street prostitution.

As in Birmingham in 1988, anti-kerbcrawling strategies are still regularly proclaimed as successes because, within a very short timescale, men caught by these different initiatives have not been apprehended for kerb-crawling again, and yet, to the frustration of police and residents in areas affected, kerb-crawling continues.

An illustration of the reasons why these 'successes' are in fact failures can be derived from the Middlesbrough report (Elliott *et al.* 2002), which states that over a six-month period, 60 kerb-crawlers had been arrested, and that 140 street workers had been identified in the area.

Assuming the ratio of clients to sex workers were no higher than 28 to one, the total kerb-crawler population would be 3,920, so if the Middlesbrough police arrested 120 over the course of a year, they would still have caught only 3 per cent of the total, and even these would be highly motivated to take evasive action to avoid 'coming to notice' a second time.

In 1991, a further 17 clients were interviewed in Birmingham,[9] of whom three had been warned or prosecuted for kerb-crawling. Only one stated that this experience had changed his behaviour, saying 'one has to be more careful in one's movements'. This survey also asked what clients would do if 'future police action were to stop you meeting working girls in your usual way?' None said they would stop paying for sex; 12 (70 per cent) said they would make contact in other ways or go to other towns.[10] One, a client of private indoor workers, commented: 'I do not think my mode of meeting them could be stopped so have not considered an alternative.'

Conclusion

This chapter has attempted to demonstrate that efforts to reduce the abuses of the sex industry, or even to eliminate the sex industry itself, by increasing the criminalisation of clients, will not only fail, but will increase levels of abuse and violence.

Estimates of the numbers of clients, based on the numbers of sex workers and the amount of business they do, indicate that at least 11 per cent of the adult male population pays for sex fairly regularly. The level of resources that would be required to police the behaviour of such a large proportion of the population is unthinkable. Police and allied agencies tasked with apprehending and monitoring violent sex offenders are already overstretched. To require them to chase after more than 2 million men who pay other consenting adults for sexual acts which would be legal if no money changed hands is absurd.

The vast majority of those who pay for sex are ordinary men, a cross-section of society, usually employed, law-abiding citizens. Clients' own accounts of why they pay for sex may have important implications for relationship counsellors but should have no relevance to the criminal justice system.

Clients who kerb-crawl cause nuisance in residential areas used by street workers, but it has been shown that both anti-kerbcrawling and anti-soliciting enforcement strategies are ineffective in that, if there is any impact at all, the problem is usually displaced to surrounding neighbourhoods or other towns. These strategies are also dangerous for sex workers, as they increase their vulnerability to violence, and may even provoke it, by provoking client anger and by legitimising attitudes of hostility towards sex workers.

Most clients are not violent, but current legislation and policy facilitates the actions of those who are: further criminalisation of clients will only make matters worse.

Notes

1 Section 71 of the Criminal Justice and Police Act 2001.
2 MP's message to vice girls, Yvette Page, *Luton Herald and Post*, 5 September 1991.
3 This and subsequent quotes come from Jacquelynne Bailey (2002) 'I don't come here for the conversation', *The Guardian*, 8 April 2002.
4 This sex worker kept a log of her clients for 16 days to assist a TV documentary-maker.

5   Campbell *et al.* (1996).
6   Kerb-crawling is not an offence in Scotland at the time of writing.
7   The latter offence came into law in May 2004, so it is too early to say how many clients will be affected by it.
8   *Birmingham Evening Mail*, 29 April 1988.
9   This was an attempt to repeat the Client Survey of 1988/9, but other project commitments prevented its completion.
10 The remainder either did not respond to the question or did not know what they would do.

References

Agustín, L. M. (2001) 'Sex workers and violence against women: utopic visions or battle of the sexes?', *Development*, 44 (3): 107–10.

Barnard, M. A., McKeganey, N. P. and Leyland, A. H. (1993) 'Risk behaviours among male clients of female prostitutes', *British Medical Journal*, 307: 7.8.

Brewer, D. D., Potterat, J. J. and Garrett, S. G. *et al.* (2000) 'Prostitution and the sex discrepancy in reported number of sex partners', *Proceedings of National Academy of Science*, USA, 97: 12385–8.

Brooks-Gordon, B. (1999) *The Criminal Careers of Kerb-Crawlers*. Paper presented to the National Police Vice Conference, June.

Brooks-Gordon, B. and Gelsthorpe, L. (2003b) 'What men say when apprehended for kerb crawling: a model of prostitutes clients' talk', in *Psychology, Crime and Law*, 9 (2): 145–71.

Brooks-Gordon, B. and Gelsthorpe, L. (2003a) 'Prostitutes' clients, Ken Livingstone and a new Trojan Horse', *Howard Journal*, 42 (5): 437–51.

Campbell, R., Coleman, S. and Torkington, P. (1996) *Street Prostitution in Inner City Liverpool: Abercromby Prostitution Project*, R. Liverpool Hope University College.

Day, S., Ward, H. and Perrotta, L. (1993) 'Prostitution and HIV: male partners of female prostitutes', *British Medical Journal*, 307: 359–61.

Elliott, K., Eland, H. and McGaw, J. (2002), *Kerb Crawling in Middlesbrough.* Safer Middlesbrough Partnership, Prostitution Task Group.

Faugier, J. and Cranfield, S. (1995) 'Reaching male clients of female prostitutes: the challenge for HIV prevention', *AIDS Care*, 7 (1).

Home Office (2004) *Paying the Price: A Consultation Paper on Prostitution.* Home Office, Communications Directorate.

Johnson, A. M., Mercer, C. H,. Erens, B., Copas, A. J., McManus, S., Wellings, K., Fenton, K. A., Korovessis, C., Macdowall, W., Nanchahal, K., Purdon, S. and Field, J. (2001) Sexual behaviour in Britain: partnerships, practices, and HIV risk behaviours', *Lancet*, 358: 1835–42.

Kinnell, H. (1989) *Prostitutes, Their Clients, and Risks of HIV Transmission in Birmingham*, Occasional Paper. Department of Public Health Medicine, Central Birmingham Health Authority.

Kinnell, H. (1990a) 'Risky business: prostitutes, clients and HIV in Birmingham', in *AIDS Dialogue*, Health Education Authority, No. 4.

Kinnell, H. (1990b) 'Prostitutes and their clients in Birmingham: action research to measure and reduce risks of HIV', in *The AIDS Letter*, Royal Society of Medicine, No. 19.

Kinnell, H. (1993) *'Wolverhampton Sex Workers Survey Report'*. Unpublished paper, SAFE Project.

Kinnell, H. and Griffiths, R. K. (1989) *Male Clients of Female Prostitutes in Birmingham, England: A Bridge for Transmission of HIV?* Poster presented at the 5th International Conference on AIDS, June (published in abstract book, ISBN 0-662-56670-X).

Lammi-Taskula, J. and Jyrkinen, M. (1995) *Clients of Prostitution in Finland.* Habitus Study.

McKeganey, N. and Barnard, M. (1996) *Sex Work on the Streets*. Buckingham: Open University Press.

McLeod, E. (1982) *Women Working: Prostitution Now*. London: Croom Helm.

Matthews, R. (1986) *Policing Prostitution: A Multi-Agency Approach*. Centre for Criminology, Middlesex Polytechnic.

May, T., Edmunds, M. and Hough, M. (1999) *Street Business: The Links between Sex and Drug Markets*, Home Office Police Research Series Paper 118. London: Home Office.

May, T., Harocopos, A. and Hough, M. (2000) *For Love or Money; Pimps and the Management of Sex Work*, Home Office Police Research Series Paper 134. London: Home Office.

Morgan Thomas, R., Plant, M. A., Plant, M. L. and Sales, J. (1990) 'Risk of HIV infection among clients of the sex industry in Scotland', *British Medical Journal*, 301.

O'Connell-Davidson, J. (1999) *Prostitution, Power and Freedom*, University of Michigan Press.

O'Neill, M. and Campbell, R. (2001) *Working Together to Create Change: Walsall Prostitution Consultation Research, Final Report*. Walsall South Health Action Zone/Staffordshire Univeristy/Liverpool Hope.

Research Centre on Violence, Abuse and Gender Relations (2000) *Kerb Crawler Re-Education Programme*. Leeds Metropolitan University, for the West Yorkshire Police Authority.

Shell, Y. Campbell, P. and Caren, I. (2001) *It's Not a Game: A Report on Hampshire Constabulary's Anti-Kerb Crawling Initiative*, Hampshire Constabulary.

Wellings, K., Johnson, A. M. and Wadsworth, J. (1994) *Sexual Behaviour in Britain: The National Survey of Sexual Attitudes and Lifestyles*. Penguin Books.

Whittaker, D. and Hart, G. (1996) 'Research note: managing risks: the social organization of indoor sex work', *Sociology of Health and Illness*, 18.

Chapter 10

Support services for women working in the sex industry

Jane Pitcher[1]

Introduction

The number of support services available to sex workers has grown substantially since the mid-to-late 1980s (Campbell *et al.* 1995). Early support projects were funded largely by health authorities as part of broader HIV prevention policies and were primarily commissioned to focus on HIV prevention, sexual health and harm minimisation (McKeganey and Barnard 1996; Ward and Day 1997; O'Neill and Campbell 2001). By the mid-1990s, a wide range of projects had been established in the UK, with an increasing range of funders (EUROPAP 1994).[2] This was accompanied by a broadening of focus in many cases beyond sexual health issues, although this continues to be a prominent focus for many projects, and primary care trusts remain important funders for many targeted sex worker services.

It is now generally recognised that agencies and projects providing support to sex workers must work holistically in order to take into account the diversity of experience and needs of those working in the sex industry (O'Neill 1997; AHRTAG 1997; Ward and Day 1997; UKNSWP 2004; Hester and Westmarland 2004). Projects may work with street sex workers, indoor workers, migrant or indigenous UK sex workers and female or male sex workers, and needs may differ according to each group, as well as being specific to individuals (UKNSWP 2004).

This chapter aims to explore some of the main issues experienced by female sex workers in the UK and the services offered by support projects. The discussion on service provision is set in the context of recent policy responses and some of the major theoretical positions concerning sex work and support services. Some general principles on effective practice in service provision are also outlined, drawing on the experience of individual projects and the literature on services to sex workers.

Support needs of sex workers: working with diversity

Sex workers may experience a number of support needs at different times during their working lives. Research studies have identified a number of issues that may be faced by female sex workers, particularly those working on the street (McKeganey and Barnard 1996; O'Neill 1997; Campbell 1995; May *et al.* 2000; Cusick *et al.* 2003; Pearce *et al.* 2002; Pitcher and Aris 2003). These include:

- violence (including early experience of domestic violence and also during their working lives, particularly for street sex workers);
- problematic drug and/or alcohol use (particularly street sex workers);
- periods of homelessness, often as a result of increasing debt and/ or drug dependency;
- low self-esteem;
- harassment from police and communities;
- experience of the criminal justice system; and
- negative experiences of accessing statutory services.

Young girls involved in sex work may also experience a number of additional 'vulnerability indicators', such as having been in local authority care, or with a background of sexual or physical abuse (Pearce *et al.* 2002; Cusick *et al.* 2003). There is also evidence that some young women become involved in the sex trade through pressure from partners or other coercive influences in their lives and that they may then be kept in the industry through dependence, for example on partners/pimps or drug dealers (May *et al.* 2000; Pearce *et al.* 2002; Cusick *et al.* 2003).

Although some of the factors outlined above may be experienced by many sex workers, this does not imply a necessary connection or causal link between any of these factors and entry into sex work, and this continues to be a matter of some dispute (Cusick *et al.* 2003). It is important not to generalise: as with members of any other profession, sex workers are a diverse group and have entered the sex industry for a range of reasons (McKeganey and Barnard 1996; O'Neill 1997). For example, the situation for women working indoors is very different from that regarding those working on the street and many women working in saunas, massage parlours, flats or independently would consider themselves to be working in the sex industry through choice (Sanders 2004a, 2004b). Some sex workers are not affected by the issues raised above and it should also not be assumed that all sex workers will want to access services. Nonetheless, these factors are clearly issues that are of relevance to support services.

As well as acknowledging relative choice, it is important also to be aware that not all indoor sex workers have entered the sex industry of their own volition, particularly those who have been trafficked (Kelly and Regan 2000). The extent to which this may be the case and in which locations is still relatively unknown and projects can play a vital role in monitoring the involvement of migrant workers in their local sex industry and the extent to which there are exploitative practices relating to migrant people. Projects are also in a position to offer confidential, non-judgmental advice and support to those being exploited (Campbell, Van Nooijen and Young 2002).

Different perspectives on sex work influencing public policy and provision

While the main focus of this chapter is on project provision, it is important to consider some of the theoretical positions and policy stances concerning sex work, as these may determine the extent to which support is given, or the type of support commissioned and offered to sex workers.

The main theoretical debates on sex work have tended to focus on women and their position in the sex industry. At one extreme, there is the 'abolitionist perspective' propounded by a particular section of feminists, which argues that all prostitution is non-consensual and an embodiment of oppressive patriarchal relations (for example, Farley 2004; also discussed in O'Connell Davidson 1998; Sanders 2004b). For many embracing this stance, the term 'sex worker' is unacceptable, because it denies the power inequalities between men and women. This position has been challenged by many of those working in the sex industry and by other writers, who argue that such a stance represents women as passive victims and denies them a sense of agency (Scambler and Scambler 1997; Mathieu 2003). Many of those who oppose the abolitionist perspective also recognise that, while some sex workers may enter the sex industry of their own volition, many women and men arrive where they are through a combination of factors. For women working in street locations in particular, some of those factors, such as coercion at an early age, increasing drug dependency and severe economic conditions, mean that choice is a relative matter (McKeganey and Barnard 1996; O'Neill 1997). For the majority of sex workers, economic necessity plays a large part in the reasons for working in the sex industry (Scambler and Scambler 1997).

Some writers have expressed concerns that the use of the term 'sex work' fails to recognise some of the factors that differentiate this from other forms of economic activity, such as vulnerability to exploitation and severe economic need which leads many into sex work (Weatherall and Priestley 2001) and it is important to acknowledge that the sale of sex is markedly different from other occupations, particularly in terms of the stigma attached (Sanders 2004b). Arguably, some of the factors which separate sex work from other forms of mainstream economic activity might be addressed through organisation within the industry and decriminalisation, as Kesler (2002) discusses.

The dominant discourses in recent years have tended to present sex workers either as passive victims or moral deviants and these are reflected in public policy and may frame the views of many professionals who come into contact with sex workers (Kantola and Squires 2004; Wahab 2003). In some instances, such views may influence support provision for sex workers, for example through limiting services only to those who wish to leave the sex industry, whereas many women who wish to remain may also have social and other needs (Sloan and Wahab 2000).

Policy responses to sex work

In order to set the work of projects in context, it is useful to consider some of the main policy responses to sex work in the UK.

While responses have sometimes differed across the country, the police role is primarily that of enforcing the law (May *et al.* 2000). In some cases, this has focused on periodic crackdowns, primarily on street sex work, in response to complaints from local communities (Hubbard 1997; Hester and Westmarland 2004; Penfold *et al.* 2004). In recent years, a more punitive approach has been taken in some areas, including the issuing of Anti-Social Behaviour Orders (ASBOs) and a 'zero tolerance' approach, particularly to outdoor sex working (Home Office 2004; Sanders 2004a). Traditional enforcement has been found to lead to geographical dispersal and also potentially reduced safety for those who continue working on the street (Campbell and Storr 2001; Hubbard and Sanders 2003; Pitcher and Aris 2003). In some instances, this has been accompanied by action from some members of local residents' groups attempting to drive out prostitution from their area, which has increased the vulnerability of street sex workers and also limited the extent to which projects can provide support (Hubbard and Sanders 2003; Sanders 2004a).

Increasingly, there has been an emphasis on a multi-agency approach to the enforcement of law (Hester and Westmarland 2004). While some local partnerships and prostitution forums include residents' representatives, some do not include representation from sex workers or support projects and is has been queried whether such approaches can be described as truly 'multi-agency' if they are not incorporating the voices of the women themselves (O'Neill 1997). The recent Home Office consultation paper *Paying the Price* (Home Office 2004) omits specific reference to the inclusion of working women or their representatives as part of local communities in decision-making processes.

Some of the recent policy debate has focused primarily on the most vulnerable groups of sex workers, particularly women working on the street and younger women, or adult women who started selling sex when they were under 18 (Home Office 2004). The needs of male sex workers and women working indoors (apart from those who are perceived as being coerced into the sex industry, for example through trafficking) have been largely ignored in this debate (Soothill and Sanders 2004; UKNSWP 2004). It has also been noted that the 'sex work discourse', which acknowledges free will, appears to be absent from many strategies concerning prostitution (Kantola and Squires 2004).

At a local level, there are examples of good working relationships between projects representing sex workers, local police and other agencies in some cities (see, for example, Campbell and Hancock 1998; Pitcher and Aris 2003; Haringey Council 2004; Penfold *et al.* 2004). In recognition that punitive responses simply serve to reinforce vulnerability and leave sex workers with little option but to continue working within the industry to support themselves, some multi-agency responses have started to consider alternative modes of provision involving sex work projects (for example, Manchester Prostitution Forum 2004). This has also been accompanied in certain cases by the development of positive relationships with local communities, which has had an impact on perceptions and behaviour.

shifting forms

Development of support projects

The primary focus of the earlier projects in the 1980s was on sexual health, HIV/AIDS prevention and harm minimisation. This was shaped by the fact that the main funding available at that time for sex worker support was from HIV prevention monies, due to concerns about the increase in HIV and AIDS, with sex worker populations among others being perceived as a 'public health risk' (Campbell *et al.* 1995; McKeganey and Barnard 1996). In contrast, many within projects and some researchers and sex worker activists pointed to the fact that the majority of sex workers were keen to practise and promote safer sex where possible (EUROPAP 1998; Campbell 2002). The philosophy of harm minimisation and a client-centred approach arising from health promotion and counselling practice has been central to much project delivery, although this sometimes sits at odds with the expectations of funders and policy-makers.

More recently, the focus of funding has been around problematic drug use, with street sex workers in particular identified as an 'at risk' group (May *et al.* 1999; Sondhi *et al.* 2002). Drug and Alcohol Action Teams (DAATs) in a number of areas now contribute funding and support to sex worker services. In 2004, the Home Office published non-statutory good practice guidance to DAATs and other authorities regarding commissioning and delivery of services to address problematic drug use among sex workers and young people being sexually exploited (Hunter and May 2004).

Although early activities focused particularly on sexual health and HIV prevention, projects found that sex workers required a number of other different services (Campbell 2004a). Many expanded their services to accommodate the diverse needs of clients, including welfare, safety, legal and housing support and advice. Constraints on funding, however, have often limited the services projects have been able to offer (Ward and Day 1997; UKNSWP 2004).

Twenty years on, the majority of projects aim to provide a range of services for their client group, linking in with other agencies as appropriate. Service provision in different areas is still variable and shaped by local needs, available funding, commissioning regimes and priorities. Increasingly, however, projects are commissioned to provide holistic services (Campbell 2004).

proįcet provides

Project activities: focus and delivery mechanisms

A number of projects have been established in local areas across the UK where sex work is known to take place, run by a variety of organisations, including voluntary sector groups, NHS Primary Care Trusts, drug services, local authorities and youth services. Support and advice are provided in relation to issues such as sexual health, violence, housing, law and the criminal justice system, education and training and related issues.

The type of services offered by projects differs according to their funding sources and also the organisational philosophy. Organisations tend to provide separate services for men and women sex workers, although some work with both men and women (for example, Streetreach 2003). Some projects focus specifically on young people (Pearce *et al.* 2002; Pitcher 2002b; Hester and Westmarland 2004). Some projects are commissioned to work with both outdoor and indoor workers, whereas others may concentrate on one group. Certain projects have a focus on particular groups: for example, one project in London works specifically with migrant workers and those who have been trafficked (Poppy Project 2004). Some support services are run by or employ staff who have worked in the sex industry (Campbell 2004a). Some projects may have a particular religious ethos and thus the type of support it is possible to offer will be influenced by the parameters of that religion (for example, some religious organisations may not permit the distribution of condoms or other forms of contraception).

Alternatives to conventional services and advocacy role of projects

Many of the services have arisen as a response to under-use of conventional services by sex workers, who are perceived as a 'hard to reach' group by many mainstream agencies. Workers in the sex industry may often not access health, drugs and social care services because of fear of discrimination if they reveal details of their lifestyle (Faugier and Cranfield 1994; Hunter and May 2004). In many cases, this fear has been justified, as sex workers have experienced judgmental attitudes from staff in many mainstream agencies (EUROPAP 1998; Brighton Oasis Project 2003; Campbell *et al.* 1995; Aris and Pitcher 2004). Indoor workers potentially face similar stigmatisation from agencies as that experienced by outdoor workers if they disclose their livelihood (Campbell *et al.* 2002; Sanders 2004b). Thus, projects

241

have worked to provide specially tailored services, or have acted as advocates for sex workers when engaging with other organisations. It is important that support services are perceived to be detached from mainstream services, even if they receive their main funding from these services (Ward and Day 1997; Pitcher and Aris 2003).

Sexual health support and advice

Despite the common perception of sex workers being a risk to public health, the majority of studies suggest relatively low rates of sexually transmitted infections (STIs) among sex working populations in the UK compared with other groups (for example, McKeganey and Barnard 1996; Ward and Day 1997; Ward *et al*. 2004). This could be attributed to the work of early support projects or to the care exercised by sex workers themselves, or a combination of the two. Nonetheless, there is seen to be a need to provide continued support, in the form of distribution of condoms and sometimes injecting equipment, facilitating health checks, distributing safer sex and drugs literature and taking other preventive action, such as encouraging Hepatitis B vaccinations, particularly as new sex workers may be less conscious of the risks (EUROPAP 1998; UKNSWP 2004). The UKNSWP (2004) argue that sexual health promotion and services are still critical, in recognition of two key issues: a range of factors inhibiting sex workers' access to mainstream sexual health services, such as fear of discrimination by health professionals and lack of knowledge about free and confidential services (particularly affecting migrant sex workers) and enduring pressures on some sex workers to maximise earnings, such as problematic drug use, pressure from coercers and the need to pay off debts or fines that may lessen resistance to offers of extra money to practise unsafe sex.

A number of projects provide targeted clinical sexual health services specifically for sex workers, such as community-based genito-urinary medicine (GUM), some within sex worker service drop-in buildings and at least one within a mobile facility, and contraceptive clinics or hospital-based clinics specifically for sex workers. Such provision enables sex workers to access a full range of sexual health information screening, advice and treatment (Ward and Day 1997; Bradford 2002; UKNSWP 2004).

In areas where they are commissioned, sexual health outreach services can be an important source of support for indoor workers (Ayres 1999; Galatowicz *et al*. 2005).

General health, welfare and legal advice

In addition to specific sexual health services, projects may give information or support on a range of other general health issues, for example advice on basic nutrition, fitness, basic first aid and health outreach staffed by nursing professionals (Campbell 2004a; Hester and Westmarland 2004). In some towns and cities a proportion of street sex workers may not have a GP and thus liaison with and referral to other health services, such as pregnancy advice services, may be an important aspect of project work.

Sex workers, particularly those working on the street who tend to be more vulnerable to arrest, are likely to require a range of other welfare and legal advice services. For example, debt, rent arrears, benefits advice and childcare needs are all issues that have been raised with services (Campbell *et al.* 1995; Pitcher and Aris 2003; Campbell 2004a). The need for legal advice has also been identified by projects working with sex workers in indoor locations (Galatowicz *et al.* 2005).

Drug and alcohol treatment and prevention services

The links between drug use and sex work, particularly for on-street workers, have been established in many studies (May *et al.* 1999; Campbell 2002; Pitcher and Aris 2003; Hester and Westmarland 2004). Concerns have been expressed over the increasing association between street sex work and use of crack cocaine, either replacing or in addition to heroin, leading to greater risk-taking and/or increased working hours (May *et al.* 1999, 2001). Drug dependency is seen to keep women in sex work and presents barriers to exiting (West Yorkshire Police 2000; Williamson and Folaron 2003; Surratt *et al.* 2004).

There are substantial differences between the needs of indoor and outdoor sex workers when considering drug and alcohol use and services. Indoor sex workers tend to be less likely than those working outdoors to be drug dependent. Working in an indoor environment requires a degree of organisation and the willingness for women to work long shifts, which can be difficult for some with problematic drug use. Many indoor employers have strict regulations about drug use, for example not permitting drug use on the premises, or not employing women who use drugs (May *et al.* 2000; Sanders 2004b; Soothill and Sanders 2004). Thus the mutual reinforcement of drug use and sex work is absent from many indoor environments (Cusick *et al.* 2003).

243

Women who are drug users may face particular barriers that restrict their access to drug treatment, including violence from clients, negative experiences of treatment services or workers, or peer pressure, for example from partners (Sondhi *et al.* 2002). Illicit drug use, as well as sex work itself, also conflicts powerfully with the traditional images of women as mothers, carers and wives, and being a drug user often makes women more culpable in the eyes of society and the law (Chan and Rigakos 2002). The expectation of disapproval and fear that their children may be taken into care can be strong disincentives to coming forward for treatment (Becker and Duffy 2002; Department of Health 2002; Pitcher and Aris 2003).

Greater accessibility to drug treatment is seen as essential towards stabilisation and services need to be available when women need them, otherwise they may disappear from services 'into chaos' (Hester and Westmarland 2004). While the picture is variable, in some areas if a sex worker wishes to be referred into drugs services there can be a considerable delay until a first assessment appointment can be secured. Aftercare and follow-up for clients who 'drop out' is also important (Hunter and May 2004).

Many support projects now provide information and advice in relation to drug and alcohol use, facilitate referral to treatment services and work closely with those services. Some have their own arrest referral or court diversion schemes, discussed in greater detail below. Certain projects offering outreach also have arrangements for specialist workers from other agencies to accompany project staff and volunteers on outreach sessions (for example, Aris and Pitcher 2004). A small number of projects now offer their own community-based 'in-house' drug treatment services, some with low threshold prescribing and maintenance services, specifically for their female sex-working clients (Campbell 2004a; Hunter and May 2004).

Violence and safety

There is considerable evidence that sex workers are at risk of violence from a range of sources, including clients, pimps/managers, drug dealers and sometimes local residents in areas of street sex work (Campbell and Storr 2001; Pearce *et al.* 2002; Pitcher and Aris 2003; Sanders 2004b). While there is evidence of violence experienced by sex workers in both indoor and outdoor settings, those working on the street are most at risk (Kinnell 2002). The exposure to violence is exacerbated when drug use is involved (May *et al.* 1999; Penfold *et al.* 2004; Surratt *et al.* 2004). It is acknowledged that further research is needed into indoor sex work and the experience of violence (Raphael and Shapiro 2004).

Some police responses give emphasis to women's safety, but many sex workers are reluctant to approach the police about violent incidents because of fear of not being taken seriously or being penalised because of their status (Campbell and Kinnell 2001). For many women the process of reporting a violent incident and following it through to its conclusion is a daunting one and often one of the most important reasons for low rates of reporting. Developing policing approaches and other interventions to address the safety of sex workers is seen to be paramount (Campbell and Storr 2001).

In response to concerns about violence, many projects have developed 'dodgy punters' or 'ugly mugs' sheets that give descriptions of violent or potentially violent customers who have been reported to the project by sex workers. These are distributed to clients working both in- and outdoors. In some cases, where projects have good links to the police, such information is used by the police to build up intelligence on violent offenders (Campbell 2002; Aris and Pitcher 2004; Penfold *et al.* 2004).

Housing and homelessness

Housing tends to be a pressing need for the majority of street sex workers and a large proportion have experienced homelessness (Stewart 2000; Campbell 2002; Aris and Pitcher 2004; Hunter and May 2004; Shelter 2004). Sex workers, particularly those who use drugs, also face particular barriers to accessing social housing because of the restrictions on entry placed by many agencies (Shelter 2004). Some hostels will not take in clients immediately after leaving prison (Campbell 2004a), which has implications for many street sex workers.

Homelessness heightens women's vulnerability to exploitation and violence and is seen to be a major destabilising factor for women in street sex work (UKNSWP 2004). It is also a barrier to accessing many services, including health, drugs and GP services, social security benefits and education or training.

Some projects have responded to this need by liaising with housing providers to facilitate referrals, accompanying clients to appointments and providing information to sex workers. Some have developed specific agreements with housing providers to provide accommodation for clients (Campbell 2004a; Poppy Project 2004; Shelter 2004). Many sex work projects, however, continue to identify serious gaps in appropriate housing for clients, including 'crisis' accommodation, supported housing for those accessing drug treatment or attempting to stabilise their use and supported housing for women trying to leave sex work (UKNSWP 2004; Campbell 2004b).

Arrest referral and court diversion schemes

In response to the situation whereby women arrested for offences related to prostitution are then forced back on the street to pay the fines imposed, an increasing number of projects are now providing arrest referral or court diversion schemes, in liaison with criminal justice and other agencies (Home Office 2004). For example, in Manchester and Coventry, women arrested for loitering or soliciting are bailed to appear in court on specific days when workers from support projects are in attendance (Davies and Pitcher 2004). The women are then given the option of engaging with the project (with a minimum number of appointments) and sometimes referral on to partner agencies in place of a fine. Offering a number of services to women in place of punitive law enforcement starts to address some of the problems faced, particularly for women working on the street. Hunter and May (2004) note the necessity for links with specialist support services in order to ensure the effectiveness of arrest referral schemes.

It is important to recognise that any changes to the lifestyle of clients will be a longer-term process. In an evaluation of an arrest referral scheme in London, it was noted that projects targeting sex workers who are an 'especially hard to reach group' need a longer period of time to bed in and win the trust of their client group (May *et al.* 2001).

One of the key gaps in provision for sex workers, particularly street workers who are more vulnerable to arrest, is when they are serving a prison sentence or on leaving prison. The need for aftercare on release from custody as well as at other points in the criminal justice system is an issue that has been noted, for example by Hunter and May (2004). Where projects can link in with criminal justice agencies, there is a possibility for integrated provision to support sex workers who have been through the system, and some projects now undertake regular prison visits. Housing is a particular problem facing many sex workers leaving prison.

Mediation activities and work with local communities

One of the issues confronting projects is the need to deal with community concerns about the impact of sex working in their neighbourhood, such as discarded needles and condoms and unacceptable levels of noise and nuisance. More recently, some projects have been gradually building links with local communities, particularly in areas where street sex work takes place. Community liaison and mediation[3] allows for a more community-focused approach and can also lead to perceptions of reduced problems and an atmosphere of greater tolerance and understanding (Aris and Pitcher 2004; Hester and Westmarland 2004; Home Office 2004). Support services also need to be aware of the need to facilitate safe and appropriate disposal of injecting equipment and condoms, which will help to address some of the major concerns of local communities (Home Office 2004).

Exiting support and strategies

Many projects offer support to women and men wishing to move out of sex work alongside broader support and harm minimisation work (Bradford 2002; Campbell 2002), and some have exiting as their main focus (for example, Routes Out in Glasgow). While some sex workers may wish to and be ready to change their lifestyle, there are also many who do not want to move on, yet who may still need other support for problematic factors in their lives. Many projects offer a more holistic service, with support for exiting being one of several interventions available, depending on what clients actually want at particular times (Campbell 2004a).

Many people working in the sex industry may feel that they have no alternative, because other occupations do not offer comparable economic benefits. Some have moved from low-paid jobs or undertake work in the sex industry to supplement low incomes (O'Neill 1997). Some sex workers, particularly those working outdoors, have relatively few qualifications and thus the alternative options available to them may be limited (Hester and Westmarland 2004; Galatowicz et al. 2005). Projects can support them in developing additional skills. Take-up of different options provided by projects will depend on the type of support women are seeking at that time and the extent to which they are ready to enter structured training (Hester and Westmarland 2004). Williamson and Folaron (2003) argue that agencies working with sex workers should identify their lifestyle phase in order to target interventions.

Entering and leaving sex work may not be single directions taken: many sex workers will move out of sex work during their life, but re-enter at particular times because of changes in circumstance (Hunter and May 2004). Some women may only work at certain times during the year when they need additional income. Projects need to support women at different stages in their lifestyle.

Other provision and delivery methods

Most projects working with sex workers offer a range of other services, including practical support such as provision of food and soft drinks, personal alarms, counselling, referral to other agencies, accompaniment to appointments and other general help (Pitcher and Aris 2003; Campbell 2004a). As well as skills and employment-related training, many projects also offer other training to sex workers around issues such as safety and self-defence (Blackwood and Williams 1999; Campbell 2004a).

Outreach, both on the streets and to indoor venues, is commonly undertaken by projects and is generally seen as one of the most important aspects of provision. In some cases, workers in mainstream agencies now undertake outreach with support projects, helping to provide a more integrated service (Aris and Pitcher 2004).

Many projects also offer a drop-in, which may sometimes be at premises outside the main street beat, or sometimes within the beat itself. In some cases, the drop-in may have specific services available through links with other agencies; in others it may be a more general space in which sex workers can just come to relax, make use of facilities and network with others in similar circumstances, in a 'non-judgemental environment' (Campbell 2004a). For some workers who are homeless, the opportunity to get food and have a space to wash is invaluable and some organisations that provide general services for homeless people will also welcome sex workers.

One-to-one access and support and individual case work are also crucial services provided by the majority of projects (Campbell 2004a). Having 'someone to talk to' is seen as a particularly important aspect of project provision (Hester and Westmarland 2004: 97).

Effectiveness and good practice principles for project delivery

There has in recent years been a substantial amount of literature considering effective practice in relation to project services. This has often grown out of service evaluations or wider research projects. It is only recently that the UK government has attempted to identify effective practice regarding drug treatment and other support for adult street sex workers (Hester and Westmarland 2004; Hunter and May 2004).

A number of international, European and national networks of practitioners have also worked to identify good practice in service delivery. For example, a European Union-funded network, EUROPAP (European Intervention Project AIDS Prevention for Prostitutes) was developed to provide good practice on sexual health promotion among sex workers and has produced a number of good practice guidance documents (EUROPAP 1998; EUROPAP 2003).

In 2002, the United Kingdom Network of Sex Work Projects (UKNSWP) was formed, developing from a previous network of agencies in the UK providing health and other services to sex workers (EUROPAP UK). The UKNSWP is an independent voluntary-sector body, which now has a membership of more than 60 projects in the UK (UKNSWP 2004). Member organisations include the main projects for sex workers in most towns and cities with a visible sex industry and those where it is less visible (for example, areas without a major street scene). Member projects cover a diverse range of provision.

The UKNSWP has facilitated discussions between members and helped to develop good practice guidelines for projects. These have emerged from debates around project practice and a substantial body of research evidence. There are thus certain principles that need to be considered in project development. The main considerations in relation to effective practice are discussed below.

User-focused and flexible services

Projects should aim to be client-focused and responsive to sex workers' needs, ideally undertaking some form of needs assessment or encouraging user feedback on a regular basis, in order that their services reflect current need. User involvement in planning and delivery of services is also an essential component of good project practice (O'Neill and Campbell 2001). In addition to regular consultation, this might include peer education and support, ensuring that sex workers are present on advisory or steering groups and offering appropriate support to facilitate their input. Internationally, there are many sex worker-led services, including SCOT-PEP in the UK.

A non-judgmental approach on the part of staff and volunteers in support projects is also vital to ensure engagement of sex workers (Brighton Oasis Project 2003; Campbell 2004a). This includes supporting the choices of individuals: for example, respecting the decisions of sex workers wishing to move on and also those who prefer to remain within the sex industry.

Many street sex workers in particular may experience difficulty in keeping appointments while they are working on the street because of competing priorities in their lives (Hester and Westmarland 2004). Services should therefore be as accessible and flexible as possible: an 'open-door' approach has been identified as essential in providing the kind of flexible services required (Pearce *et al*. 2002).

Provision of a safe space

Having a safe and supportive space to visit regularly is important to many sex workers. This might be an outreach van, where sex workers can visit in the knowledge that they will not encounter harassment from others (Sanders 2004b). Many projects have a drop-in, which might be available for informal meetings, appointments with specialists or project staff, or simply somewhere sociable where sex workers can just 'be themselves'.

Outreach services

National current good-practice guidance stresses the importance of community-based outreach with sex workers (Hester and Westmarland 2004). The Home Office guidance on drug problems and street sex markets (Hunter and May 2004) advises that outreach should be an integral part of drug service provision for street sex workers. Outreach is identified as a means of contacting a potentially 'hard-to-reach' group and offering a range of on-the-spot help, including harm minimisation, advice and information, condoms, needle exchange, information about drug treatment, sexual health and other services. It also offers an opportunity for health and other professionals to understand the working conditions of women clients and to tailor services to the needs of sex workers (EUROPAP 2003).

Holistic approaches

An integrated or holistic service is generally considered to be optimum in supporting sex workers. This can take a range of forms. For example, projects can themselves provide a wide variety of services, including ones that meet basic needs such as food, personal hygiene, childcare, etc. through to more specialised provision such as drug treatment, housing and sexual health services. Many projects are not resourced to undertake the full range of services, or may wish to focus on certain issues and thus may work in partnership with other organisations.

Many sex workers visiting services do not wish to be categorised merely as 'sex worker', 'drug user' or other labels, but wish to be seen as individuals (Ward and Day 1997; Pitcher and Aris 2003). There is evidence that a focus on one particular issue, such as drug prevention or exiting, will deter some potential clients of support projects (Ward and Day 1997; National AIDS Manual 1993).

One of the most important issues is that projects and agencies should recognise and respect the diversity of service users and their support needs. Similarly, some venues may not be appropriate for some clients (for example, Ward and Day 1997, cite examples of some women being averse to going to a 'drop-in' because of their fear of being categorised as one of a group of prostitutes). Thus it is important that while services take a holistic approach, they also offer a range of flexible provision, including outreach, drop-in services and also one-to-one support (Hester and Westmarland 2004).

Increasingly, projects in some of the larger cities are now working with migrant sex workers. This requires a range of additional provision and skills for staff, including language skills (Ayres 2005).

Working in partnership

Building links with other agencies and services is also necessary for projects in order to raise awareness among staff in those agencies and to provide an integrated service (Aris and Pitcher 2004). These could include police, probation, other criminal justice agencies, housing providers, social services, health services and other public or voluntary services that sex workers might encounter during their working lives.

Projects are not able to cater for all necessities and thus are likely to need to refer sex workers on to other agencies for support. Building close links with these organisations and sometimes undertaking an advocacy role, particularly in the initial stages of contact for the individual, are also important components of support (Hunter and May 2004).

Having a working partnership which includes not only projects and agencies but also members of local communities can help to increase information and intelligence-gathering to address issues such as violence against sex workers (Hester and Westmarland 2004). Through taking on some form of mediation role between local communities and sex workers, projects can also help to reduce tension in local areas.

Information-sharing

Information-sharing can also be a positive development: for example, projects can help to provide evidence of violent clients to the police through supporting sex workers who report incidents and passing on information. Specialist services to sex workers can be invaluable when linking with police, for example in supplying information on men exploiting young people and helping to secure convictions against coercive and violent pimps (May *et al*. 2000; Streetreach 2003). Project and agency support, counselling and encouragement for witnesses is also essential.

Client confidentiality and preservation of anonymity has been identified as a key component of project support (EUROPAP 2003). It is important, therefore, that confidentiality is maintained as far as possible, although there will also be times when this has to be balanced against issues of health and safety of clients (EUROPAP 1998). As projects and other agencies work more closely together and share information, data-sharing protocols should be established between projects and partner agencies and projects need to ensure that they have the agreement of clients before they disclose information relating to them.[4]

Staff training and support

In addition to the training of staff in external agencies and education and training courses for clients, project staff and volunteers themselves also need ongoing support, training and supervision (Pearce *et al*. 2002). For example, sexual health and drugs awareness courses and updates on legislative and policy changes are all vital to ensure staff are fully informed in their work. The UK Network of Sex Work Projects now provide training in a range of issues, such as crack awareness, sexual health, safety and other areas (UKNSWP 2003).

Harm reduction

The philosophy of harm minimisation and a client-centred approach have tended to inform the culture of many projects (O'Neill and Campbell 2001). Projects and supporting agencies need to be realistic in their expectations and not expect that change will happen within a short time. For some sex workers with a number of serious issues to contend with, moving into a situation where they feel more in control of their lives may take a year or more. Some women may not want to move out of sex work and a user-focused approach needs to acknowledge such diversity (Campbell 2004a). Among other services, therefore, it is important that projects provide harm reduction materials and advice, for example in relation to safer sex or drug and alcohol use (Hunter and May 2004).

Monitoring of project provision

In order to assess the effectiveness of projects, it is important for projects themselves to monitor activities and ensure regular feedback, as well as considering wider evaluation to examine project processes as well as outcomes (Hunter and May 2004).

Projects need to be realistic in their aims and monitor a range of factors. For example, given that individual change may take place very slowly in some cases, it is important that incremental stages in personal development are considered. These might include steps such as return visits to the project and attendance at appointments, which in another setting might be considered minor developments, but in the context of working with vulnerable groups can be major milestones (Pitcher 2002a).

Barriers and challenges to provision

The majority of projects work closely with other agencies in their locality, although some projects, particularly in their early stages, have encountered limited support from mainstream agencies. Many have attempted to address this through training agency staff in order to build awareness of their services and also the issues affecting sex workers (UKNSWP 2003; Aris and Pitcher 2004; Campbell 2004a). Many sex workers have had negative experiences of agencies in the past, where they have often encountered judgmental attitudes if they divulge details of their work. Thus projects have a significant role in challenging attitudes of agency staff towards sex workers, as well as addressing the suspicion of those agencies held by many of their clients.

Projects need to deliver awareness and/or training activities to agencies on an ongoing basis because of staff changes. Although projects may have links with one branch of an organisation, this does not necessarily mean that another section of the same organisation will also be aware of the project's activities. For example, police in one sector covering the main street sex work beat may have protocols with a project, but if the beat moves or sex workers are picked up in another area, police in that sector may not know about the project or agreements with other parts of the organisation (Galatowicz *et al.* 2005).

One of the key issues for projects is the difficulty of delivering services in a context of criminalisation, which is more strictly enforced in some areas than others. While this has an impact on street workers in particular, within the existing legal framework there is also a constant threat of criminalisation for owners and managers of indoor premises, as well as stigma for sex workers (Campbell *et al.* 2002). The current enforcement and legislative framework creates a difficult climate in which to contact sex workers and deliver services and enforcement can directly disrupt service provision, particularly for street sex workers (Campbell 2004a; UKNSWP 2004; Galatowicz *et al.* 2005).

Not all sex workers will engage with projects, or may be initially cautious, and projects need to consider how non-engagement should be handled. For example, if some sex workers referred through court diversion schemes are reluctant to engage with support projects this may result in a more punitive approach by criminal justice agencies to those sex workers. Clearly parameters need to be agreed to ensure that the same person is not referred on several occasions without engaging, but consideration might be given to reassessing the situation should that person be arrested in future, to ascertain whether she might be more amenable to engagement. Projects have also sometimes encountered problems when a sex worker *does* engage with them but is still rearrested on the street (Davies and Pitcher 2004). Protocols need to set in place realistic timescales for individual development: lifestyle changes will take a significant amount of time and in the interim, while individuals are receiving support from services, changes to behaviour and situation may be relatively imperceptible.

Some projects, particularly those working with street sex workers, have encountered opposition from members of local communities (Hubbard and Sanders 2003). While some have been able to address concerns through undertaking the mediation role discussed above, in certain cases residents have responded very negatively to project activities. In some more extreme instances, residents have perceived sex work projects as contributing to the problem and encouraging sex work in their area and have actively set out to oppose the work of support projects. In some local areas, residents have taken their own direct action against both sex workers and support projects and this has also tended to determine official responses to street sex work (Sanders 2004a). This can obviously make it much more difficult for projects to deliver services within a multi-agency framework. This raises the question of the extent to which community action can be considered a positive development, if it is constraining the activities of others in the locality and creating an environment which prohibits the delivery of services to groups who are particularly vulnerable and in need of support from those services.

One of the results of continued enforcement by police and organised residents' groups to address street sex work in local areas is likely to be displacement to other areas (Gordon-Thomas 2004; Clark *et al.* 2004). As well as dispersing street sex work to other communities, who may then experience problems from the nuisance associated with sex work that projects have attempted to reduce in other areas, the other potential impact is that projects will then lose touch with their clients, who have once again isolated themselves from services in an attempt to protect themselves from harassment. This can put heavy demands on projects if they have to start anew in building up relationships with local communities, agencies and sex workers and can be severely detrimental to service delivery.

In order to deliver services to meet local needs, some have been reliant on volunteers to a lesser or greater extent. Encouraging volunteers to participate in services is a positive aspect of project provision, particularly if they are from the local communities in which the project is delivered. There are also implications for ongoing training and support of volunteers and it has to be borne in mind that many volunteers also have other commitments and thus may have to prioritise these at times. Volunteer turnover can sometimes be a serious problem, creating barriers to service continuity. It is thus important that projects do not become over-dependent on volunteers, but build their engagement around the activities of more permanent, paid staff.

One of the main barriers to expanding provision and continuity of delivery has been the limited resources available to projects, particularly those in the voluntary sector. Campbell (2004a) reported that operating in a climate of short-term and often inadequate funding was one of the key challenges identified by sex work projects. The short-term nature of much funding available to projects can lead to difficulties in recruiting and retaining paid staff. The nature of funding available may also limit the kinds of services that can be provided if there are particular conditions set on type of provision. Project delivery has to link in with the priorities or focus of funders, but this can present problems, for example when national priorities and concerns change, which can hamper forward planning. In some instances, lack of sustained funding may lead to project closures even when there is an identified need for services. This has serious implications for project clients, who may find themselves suddenly without the support they have been led to expect over a number of years (Pitcher 2002a). There is currently no statutory obligation for local authorities to provide funding for targeted sex worker support services (Campbell 2004a).

Conclusions

This chapter has outlined the range of project provision, the body of knowledge concerning effective practice and the difficulties of providing services in a culture of short-term funding and policy changes.

The importance of independent projects delivering holistic and user-focused services to sex workers has been recognised in much of the good practice guidance emerging in recent years.

A user-focused approach has tended to inform much project provision, but it is also important that services continue to seek feedback in order to reflect the needs of their client group. Ideally, sex workers should be involved at all stages in project development and implementation.

Flexibility in service delivery and provision of a range of services in order to meet different requirements continue to be vital elements of project provision and where possible these principles should extend to mainstream agency provision for sex workers.

The need for a multi-agency approach to tackling some of the problems faced by many women sex workers, particularly those working on the street, has also been acknowledged in much of the policy literature. Many projects work in partnership with other agencies in order to facilitate referrals and also provide training to those agencies. In some areas formal court diversion schemes have been established and these are recognised as an effective means of breaking the cycle of fining and reoffending faced by many women working on the street. Such schemes are relatively new, however, and their effectiveness needs to be monitored over a longer period.

3 For example, communicating community concerns to sex workers and working with local communities to develop understanding of the issues faced by street sex workers.
4 Obviously child protection legislation may have a bearing on the need to disclose, but it is still good practice to ensure that clients are informed of each step if projects have to release certain information.

References

AHRTAG (1997) *Making Sex Work Safe*. Network of Sex Worker Projects.

Aris, R. and Pitcher, J. (2004) *Evaluation of Coventry SWISH Arrest Referral Scheme for Sex Workers: Final Report*. London: Terrence Higgins Trust.

Ayres, L. (1999) *Results of Needs Assessment of Women Sex Workers in South Cheshire*. Crewe: South Cheshire Drug Service.

Ayres, J. (2005) *Developing Services for Migrant Sex Workers*. Presentation to UKNSWP conference 'Working with Diversity in Sex Work', Liverpool 25 February.

Becker, J. and Duffy, C. (2002) *Women Drug Users and Drugs Service Provision: Service Level Responses to Engagement and Retention*, DPAS Briefing Paper 17. London: Home Office.

Blackwood, S. and Williams, K. (1999) *Assess Your Weapons: Client-led Self-defence Training with Women Sex Workers 1994–1999*. Southampton: Resistance/South West Health Alliance.

Bradford, M. (2002) *Developing Exit Strategies for Female Outdoor Sex Workers in Barnet, Enfield and Haringey*. Sexual Health on Call (SHOC).

Brighton Oasis Project (2003) *Evaluation of Outreach to Sex Work Establishments*. Brighton: Brighton Oasis Sex Workers Outreach Project.

Campbell, R. (2002) *Linx Project Development, Service Provision and Evaluation*. Liverpool Hope University/Nacro.

Campbell, R. (2004a) *Celebrating the Work of Sex Work Projects*. Paper presented at Manchester Prostitution Forum Conference, Manchester 14 October.

Campbell, R. (2004b) *Housing Needs of Street Sex Workers: National Issues and Some Responses*. Presentation at 'Beat the Streets', Society of St James, Southampton 20 April.

Campbell, R. and Hancock, L. (1998) *Sex Work in the Climate of Zero Tolerance: Hearing Loud Voices and the Silence of Dissent*. Paper presented at 'Sex Work Reassessed', University of East London, 9 September.

Campbell, R. and Kinnell, H. (2001) 'We shouldn't have to put up with this: street sex work and violence', *Criminal Justice Matters*, 42 (Winter): 12.

Campbell, R. and Storr, M. (2001) 'Challenging the kerb crawler rehabilitation programme', *Feminist Review*, 67 (1): 94–108.

Campbell, R., Coleman, S. and Torkington, P. (1995) *Street Prostitution in Inner City Liverpool*. Liverpool City Council/Liverpool Hope.

Campbell, R., Van Nooijen, L. and Young, C. (2002) *Sexual Health Promotion with Parlour Sex Workers: The Enduring Impact of Criminalisation and Stigma on Access to Sex Health Care*. Paper presented at 'Sex Work and Health in a Changing Europe', EUROPAP Conference 18–20 January, Milton Keynes.

Chan, W. and Rigakos, G. S. (2002) 'Risk, crime and gender', *British Journal of Criminology*, 42 (4): 743–61.

Clark, P., Bellis, M., Cook, P. and Tocque, K. (2004) *Consultation on a Managed Zone for Sex Trade Workers in Liverpool: Executive Summary*. Liverpool John Moores University.

Cusick, L., Martin, A. and May, T. (2003) *Vulnerability and Involvement in Drug Use and Sex Work*, Home Office Research Study 268. London: Home Office.

Davies, J. and Pitcher, J. (2004) *Criminal Justice and Sex Workers*. Workshop presentation delivered at Manchester Prostitution Forum Conference, Manchester 14 October.

Department of Health (2002) *Models of Care for Substance Misuse Treatment: Promoting Quality, Efficiency and Effectiveness in Drug Misuse Treatment Services*, full report for consultation. London: DoH.

EUROPAP (1994) *Final Report: European Intervention Projects AIDS Prevention for Prostitutes*. Ghent, Belgium: Department of Public Health.

EUROPAP (1998) *Hustling for Health: Developing Services for Sex Workers in Europe*. EUROPAP, Imperial College, London.

EUROPAP (2003) *Practical Guidelines for Delivering Health Services to Sex Workers*. EUROPAP, European Commission DVG.

Farley, M. (2004) '"Bad for the body, bad for the heart": prostitution harms women even if legalized or decriminalized', *Violence Against Women*, 10 (10): 1087–125.

Faugier, J. and Cranfield, S. (1994) *Making the Connection: Health Care Needs of Drug Using Prostitutes: Information Pack*. School of Nursing, University of Manchester.

Galatowicz, L., Pitcher, J. and Woolley, A. (2005) *Report of the Community-led Research Project Focusing on Drug and Alcohol Use of Women Sex Workers and Access to Services*. Coventry: SWISH, for University of Central Lancashire and Department of Health.

Gordon-Thomas, R. (2004) *Edinburgh Zone and the ASBO Experience*. Paper presented at the Manchester Prostitution Forum conference, Manchester 14 October.

Haringey Council (2004) *Review of Street Prostitution*. Crime & Community Safety Scrutiny Panel.

Hester, M. and Westmarland, N. (2004) *Tackling Street Prostitution: Towards a Holistic Approach*, Home Office Research Study 279. London: HMSO.

Home Office (2004) *Paying the Price: A Consultation Paper on Prostitution*. London: HMSO.

Hubbard, P. (1997) 'Red-light districts and toleration zones: geographies of female street prostitution in England and Wales', *Area*, 29: 129–40.

Hubbard, P. and Sanders, T. (2003) 'Making space for sex work', *International Journal of Urban and Regional Research*, 27: 75–89.

Hunter, G. and May, T. (2004) *Solutions and Strategies: Drug Problems and Street Sex Markets. Guidance for Partnerships and Providers*. London: Home Office.

Kantola, J. and Squires, J. (2004) 'Discourses surrounding prostitution policies in the UK', *European Journal of Women's Studies*, 11 (1): 77–101 (regarding contrast between sex worker as 'public nuisance' v. 'innocent victim').

Kelly, L. and Regan, L. (2000) *Stopping Traffic: Exploring the Extent of, and Responses to, Trafficking in Women for Sexual Exploitation in the UK*, Police Research Series Paper 125. London: HMSO.

Kesler, K. (2002) 'Is a feminist stance in support of prostitution possible? An exploration of current trends', *Sexualities*, 5 (2): 219–35.

Kinnell, H. (2002) *Tackling Violence in Sex Work*. Paper presented at: 'What Future Sex Workers? Reducing the Impact on the Community Through a Multi-Agency Approach', 28 May, Barbican Centre, Silk Street.

McKeganey, N. and Barnard, M. (1996) *Sex Work on the Streets: Prostitutes and Their Clients*. Buckingham: Open University Press.

Manchester Prostitution Forum (2004) *Manchester Actions on Prostitution: MAP Working Document*, Key Recommendations, July 2004–July 2007.

Mathieu, L. (2003) 'The emergence and uncertain outcomes of prostitutes' social movements', *European Journal of Women's Studies*, 10 (1): 29–50.

May, T., Edmunds, M. and Hough, M. (1999) *Street Business: The Links between Sex and Drug Markets*, Police Research Series Paper 118. London: Home Office, PRCU.

May, T., Harocopos, A. and Hough, M. (2000) *For Love or Money: Pimps and the Management of Sex Work*, Police Research Series Paper 134. London: HMSO.

May, T., Harocopos, A. and Turnbull, P. J. (2001) *Selling Sex in the City: An Evaluation of a Targeted Arrest Referral Scheme for Sex Workers in Kings Cross*. London: South Bank University.

Morgan-Thomas, R. (2004) *SCOT-PEP: The Edinburgh Zone and ASBO Experience*. Paper presented at the Manchester Prostitution Forum Conference 14 October.

O'Connell Davidson, J. (1998) *Prostitution, Power and Freedom*. London: Polity Press.

O'Neill, M. (1997) 'Prostitute women now', in G. Scambler and A. Scambler (eds), *Rethinking Prostitution: Purchasing Sex in the 1990s*. London: Routledge.

O'Neill, M. and Campbell, R. (2001) *Working Together to Create Change: Walsall Prostitution Consultation Research*. Walsall: Staffordshire University/Liverpool Hope University/Walsall Health Authority.

Pearce, J. with Williams, M. and Galvin, C. (2002) *'It's Someone Taking a Part of You': A Study of Young Women and Sexual Exploitation*. London: National Children's Bureau for Joseph Rowntree Foundation.

Penfold, C., Hunter, G., Campbell, R. and Barham, L. (2004) 'Tackling client violence in female street prostitution: inter-agency working between outreach agencies and the police', *Policing and Society*, 14 (4): 365–79.

Pitcher, J. (2002a) 'Policies and programmes to address disadvantage among young people: issues for evaluation', *Evaluation*, 8 (4): 474–95.

Pitcher, J. (2002b) *Community Safety Regeneration 4 Birmingham: The First Three Years*. Community Safety Regeneration 4 Birmingham/Advantage West Midlands/Nacro.

Pitcher, J. and Aris, R. (2003) *Women and Street Sex Work: Issues Arising from an Evaluation of an Arrest Referral Scheme*. London: Nacro Research Briefing.

Poppy Project (2004) *Poppy Project Newsletter*, Issue 1. London: Eaves Housing.

Raphael, J. and Shapiro, D. L. (2004) 'Violence in indoor and outdoor prostitution venues', *Violence Against Women*, 10 (2): 126–39.

Sanders, T. (2004a) 'The risks of street prostitution: punters, police and protesters', *Urban Studies*, 41 (9): 1703–17.

Sanders, T. (2004b) *Sex Work: A Risky Business*. Cullompton: Willan Publishing.

Scambler, G. and Scambler, A. (eds) (1997) *Rethinking Prostitution: Purchasing Sex in the 1990s*. London: Routledge.

'Services for sex workers', in *National Aids Manual* (1993).

Shelter (2004) *Off the Streets: Tackling Homelessness among Female Sex Workers*, Review summary. London: Shelter.

Sloan, L. and Wahab, S. (2000) 'Feminist voices on sex work: implications for social work', *Affilia*, 15 (4): 457–79.

Sondhi, J., O'Shea, J. and Williams, T. (2002) *Arrest Referral: Emerging Findings from the National Monitoring and Evaluation Programme*, DPAS Paper 18. London: Home Office.

Soothill, K. and Sanders, T. (2004) 'Calling the tune? Some observations on *Paying the Price: A Consultation Paper on Prostitution*', *Journal of Forensic Psychiatry and Psychology*, 15 (4): 642–59.

Stewart, A. (2000) *Where is She Tonight? Women, Street Prostitution and Homelessness in Glasgow*, Base 75/Rough Sleepers Initiative, Glasgow.

Streetreach (2003) *Annual report, April 2002 – March 2003*. Doncaster: Streetreach.

Surratt, H. L., Inciardi, J. A., Kurtz, S. P. and Kiley, M. C. (2004) 'Sex work and drug use in a subculture of violence', *Crime and Delinquency*, 50 (1): 43–59.

United Kingdom Network of Sex Work Projects (2003) *1st Annual Report, June 2002 to November 2003*. Manchester: UKNSWP.

United Kingdom Network of Sex Work Projects (2004) *Response to 'Paying the Price' (Home Office Consultation Document)*. Manchester: UKNSWP.

Wahab, S. (2003) 'Creating knowledge collaboratively with female sex workers: insights from a qualitative, feminist and participatory study', *Qualitative Inquiry*, 9 (4): 625–42.

Some sex work support projects now provide a form of mediation between local communities and sex workers, particularly those working on the street, and this is seen as a vital role for future project development. The effectiveness of such a policy, however, is dependent on the cooperation and support of Crime and Disorder and other strategic partnerships. The inclusion of support projects and sex workers themselves in strategic partnerships focusing on sex work has not always been considered, but should be seen as an essential feature of strategy development in relation to sex work at both national and local levels.

One of the major barriers to project provision has been lack of sustained funding, leading to limited services in some cases or closure of projects in more extreme instances. Funding remains one of the key challenges for projects and sustainability of services to sex workers is an issue for policy consideration.

Increased use of enforcement can present major difficulties for projects in providing services and accessing clients. Continued dialogue between policy-makers and sex worker support services is thus essential if some of the recent national policy guidance is to be implemented effectively at a local level.

Finally, it is important to note that much of the literature on support services to women working in the sex industry relates to women working on the street, partly because of the greater likelihood that they will experience a multiplicity of issues during their working lives. In order to develop good practice guidance for services to women working indoors, further exploration of the support needs of indoor workers may be required.

Notes

1   This paper draws on examples of good practice from a number of sources. It also reflects personal experience of particular projects and recent research into project practice. Reference is made to a number of initiatives, based on available individual evaluation reports and recent UK guidance on project practice (including Campbell 2004; Hester and Westmarland 2004; and Hunter and May 2004). It should be noted that many other projects may not publicly document their activities yet may also be working to recognised principles of effective practice.
2   EUROPAP identified 81 projects working with prostitutes in the UK in 1994, of which 59 per cent were funded by local health authorities.

Ward, H. and Day, S. (1997) 'Health care and regulation: new perspectives', in G. Scambler and A. Scambler (eds), *Rethinking Prostitution: Purchasing Sex in the 1990s*. London: Routledge.

Ward, H., Day, S., Green, A., Cooper, K. and Weber, J. (2004) 'Declining prevalence of STI in the London sex industry 1985 to 2002', *Sex Transm Infect*, 80: 374–6.

West Yorkshire Police (2000) *The Kerb Crawlers Rehabilitation Programme: An Evaluation from the Police Perspective*. Leeds: West Yorkshire Police.

Weatherall, A. and Priestley, A. (2001) 'A feminist discourse analysis of sex "work"', *Feminism and Psychology*, 11 (3): 323–40.

Williamson, C. and Folaron, G. (2003) 'Understanding the experience of street-level prostitutes', *Qualitative Social Work*, 2 (3): 271–87.

Chapter 11

Sex workers in the Labour Movement

Ana Lopes

Introduction

This chapter outlines the foundation and development of the International Union of Sex Workers (IUSW). The first section retraces the development of this sex worker activist organisation from a small and local coalition to an international rights group well established within the international movement for sex workers' rights.

Recognition of sex workers' rights to form and join official unions has always been a prominent demand of the IUSW. The second section of this chapter outlines the process by which a small grass-roots organisation became an official branch of the GMB union, a major general workers' union in the UK.

Founding the organisation

My PhD research was based on an anthropological study of the sex industry. I started by conducting pilot interviews with sex workers from different sectors of the industry. Analysis of these interviews revealed that my interviewees had made an informed decision to work in the industry and did not find anything inherently exploitative or immoral in the work they did per se. However, they experienced exploitation and felt a lack of a platform from which to address problems faced in the course of their work. They also felt that the public had a distorted view of what their work really was about.

It's not great, but I like it. I'm not sleazy. Yes, I think we need an organisation to say that. (Sex worker)

I have also entered the sex industry myself, by taking a part-time job as an adult chatline operator. My experience has been similar to those expressed by my interviewees. I had no complaints about the work itself, but I felt the need to keep the true nature of my job a secret from many people – either because I feared their stigmatisation, or because I feared for my personal safety.[1]

Furthermore, and perhaps more importantly, not knowing any other similar company and being new in the industry I feared I was being taken advantage of by my manager. Were the working conditions I was offered acceptable or standard practice? Was my pay within the legal requirements? Where could I be informed?

My initial research into campaigning groups within the sex industry introduced me to the English Collective of Prostitutes (ECP). The ECP emerged in 1975 and set up a legal service where female sex workers engaged in prostitution can access advice about the law, the courts and the police.

However, in my field research it soon became apparent that my interviewees did not feel that the ECP responded to their needs. On the one hand the ECP only represented female sex workers, while my interviewees included male and female sex workers from several different sectors of the industry. And on the other hand, those interviewees who had come across the ECP in the past were disillusioned with the group and objected to their abolitionist stance.

Thus, encouraged by friends and supporters of the sex workers' rights cause, I called a meeting in February 2000, which was attended by sex workers and some supporters – members of the campaigning group Sexual Freedom Coalition, academics and students who supported sex workers' rights activism. At this first meeting, participants agreed to form an organisation to campaign for sex workers' rights. At a following meeting we agreed to organise an action in Soho on International Women's Day 2000.

The Soho March

The Wages for Housewives Campaign in conjunction with the ECP called a global women's strike on International Women's Day 2000. Similarly, the ECP called a strike of sex workers operating from Soho,

London's most famous red light district, over attempts by the local authorities to remove sex work from the area.

This was an opportunity to show our support for those sex workers going on strike. Furthermore, we wanted to add a carnival atmosphere to the event. A students' samba band was invited and an evening parade through the streets of Soho took place. The small group of organisers, under the name of the International Union of Sex Workers (IUSW) took to the streets in flamboyant costumes, accompanied by drummers, members of the Sexual Freedom Coalition and students.

Leaflets about the new group, prostitution laws and the sex workers' strike were distributed as members of the public joined the parade. The event also saw the first outing of the banner that became famous and seen in numerous other demonstrations – the International Union of Sex Workers' banner, with its picture of exotic dancers standing in line in a defiant attitude, and the slogan 'Sex Workers of the World Unite!'

The success of the event and the media attention it generated encouraged the group to meet regularly and formalise the organisation. At this stage I rearranged my PhD research proposal, and my project became an Action Research Investigation. I set myself not only to understand a situation but also to act on it – helping to found and develop the International Union of Sex Workers. My role would be that of a researcher/observer but also that of activist.

My PhD project has consisted of an action research project and, contrary to most orthodox ethnographic research, my role as researcher was not that of an expert who studies a certain situation but that of a resource, a participant who acts as a catalyst, who stimulates change – in this case a person who spearheaded a group of sex workers to unionise.

My experience as researcher and activist within the sex workers' rights movement has led me to reject efforts to separate the researcher from the activist. Such separation is not only arguably impossible to achieve but may actually be detrimental to the research and the activist outcomes sought. In fact, retaining both an academic and an activist persona has enabled me to diminish the gap between action and theory.

There is an urgent need to investigate sex worker organisations in order to improve the efficacy of sex worker activism and advocacy and enhance our struggle for sex workers' rights. Such investigation should mainly be done by sex worker activists with self-reflecting and analytical skills, since social researchers with no personal involvement in the industry are likely to miss those points which are of most relevance to sex worker activists ourselves.

Very little research exists in the field of sex worker activism. Jennes (1993) offers a good in-depth look at COYOTE, a sex worker organisation often cited as the pioneer of the western sex worker movement. However, Jennes' work was written several years after the foundation of the organisation and Jennes is neither a sex worker nor a sex worker activist.

Although sex worker activists themselves have seldom shared their knowledge and expertise in this field, their voices have been represented in essays edited by authors such as Nagle (1997) and Kempadoo and Doezema (1998). Nevertheless more self-reflection within the movement is needed.

Developing the International Union of Sex Workers

The name International Union of Sex Workers emerged in a discussion with a co-founder of the organisation. It had been agreed in the first meeting that the group's main aim would be to establish sex work as legitimate work. Thus we called ourselves a union – an association of workers in a particular industry. The word international came from our perception that the industry has gone global and therefore a successful mobilisation of workers should overcome national borders too. And finally we chose the term sex workers as a general term that includes all those who work in all the various sectors of the industry.

During the first months of the organisation's existence our actions focused on recruiting new members, working on a manifesto type of document (our list of demands) and developing a publication that would voice our demands and work as a networking tool for sex workers. Our list of demands has since been distributed in leaflets at several events and reads as follows:

We demand:
- Decriminalisation of all aspects of sex work involving consenting adults.
- The right to form and join professional associations or unions.
- The right to work on the same basis as other independent contractors and employers and to receive the same benefits as other self-employed or contracted workers.

- No taxation without such rights and representation.
- Zero tolerance of coercion, violence, sexual abuse, child labour, rape and racism.
- Legal support for sex workers who want to sue those who exploit their labour.
- The right to travel across national boundaries and obtain work permits wherever we live.
- Clean and safe places to work.
- The right to choose whether to work on our own or co-operatively with other sex workers.
- The absolute right to say no.
- Access to training – our jobs require very special skills and professional standards.
- Access to health clinics where we do not feel stigmatised.
- Re-training programmes for sex workers who want to leave the industry.
- An end to social attitudes which stigmatise those who are or have been sex workers.

The magazine *Respect!*

The first issue of the union's magazine was published in July 2000. One of the co-founders of the association was responsible for the invention of its title *Respect!* – Rights and Equality for Sex Professionals and Employees in Connected Trades.

This first issue argues why sex workers should unionise.

> Yes it is a profession – I believe a perfectly respectable profession, and should be viewed as such in the same way as a teacher, accountant or anyone else. I believe that the first step is to obtain recognition for sex workers as legitimate workers in a legitimate industry and profession. The first move is to form a union and then press for the same rights as other workers enjoy. (Rona 2000: 4)

Writing and publishing this issue has helped us establish some important links. Two members of the group have travelled to Amsterdam in order to learn about the legal situation in Holland – which was at that time about to change – and to meet fellow sex worker activists. We have since been in contact with Dutch organisations like the Red Thread and the Prostitution Information Centre.

Participating and reporting on the May day demonstration that took place in London in May 2000 made us reflect on issues of pride and ways to break up the stigma attached to sex workers. We wrote:

> Carnival dancers display their sexual signals in their own terms, in solidarity rather than in competition. They do not feel isolated or marginalized, but proud of their sexuality and empowered by its collective display. Sexy carnival parades help to break down the division between good girls/bad girls. (*Respect!* 2000: 8)

The publication of *Respect!* has also encouraged participation of members and sex workers in renewed activism. The editorial team is an open and equalitarian sub-group of the organisation. It is a fluid team where members can choose to be more or less active, according to their time availability, resources, skills and will to contribute.

Celebration and pride

From its inception the IUSW has marked a presence in several demonstrations and parades. Our participation signals support for the events or causes they represent and also that we are not ashamed of ourselves. Our banner has been present in events such as Gay Pride, anti-war demonstrations and International Women's Day marches.

Often sex workers, either members or supporters of the union, have expressed their solidarity with a certain demonstration but turned down our invitation to join us on the day. This is understandable, since being seen in public carrying the union's banner may identify them as sex workers, something they may want to keep secret from family, friends and others. This problem has been dealt with by other sex worker organisations (in the UK and worldwide) by both sex workers and non-sex worker participants wearing masks.

This has never been a practice encouraged by the IUSW since it reinforces feelings of shame among activists. Emphasising pride, we work on the basis that empowered sex workers will not need masks. According to an international sex workers rights advocate, the movement has moved on from the mask-wearing stage:

There was a big thing in the old days that you had to wear a mask. You don't really have to anymore. But, so the idea of a mask ball, a masquerade was essentially, at that time, because you couldn't go public. Now a lot of people go public without masks. So there are some differences. (Sex workers' rights advocate)

Those of us who are empowered enough to do so, plus our supporters who are not sex workers, march without shame in the events the IUSW has participated in. To symbolise our identity and that we are not ashamed of what we are, we have used feather boas in public demonstrations. Non-sex worker supporters have also worn them in solidarity. Note that there is a symbolism at play here – the feather boa is used as a symbol of sex work because this is an accessory that our Western culture associates with the sex or glamour industry. There is in our culture a 'stronger' symbol – the fishnet stocking – however, there is more visibility in colourful feather boas worn around demonstrators' necks.

Being widely seen in such events, as well as being noted by the mainstream and alternative media covering them, has increased the visibility of the union. This in turn has increased awareness in the sex worker population of the union's existence and thus increased the number of members in the union.

I think it has been great at attracting attention to the existence of the union – to make people think 'sex worker' and 'union' in the same sentence – and to let sex workers know we exist – the wide publicity you get is an amazing way to disseminate this simple announcement – there is a sex workers' union. (Union member)

By representing sex workers in such events as anti-war demonstrations, marches and protests, the IUSW has also given a voice to sex workers in issues other than those that most directly concern us. Our participation has shown that, like any other group of citizens, sex workers have a position on wide and general issues, such as the morality (or lack of) of waging a war against Afghanistan or Iraq.

Fundraising parties

Funding has always been a limitation to the IUSW growth and activities. The organisation is mainly funded by members' donations. However, several fundraising parties have been organised. Advertised as 'Sex Workers' Parties', they were open to the general public too. We intended to create a sex worker-friendly environment, where sex workers feel celebrated and honoured. Simultaneously, we hoped to educate the general public and to provide them with an opportunity to socialise with workers in the sex industry. We realise that often, negative social attitudes stem from ignorance.

Helping to organise a party has been an accessible way in which members – especially new members – are able to participate in the life of the organisation. By giving members responsibility over certain tasks we intended to encourage sex workers' and other members' sense of ownership of the organisation and the event being organised.

Defining policy

In July 2000 the Green Party contacted the Sexual Freedom Coalition (SFC) and requested their recommendations on policies relating to prostitution. We were in turn invited by the SFC to help write and present such recommendations. Dr Tuppy Owens, coordinator of the SFC, and myself researched the document and in the process interviewed several sex workers and solicitors. The recommendations document became the basis for the IUSW policy. It covers issues such as the legislation on prostitution, trafficking and pornography, and it is displayed at the IUSW's web page (www.iusw.org).

After the document was written, we presented our recommendations to a group of Green Party delegates. Our team consisted of the document authors, a sex worker, a member of the SFC, an academic member of the IUSW and a women's rights activist. The Green Party has since accepted our recommendations.

Open forum

In an attempt to confirm that the founding of the union, its policies and immediate plans were in accordance with other sex workers' and sex workers' allies' wishes, an open meeting was called by the

IUSW. The event took place on 13 September 2000 in Conway Hall, London.

The invitation states that the aim of the meeting, entitled 'Organising in the Sex Industry', was to 'informally debate which directions the IUSW should take'. The meeting was attended by around 30 people from several backgrounds: individual sex workers, sex work project workers and international sex work activists. All participants welcomed the initiative of founding a union for sex workers and possible future plans were discussed, including gaining recognition from the TUC (Trades Union Congress), liaising with local sex work projects through the UK Network of Sex Work Projects (UKNSWP) represented at the meeting by Hilary Kinnell and liaising with the international sex workers' umbrella organisation, the Network of Sex Work Projects (NSWP), which was represented at the meeting by Cheryl Overs and Jo Doezema.

The IUSW has maintained close links to these two umbrella organisations – one national and the other international – and has a place in both organisations' directive boards. This has ensured that the IUSW is integrated in the wider international movement for sex workers' rights – we keep abreast of the realities of sex workers' lives and sex workers' activism internationally.

Nationally, our relation to the network of service providing agencies has been crucial, as the network has proved to be a great ally of sex workers in our fight for rights. Furthermore, service providers and outreach workers are in regular contact with a large number of sex workers. Their work entails the establishment of a trusting relationship, which is used to pass on information about health, HIV/AIDS and STI prevention, violence against sex workers, as well as information about local and regional changes in policy and practice. Many have incorporated information about the union and labour rights as part of their services.

Website and list

The development of the website has had major implications for the growth of the IUSW, since sex workers and friends across the world were able to join the organisation on-line.

In 2003, the amount of postings to the list became so high that some members complained. Thus a member of the team has been assigned the task of moderating the list. The moderator ensures that the amount and contents of the postings are balanced. Furthermore she ensures that basic rules of politeness are maintained, does not allow personal attacks of any kind on the list and ensures that discussions focus on sex work issues or issues that are relevant to the organisation's aims.

Since it has been set up, the list has been used by members from different countries to discuss working conditions (in strip clubs, brothels, etc.). Comparing working conditions between establishments in the sex industry contributes to the empowerment of sex workers. Often, sex workers are isolated and do not know that the exploitation they suffer is not universal and that there are other establishments where workers have more rights and are treated with more dignity.

Some members have also posted questions on the list about the legality of sex work in a country where they intend to migrate to. The gathering of this type of information greatly contributes to the safety and well-being of migrant sex workers. In the IUSW list, this type of information is requested and also offered by sex workers themselves, although sometimes members who are service providers do contribute as well.

Other ways in which the list has been used include increasing our reciprocal knowledge of several sex worker grass-roots organisations in different countries. This is done by members posting up reports, press releases and press clippings relating to the actions of their local organisations. Furthermore, on several occasions, members have posted up the electronic addresses of web pages containing useful resources for sex workers.

Police liaison

Police actions have a major impact on sex workers' lives and work. In some countries, the police are the main source of violence against sex workers, guilty of bribing and extorting money from sex workers. On the other hand, the police may have a major role in protecting sex workers from violence.

The importance of sex workers' relationship with the police is highlighted by most sex workers' organisations. The relationship between sex workers communities and police forces is very much related to the nature of the legal system in place and the role of the police in enforcing legislation. According to the Scarlet Alliance, the network of sex work organisations in Australia:

The nature of sex workers' contact and interaction with police determines whether they feel confident making complaints to police regarding crimes of violence. Better relationships with the police were apparent in those [Australian] States and Territories where the majority of the sex industry was legalised and where the police had no role in regulating the sex industry. (Scarlett Alliance 1999: 14)

Parallel to the IUSW lobbying activities and campaigns to change the legislation on sex work, in particular prostitution, the union has maintained that establishing communication channels and links between sex workers and police forces is crucial to the improvement of sex workers' rights. Since July 2001, the IUSW has had representing members at the Lesbian, Gay, Bisexual and Transgender (LGBT) advisory group to the Metropolitan Police. The LGBT advisory group is an independent body made up of representatives of the LGBT community that has as its remit to advise the Metropolitan Police forces on issues relating to that community.

Policing of the LGBT community in London has radically changed in the past decade, from active harassment of members of the community to a recognition by the police that the community has certain and unique policing issues and they, the police, have a commitment to address such issues. It is such a shift that we look for when it comes to policing the sex industry.

The Sex Workers' Project of the LGBT advisory group remit is to work for fair and just policing, harm reduction, as well as collecting and making available information about sex workers' civil, legal and human rights.

Since its inception this project has met with the Vice Squad to discuss issues of security and safety of sex workers. The group has also discussed funding for a possible 'drop-in' centre for sex workers, to be run by the IUSW, and it has observed court case hearings.

The Sex Workers' Project's most prominent action has been the organisation of a Training Day for the Metropolitan Police, aiming to inform the police of the number of organisations, both statutory and voluntary, which offer help, support and advice to sex workers. The event took place in September 2003 and was attended by representatives of all London boroughs involved in policing the sex industry.

The training included presentations given by sex worker members of IUSW. Initially, the organising team intended to include in the programme a session on street prostitution, led by a street prostitute, as well as a transgender session, led by a transgender sex worker. Despite the large number of possible speakers contacted, the team could not fulfil its intentions. This shows that although the event was groundbreaking, with sex workers speaking directly to the police about issues of policing they faced daily, there is still a lot of fear and mistrust from sex workers. This, of course, is related to the police's role in enforcing legislation around prostitution (e.g. soliciting, etc.).

International activities

The IUSW membership has expanded both in numbers and countries covered. Sex workers and allies in Europe, Asia, Africa and Oceania have joined the organisation. However, there are no IUSW-led activities in these countries. Members keep in touch through the website, e-mail list and occasionally by post or telephone.

In Canada, however, there has been an attempt to create a formal branch of the IUSW. Although it has not yet been made formal, there is a growing number of sex workers and allies who have adhered to the IUSW. They have, for example, represented the IUSW in the organisation of a festival for sex workers' rights that took place in February 2003.

The IUSW's integration within the international movement for sex workers' rights is strengthened through our participation in international conferences and events. The IUSW has been present at important conferences such as 'Sex Work and Health in a Changing Europe'. At this conference, held in January 2002, the IUSW in conjunction with the NSWP organised a fringe session for sex workers only. From this session we took a statement that was then accepted by the whole conference. The statement called for those present at the conference to condemn the legislation passed recently in Sweden that penalised sex work clients.

Through several of our members, the IUSW has also had a presence in various international conferences. For example, IUSW members have presented at international conferences such as the International HIV/AIDS Conference held in Barcelona, Spain in July 2002 and at the International Harm Reduction Conference held in Bangkok in 2003. One of our members led a training session at an international event organised by the ENMP (European Network of Male Prostitution) and we have received invitations to address sex-worker organised meetings and conferences in Sweden, Taiwan and Hong Kong.

Affiliating with the GMB

Gaining official recognition as a union has always been a priority for the IUSW. Various agencies have been helpful in attempts at achieving such recognition. In July 2001, the Labour Campaign for Lesbian and Gay Rights invited two members of the IUSW to the Gay and Lesbian TUC conference that took place in London. The IUSW took the opportunity to meet with union gay and lesbian officers and flag the idea of getting TUC recognition for a recently formed sex workers' union.

The rationale behind the move was that gay and lesbian officers would be more likely to be sympathetic to our cause than other union officers, given the parallels between the sex worker and gay population – the stigma attached to both and the history of the movement for gay rights. Although the conference was fruitful in terms of networking with different unions no TUC recognition came of it. Most officers approached were interested in our case and sympathetic on an individual level, but no headway was made in terms of getting unions interested in representing our group of workers.

In November 2001, I attended the No Sweat annual conference. No Sweat is a worldwide campaigning organisation that stands against sweatshop labour. Sweatshop is a term originally coined in the nineteenth century, but it is used today to refer to unsafe working places where workers labour for very long hours and for very low pay. No Sweat aims to publicise, expose and eradicate sweatshop employment. They claim that the way forward is to help unionise sweatshops. Joining a union is the way to enforce existing laws and extend labour rights.

At this conference, a GMB London region officer presented a new GMB campaign to unionise sweatshop labourers working in East London. This campaign counted with the support of No Sweat. The officer argued that it was the duty and responsibility of a general union like the GMB to organise sweatshop workers and play an important role in helping to minimise their exploitation and improve their working conditions The similarities with the sex industry became obvious to me. In fact, No Sweat's website reads:

> Sweatshop labour is modern, global capitalism stripped bare. From the small, back street sweatshop to some of the biggest corporations in the world – child labour, forced overtime,

poverty wages, unsafe conditions, harassment of women and intimidation of trade unionists are commonplace.

Abhorrent working conditions are also commonplace in the sex industry – and we could add violence, rape and trafficking. No Sweat and GMB's approach was pragmatic. They called for unionisation in order to raise working conditions and exert pressure on bosses and managers. The ultimate aim of the campaign was to eradicate sweatshop labour, not the whole garment-making industry (or other industries where sweatshops can be found). Likewise, the IUSW campaigns for the establishment of labour rights in the sex industry, protection from exploitation and the eradication of violence and harassment, not the eradication of the whole sex industry.

Thus at the end of the conference I approached the GMB officer, introduced the IUSW and requested the GMB's help in unionising our organisation. Talks and negotiations between the IUSW and the GMB London region started soon afterwards. The GMB committed itself to establish a branch within the London region to represent sex workers.

We would have to work together. The IUSW team was familiar with the realities, issues and problems faced by sex workers, but we had no knowledge of organising in the context of the mainstream trade union movement. The GMB union and its officers were happy to provide us with support and knowledge in that area, but on the other hand they were not familiar with the sex industry and did not know to what extent it differed from other industries. Nowadays, several GMB officers, and not only those based in London, are able to accompany us on our campaigns and represent our members when needed.

Historical antecedents

Since the publication of Delacoste and Alexander's (1987) *Sex Work*, the concept of sex work as ordinary work or labour has been central to the movement for sex workers' rights. Thus, there have been several attempts to align sex workers with other workers by unionising. In fact, sex workers have succeeded in achieving a place within the mainstream trade union movement in countries such as Greece, Cambodia, Argentina, the Netherlands and the USA. In the UK, unionisation within the sex industry has become a reality in

2002 through the affiliation of a sex worker grass-roots organisation (the IUSW) to a major national union, the GMB.

The GMB Union as we know it today originated from the Gas Workers and General Union. It was formed in 1889 in East London, by Will Thorne, a pioneer in the labour movement and new unionism. The union's first battle resulted in the reduction of gas workers' working hours from 12 to 8 and the success of the battle resulted in a growth of the union that counted 77,000 members in 1911.

In 1924, the union amalgamated with the Municipal Employees Association and the National Federation of Women Workers and this amalgamation resulted in the formation of the National Union of General and Municipal Workers. Since 1924 many other amalgamations have taken place. In 1989 the union adopted the letters 'GMB' as its name. Although the G stands for General, the M for Municipal and the B for Boilermakers, the union is known as Britain's General Union and is registered solely as GMB. In 2003, the GMB has around 1 million members, 40 per cent of which are women. The GMB defends general unionism thus:

> The particular strength of a general union is that it gives to workers in any industry, however large or small, the combined support of all its members in all industries and services. (GMB website)

The Gas Workers and General Union was unique in the fact that it was 'new', that is it organised workers who had not been hitherto in other trade unions. Furthermore, the union was 'general' – it covered a variety of industries not only for the practical reason of maximising bargaining power but also due to Thorne's socialist ideals of solidarity among workers previously broken up and divided (Radice and Radice 1974).

There is a parallel then, between the pioneer gas worker unionists and sex worker activists demanding a place in the trade union movement. In fact, gas workers were rejected by the unions of the time. It was feared that connections with such low-status workers would give the unions a bad name. They were considered different from other workers who were welcome in the unions. They did not fit with the contemporary unions' idea of a decent worker. Gas workers had to form their own union. Nowadays, gas workers do not seem different from other workers.

Almost 100 years later, Bindel, writing in the *Guardian*, claims that the GMB should not take sex workers into membership because 'sex workers are different', as she entitles her article (Bindel 2003). But the improvements achieved by the GMB as well as the growing empowerment of sex workers in Britain through the union's voice is showing that sex workers are not different – just as gas workers are not different from other workers.

Open meeting

Given the opportunity to join one of the biggest mainstream unions in the UK, the IUSW invited its members to an open meeting in order to discuss whether this was a move that would benefit sex workers. A great effort was put into publicising the meeting, so our decision could be more representative of the will of most sex workers.

The meeting took place on 2 March 2002 and was attended by around 70 people. There were representatives from most sectors of the sex industry: prostitution, strip tease, pornography and phone sex – and several representatives of service-providing agencies, as well as clients of sex workers.

The meetings' special guest was Sietske Altink, a representative of the Dutch sex worker organisation the Red Thread (De Rode Draad). This contribution to the meeting was very useful since the government of the Netherlands had just legalised the sex industry, which gave the Red Thread – a collective of sex workers and allies established in 1985 – the opportunity and impetus to enter into talks with a recognised union with a view to affiliation. Thus we had a lot to gain in the UK from hearing about the Dutch experience. Some of the difficulties highlighted at the meeting were soon to be faced in the UK, e.g. barriers to recruitment such as fear of overriding anonymity.

The meeting also had presentations by the first of a long list of sex workers to be served with an Anti-Social Behaviour Order (ASBO) in London. The ASBO was created within the legislation in order to target nuisance in neighbourhoods, for example neighbours and youth who display anti-social behaviour disturbing their local communities. The order may ban young people from being in a certain neighbourhood after a certain time. However, it has been used to target street-based sex workers. The assignment of ASBOs has led sex workers out of beat areas (where they can work alongside other workers for safety and access support services such as outreach programmes) to unfamiliar areas where their safety is at risk and where they cannot be reached by support services. The assignment of such orders has been contested by sex worker activists and sex work projects on the grounds of its unfairness; street soliciting is not in itself an imprisonable offence, but the breach of an ASBO may result in five years' imprisonment.

Sex workers in the labour movement

By joining the GMB, the International Union of Sex Workers has achieved two of its main goals in just two years of existence: the establishment of the right for any sex worker to join an official trade union and the acceptance of sex work as legitimate employment. This has aligned sex workers in the UK with other workers. It has also been a step forward in the direction of eliminating – or at least minimising – stigma towards sex workers.

The mainstream labour movement did not immediately welcome sex worker activists/unionists. However, there has been a gradual improvement in the levels of acceptance. Shortly before the IUSW affiliated to the GMB in 2002, a TUC spokesperson was quoted in the media as saying:

> I'm not sure that the unions would represent people who are working illegally or on the black economy and who are not part of the tax system. It would be highly unlikely that a sex workers' union could affiliate with the TUC unless prostitution was legalised. (TUC spokesperson, quoted in Auerbach, 2002)

Soon after joining the GMB and the mainstream labour movement, we intended to celebrate and publicise the affiliation on Mayday, Labour Day 2002. We wrote to the Mayday Committee, who organise the trade union march and speeches in central London, requesting that one of our representatives be allowed to speak at the event. Their reaction has been recorded in the branch meeting minutes of 6 April 2002:

> Lisa has written to the Mayday committee to request that we have a speaker at the Rally – but they declined on the basis that what the GMB is trying to do is illegal.

Moreover, many trade unionists assumed that the sex workers' affiliation had been triggered and instigated by GMB recruitment officers – they were unaware that in reality it was the IUSW that approached the GMB and not the other way around. At the time of the merge, GMB recruitment officers were criticised for looking for controversy for its own sake.

This apprehension was to gradually change. As a GMB branch, we have attended and passed a motion at the TUC (Trades Union Congress) Women's Conference in March 2003. The motion, drafted by branch members, called for trade union movement support for sex worker unionists and for the TUC's commitment to demand from government a full review of the legislation on sex work. The motion was passed with four abstentions, from around 600 delegates.

Furthermore, in 2003, the branch was invited to speak at two events organised by the mainstream trade union movement. The first event was a panel of speakers organised at the annual Glastonbury Festival. Other panellists included a senior representative of the FBU (Fire Brigades Union) and Billy Bragg – the famous musician and campaigner who launched a GMB campaign to unionise road crew workers.

The second event was the Tolpuddle Festival, an annual event that celebrates the Tolpuddle martyrs, pioneers of trade unionism. In the early nineteenth century, a small group of agricultural workers from a small village in Dorset were harshly punished and transported to Australia for forming a trade union (Monks 1999). Ever since they have been remembered by trade unionists in an annual march, which has now extended into a three-day festival in the village of Tolpuddle.

At this event the IUSW led a workshop and also spoke, from the main stage, to thousands of trade unionists. Both talks were very well received and it was clear that most union activists accepted sex workers as part of the mainstream labour movement. The IUSW presence at the festival was also noted as symbolic and a parallel was drawn with the Tolpuddle Martyrs. After all, the event is a celebration of workers' rights to organise and we, sex workers, had just established that right for ourselves.

In fact, the same development has happened within the GMB union itself. In March 2002, when sex workers officially joined the union, at least two members returned their membership cards on the grounds that they refused to be part of a union that represented prostitutes. But representing the branch at a series of meetings and conferences has helped to shift the way GMB members see the new sex workers' branch.

In June 2002 history was made when a sex industry branch representative addressed the Biannual National Congress of the

GMB, held at Blackpool. The motion presented called for the union's support for sex workers' campaigns, especially the decriminalisation of prostitution. The motion was passed unanimously, a show of the level of support the branch has secured from all regional sections of the GMB, after such a controversial affiliation.

Union branch organisation

The purpose of each Branch is to help the Union achieve the objectives set out in these Rules, giving priority to recruitment, organising, servicing and retention. As the basic unit of the Union, the Branch shall encourage members to participate in its democracy. (GMB 2001: 43)

Apart from clearly setting the purpose of a branch, the GMB rulebook provides guidance on how to organise regional branches. This guidance is only loose, since the rulebook has been composed of the sets of rules of the major unions that amalgamated in the past to form what today is the GMB. Such looseness works to the advantage of the sex industry branch and has contributed greatly for the successful 'marriage' of a grass-roots organisation and a union.

Thus GMB rules have often been adapted to suit the reality and needs of sex workers – which may vary from other workers. For example, we have established that any person wishing to join the sex industry branch can do so under a false or work name. We have also made sure that branch officials' addresses are not given out to anyone, not even branch members. This is a security measure that other branches feel is not appropriate for them. On the contrary, postal addresses are provided to any new member so that they can post letters directly to their branch officials (secretary, president, etc.). However, in our branch we have decided to change this policy to ensure the physical safety of our branch officials.

Although the rulebook suggests that branch meetings be quarterly, the sex industry branch has decided to meet once every two months. The GMB London region offices are located in Hendon. Our first meetings were held there but soon it became apparent that a considerable number of members faced difficulties in accessing the meetings. Thus since September 2002 meetings have been held in Central London, at a project that offers support to young male sex workers.

Union benefits

Members of the sex workers branch enjoy all the benefits offered by the GMB to its other members. The most popular benefit among our branch's members is the free legal advice and legal representation offered by the GMB. This is easily explained by the semi-legality of some sectors of the sex industry (e.g. prostitution). Sex workers also often feel discriminated against by the justice system. Often, those sex workers who are arrested by the police, caught up in raids or assaulted by a client do not know what rights they are entitled to.

Likewise, tax advice is sought by sex workers and our allies. The tax situation is confusing; many sex workers would like to pay tax but they cannot do so under their real occupation. Furthermore, many fear that by expressing the will to pay tax, they will be forced to pay exorbitant tax in arrears.

Training and development are also offered as membership benefits. Training is of advantage to those who would like to acquire new skills in their line of work as well as for those who would like to leave the industry all together. Training available includes CV writing, computer skills, self-defence and trade union skills. In addition, members can apply for subsidised training in dancing and striptease skills.

The GMB offers professional, free and confidential advice on employment rights and domestic violence. Money benefits such as the money club (that finds the cheapest products on request) and discount insurance policies are also attractions to potential members.

In addition, there are other reasons why sex workers join the GMB. Firstly, the GMB works to limit the stigma surrounding sex work:

> One of the reasons why I am with something like the GMB is because it's about the destigmatisation of the business. And that's a really important one for me. (Union member)

Secondly, union activities and meetings become a safe place where sex workers can talk freely about their working life and life style. In a stigmatised sector where most workers keep the nature of their work secret from their friends and family, this has quite an important value.

> So it [the union] actually represents a support network in a sense. Who do you talk to when you get a problem? There's no one to talk to … That had certainly been a problem in the past.

That's something I get from the union – you can talk. (Union member)

Union recognition agreements

One of the main benefits of joining a union is to be represented by that union in disputes and negotiations on pay and conditions? Can the GMB do this for its sex worker members? In an article of 7 June 2003, Bindel dismisses the usefulness of organising workers in the sex industry on the grounds that negotiating on behalf of sex workers is legitimising pimps:

> If prostitutes are the workers, who are the bosses? Pimps and brothel keepers? Is it really acceptable to legitimise these people and call them managers? (Bindel 2003)

Bindel ignores the fact that, in reality, those who run businesses in the sex industry have a great impact on the lives of sex workers. Negotiating with them is crucial to improving working conditions in the sex industry. In order to do this across the whole of the sex industry, the GMB has to lobby for changes in the law – for the removal of laws that place businesses in illegality.

Bindel also ignores the fact that the sex industry does not operate illegally in its entirety. Many sectors and establishments are perfectly legal and licensed. Those places are working places like any others where the main functions of the union can be performed just as they are in any other member industries. The following section will show how.

In principle, there is a conflict of interest between the union representing sex workers and business managers operating in the sex industry, since ultimately the union's aspiration is to establish workers' control over their own industry. However, in some cases, it is very much in the interests of managers to support the union. In the sex industry, this is the case when an employer is victimised or affected by the stigmatisation attached to the industry in general – that is, when an employer suffers the same stigmatisation that sex workers endure.

In 2002, in the early days of the sex workers union branch, we were approached by one of the managers of a new table-dancing club in the Docklands area, London, requesting the union's involvement in the new club. It is important to note that it is not at all common for the management to look for the unionisation of workers, since unionisation is in the workers' interests and often in conflict with the management's interests. Thus the sex industry branch challenged this request and speculated as to whether there was a genuine interest in sex workers' rights. Perhaps the reason behind this unusual request was that with union recognition this particular table-dancing club would attract more clients – who would feel 'less guilty' of visiting a table-dancing club knowing that those who work there were given proper labour rights. Nevertheless, we investigated the request and did not find a reason why we should not organise the workers of this table-dancing club.

Thus before the opening of the club a union recognition agreement was signed by the table-dancing club and the GMB. Majingo's was the first table-dancing club to recognise the union in the UK. The recognition agreement contains important clauses that secure the union's powers within the club and ensures that workers are given resources to run union activities rather than being penalised for their part in such activities.

The agreement establishes the right of the GMB to represent and negotiate on behalf of its members who work in this table-dancing club. It also recognises the GMB as the sole bargaining agency for collective issues concerning conditions.

All new dancers receive a union membership form. Union representatives are elected regularly and facilities to arrange meetings between workers and union officials are granted by management. The union also agreed the code of conduct (for dancers, managers and clients). It is agreed that management cannot make changes to this code or any of the club rules (e.g. stage fees) without informing the union.

In August 2002, another table-dancing club approached the GMB office. This Bristol club is run by a woman, a former table dancer herself. This manager has encouraged a large number of workers to join the union. Again, a code of conduct was agreed and a union recognition agreement signed. The club's managers and dancers have recently requested our help in setting up a Bristol forum consisting of dancers, club managers, council members, members of the police and members of the local community.

Thus we have shown that it is possible for unions to organise sex workers (as they have organised workers in many other industries) and that union organisation can indeed result in the improvement of working conditions within the sex industry.

Barriers to recruitment

Recruitment is fundamental to the branch since our continued union status could be threatened if affiliate numbers drop below a certain minimum. Although membership has grown steadily since March 2002, we have recognised reasons why some sex workers are reluctant to join.

The vast majority of sex workers, out of necessity, would rather remain anonymous and therefore their privacy precludes union membership. Although confidentiality has been assured by the GMB union, it is understandable that many prefer not to take any risks at all.

> It's a Catch 22 situation. They simply don't want to join a union, they don't want to join anything where their names get put down on paper. While there's the stigma … (Union member)

Furthermore, joining a recently created union branch which is so involved in campaigning requires a certain level of commitment to the struggle for better labour conditions. In reality many sex workers are not politicised at all and are rather just interested in working.

> Most people aren't interested in a cause. Most people want to wake up in the morning, go to work … And then you have a small group of people who want to change the world. And that's when activists come in. That's us. (Union member)

Moreover, many men, women and transgender sex workers do not identify as sex workers. In fact, many exotic dancers, masseuses, sex phone operators among others working in the industry do not classify their work as sex work. This may be because they understand the term sex worker as signifying prostitute. Or it may be based on the ground that they have no physical contact with their clients.

Since many people who work in the sex industry do not identify as sex workers, the name of our branch may be a barrier to recruitment in itself. Many sex workers who do not work independently, especially those who work in flats or clubs, have mentioned their fear of reprisals by their managers.

> The problem if you go to the clubs, like I said, is that a lot of the owners will say, what do we need it [the union] for? Why?

It's only going to cause problems! There needs to be something more because otherwise what will happen is that the clubs won't take in girls that are in the union. I know this. That's what will happen. (Former sex worker)

Furthermore, many workers expect their time in the industry to be brief and as a result they do not see it as worthwhile becoming active or taking part in union activities.

It's a transit occupation; people are always coming and going; they don't think of it as a lifetime occupation. So, they think 'I'm just doing this for a couple of years'. So, it's difficult to organise. But maybe it's difficult to organise in any industry too, because people don't work in one place for lifetime anymore. (Sex worker rights advocate)

These barriers are caused by the marginalisation of sex workers and the stigma attached to our industry. Once we claim our rights, there will be no reason why sex workers should not be proud of themselves and join a union or professional association. One of the aims of any sex worker organisation should be, thus, to promote self-respect and pride, without which no one is able to stand up for their rights.

Union branch development

At the time of writing (December 2003), the branch has enough members to secure its existence. Furthermore, there is enough support from the GMB union, the trade union movement in general and the most important agencies that work around sex work. The branch is therefore entering a new stage in its existence.

Elections took place in December 2003 to ensure that there is a greater division of labour among active branch members and that leadership is shared. As the branch grows and publicity reaches sex workers in other areas of the country, difficulties arise in providing a satisfactory service to members outside the London region. Thus a short-term priority of the GMB is to establish other regional branches representing sex workers.

Another improvement, within the London branch, has been the creation of a Dancers Section. This will ensure that the issues faced by dancers – striptease, pole and lap dancers – are given full attention. On the other hand, it is hoped that some dancers who have been reluctant to join the union on the grounds that they do not identify themselves as sex workers will feel more comfortable to come forward and join.

Combining different types of activism

In my literature search on types of activism I have found either discussions of strategies such as lobbying and striking 'traditional' of old social movements, or discussions of strategies such as direct action and art as protest common among 'new' social movements – but never both. A new social movement's strength comes from, among other factors, the use of new strategies such as direct action. However, the skills acquired by old social movements of organised political action are not to be ignored. I argue that a strong and effective sex workers' rights movement should combine both types of strategies. Activists and social researchers should pay attention to the need to be familiar with both approaches and provide guidance on how to achieve success on both 'fronts'.

Sex worker organisations have displayed different styles of activism – sometimes emphasising cultural activities, celebration and pride, at other times leaning towards a more bureaucratic approach aimed at achieving change through established political channels. The international movement for sex workers rights has seen expressions of both types and that is usually accepted as one of the strengths of the movement.

> I have no objections if a group of sex workers want to see themselves as professionals, as employees, or as anti-capitalists or informal labourers, or if they join a union. I think all of those perspectives form the movement. (Sex worker activist)

Throughout the life of the IUSW/GMB branch we have practised both styles of activism as our members see the relevance and appropriateness of both and the strength of combining them.

> That engine for change is a political one. I'm not saying there isn't a place for grassroots activism to call for a change … It's got to be in both directions. (Union member)

> I do see my role in the movement often as a liaison between the grey side and the fun, flamboyant, taboo breaking side. I think I enjoy being the grey person to the nude protests, and the naughty boa wearer to the lawyers. (Union member)

The advantage of joining forces is clear. On the one hand unions or other organisations (such as political parties) have the structure and resources to reach dispersed work forces and to lobby on a large scale. On the other hand, grass-roots organisations have the knowledge of the 'ground' and moreover they often present a less intimidating, friendlier and familiar face to those who seek support.

However, the integration of such different types of organisation has not been easy. The approach of a grass-roots organisation is necessarily different from that of a general union. Nowadays, big unions resemble business enterprises, and activities and campaigns are often accepted or rejected on the basis of their monetary outcomes. On the other hand, while grass-roots organisation's activities are limited by the amount of funds available to them, they tend to remain more faithful to its aims. Moreover, while unions are very structured and hierarchical institutions, a grass-roots group like the IUSW has a much more egalitarian configuration, in which each member's voice has the same weight.

The future

By aligning ourselves with other workers in the mainstream trade union movement, the IUSW/GMB sex workers' branch actually aligns sex worker activists with a very strong movement – the labour movement. Our successful unionisation has inspired sex worker activists in other countries. In Sweden, an informal network of sex workers has recently requested the assistance of the UK union in attempting to unionise. The process is under way and the network will soon be affiliated to a fully recognised union. French activists have also sought our advice on how to approach French national unions. We hope sex workers in other countries will take our example and establish their labour rights, starting with the right to unionise, although it is important to note that this is not an aspiration of all sex worker organisations.

An organisation has a life of its own and it is not possible to predict where it will go. The aspiration of an organisation that arose out of the need to protect a group of people by establishing their rights is to become obsolete.

> I would like it to wither away, except as one of the banners in the union march ... I would like to see unions becoming ornamental, social organisations, because labour is so well treated! (Union member)

Conclusion

In only two years the IUSW achieved one of its main demands – the establishment of the right for any sex worker to join a recognised union. The acceptance of sex workers by fellow members of the GMB and the labour movement was not immediate but conquered by networking efforts.

Several barriers prevent sex workers from joining the union, mostly arising from unfair legislation (especially connected to prostitution) and social attitudes towards sex workers. Nevertheless, the branch is well established and its activities have shown that sex workers are not different – like other workers, we benefit from union organisation. Clearly, union activism can make a difference in sex workers lives and working conditions.

Note

1   I mostly feared verbal abuse, but physical violence was also in my mind, since unfortunately, the 'whore stigma' is such that sex workers suffer high levels of violence.

Bibliography

Auerbach, A. (2002) 'Meet Britain's most unlikely shop steward', *Evening Standard*, 25 January.

Bindel, J. (2003) 'Sex workers are different' *Guardian*, 7 July.

Delacoste, F. and Alexander, P. (eds) (1987) *Sex Work: Writings by Women in the Sex Industry*. Pittsburg: Cleis Press.

GMB (2001) *GMB Rulebook*. GMB internal publication.

Jennes, V. (1993) *Making It Work: The Prostitutes' Rights Movement in Perspective*. Hawthorne, NY: Aldine de Gruyter.

Kempadoo, K. and Doezema, J. (eds) (1998) *Global Sex Workers: Rights, Resistance, and Redefinition*. New York and London: Routledge.

Monks, J. (1999) 'Introduction', in Trade Union Congress, *1934 The Martyrs of Tolpuddle*. London: Peter Gill & Associates.

Nagle, J. (1997) *Whores and Other Feminists*. New York: Routledge.

Radice, E. A. and G. H. (1974) *Will Thorne: Constructive Militant – A Study in New Unionism and New Politics*. London: George Allen & Unwin.

Respect! (2000) Issue 1.

Rona (2000) 'Why we need a union', *Respect!*, Issue 1: 4.

Index